M000237732

Social Organization

Select Social Science Classics

Vilhelm Aubert, *The Hidden Society*
Herbert Blumer, *Critiques of Research in the Social Sciences*
G.D.H. Cole, *Guild Socialism Restated*
Charles Horton Cooley, *Human Nature and the Social Order*
Charles Horton Cooley, *Social Organization*
Benedetto Croce, *Historical Materialism and the Economics of
   Karl Marx*
Albert Venn Dicey, *Lectures on the Relation between Law
   and Public Opinion*
Adam Ferguson, *An Essay on the History of Civil Society*
Moses I. Finley, *Studies in Land and Credit in Ancient Athens*
Ruth Fischer, *Stalin and German Communism*
G.S. Ghurye, *The Scheduled Tribes of India*
Ludwig Gumplowicz, *Outlines of Sociology*
Everett C. Hughes, *The Sociological Eye*
Helen MacGill Hughes, *News and the Human Interest Story*
Kurt Koffka, *Growth of the Mind*
Walter Laqueur, *Young Germany*
Harold J. Laski, *The American Presidency*
Gustave LeBon, *The French Revolution and the Psychology of Revolution*
Gustave LeBon, *The Psychology of Socialism*
Walter Lippmann, *A Preface to Morals*
Helen Merrell Lynd, *England in the Eighteen-Eighties*
Henry de Man, *The Psychology of Marxian Socialism*
Harriet Martineau, *Society in America*
Vilfredo Pareto, *The Transformation of Democracy*
Joseph A. Schumpeter, *The Theory of Economic Development*
George Bernard Shaw, *The Intelligent Woman's Guide to
Socialism and Capitalism*
Werner Sombart, *The Jews and Modern Capitalism*
Pitirim Sorokin, *Social and Cultural Dynamics*
William Graham Sumner, *Earth-Hunger and Other Essays*
Jacob L. Talmon, *Myth of the Nation and Vision of Revolution*
John W. Thibaut and Harold H. Kelley, *The Social Psychology of Groups*
de Tocqueville, Alexis, *Recollections: The French Revolution of 1848.*
Thorstein Veblen, *The Engineers and the Price System*
Thorstein Veblen, *The Theory of Business Enterprise*
Graham Wallas, *Human Nature in Politics*
Max Weber, *General Economic History*
Florian Znaniecki, *Cultural Sciences*
Florian Znaniecki, *The Social Role of the Man of Knowledge*

Second Printing 1993
Transaction edition 1983. Original edition copyright
1909, 1937 by Charles Scribner's Sons, 1962 by
Schocken Books, Inc.

All rights reserved under International and Pan-
American Copyright Conventions. No part of this book
may be reproduced or transmitted in any form or by
any means, electronic or mechanical, including
photocopy, recording, or any information storage and
retrieval system, without prior permission in writing
from the publisher. All inquiries should be addressed
to Transaction Publishers, Rutgers—The State
University, New Brunswick, New Jersey 08903.

Library of Congress Catalog Number: 91-32498
ISBN: 0-87855-824-1
Printed in the United States of America

Library of Congress Cataloging in Publication Data

Cooley, Charles Horton, 1864-1929.
    Social organization: a study of the larger
mind/Charles Horton Cooley; introduction by Philip
Rieff.
    p.   cm—(Transaction social science classics)
    Includes bibliographical references and index.
    ISBN 0-87855-824-1
    1. Sociology. 2. Social psychology. 3. Social
structure. I. Title. II. Series.
[HM251.C85   1983b]
301—dc20   91-32498
                                                CIP

EX LIBRIS
James H. Mahon

Social Organization
A Study of the Larger Mind

CHARLES HORTON COOLEY

Introduction by Philip Rieff

Transaction Publishers
New Brunswick (U.S.A.) and London (U.K.)

CONTENTS

INTRODUCTION   xv
PREFACE   xxxi

PART I—PRIMARY ASPECTS OF ORGANIZATION

CHAPTER I

SOCIAL AND INDIVIDUAL ASPECTS OF MIND

PAGE

Mind an Organic Whole—Conscious and Unconscious Relations
—Does Self-Consciousness Come First? *Cogito, Ergo Sum*
—The Larger Introspection—Self-Consciousness in Chil-
dren—Public Consciousness   3

CHAPTER II

SOCIAL AND INDIVIDUAL ASPECTS OF MIND—(CONTINUED)

Moral Aspect of the Organic View—It Implies that Reform
Should Be Based on Sympathy—Uses of Praise and Blame
—Responsibility Broadened but Not Lost—Moral Value of
a Larger View—Organic Morality Calls for Knowledge—
Nature of Social Organization   13

CHAPTER III

PRIMARY GROUPS

Meaning of Primary Groups—Family, Playground, and Neighborhood—How Far Influenced by Larger Society—Meaning
and Permanence of " Human Nature "—Primary Groups the
Nursery of Human Nature   23

CHAPTER IV

PRIMARY IDEALS

Nature of Primary Idealism—The Ideal of a "We" or Moral
Unity—It Does Not Exclude Self-Assertion- -Ideals Springing from Hostility—Loyalty, Truth, Service—Kindness—

v

CONTENTS

PAGE

Lawfulness—Freedom—The Doctrine of Natural Right—
Bearing of Primary Idealism upon Education and Philanthropy   32

CHAPTER V

THE EXTENSION OF PRIMARY IDEALS

Primary Ideals Underlie Democracy and Christianity—Why
They Are Not Achieved on a Larger Scale—What They Re-
quire from Personality—From Social Mechanism—The
Principle of Compensation   51

PART II—COMMUNICATION

CHAPTER VI

THE SIGNIFICANCE OF COMMUNICATION

Meaning of Communication—Its Relation to Human Nature
—To Society at Large   61

CHAPTER VII

THE GROWTH OF COMMUNICATION

Pre-Verbal Communication—The Rise of Speech—Its Mental
and Social Function—The Function of Writing—Printing
and the Modern World—The Non-Verbal Arts   66

CHAPTER VIII

MODERN COMMUNICATION: ENLARGEMENT AND ANIMATION

Character of Recent Changes—Their General Effect—The
Change in the United States—Organized Gossip—Public
Opinion, Democracy, Internationalism—The Value of
Diffusion—Enlargement of Feeling—Conclusion   80

CHAPTER IX

MODERN COMMUNICATION: INDIVIDUALITY

The Question—Why Communication Should Foster Individuality—The Contrary or Dead-Level Theory—Reconciliation of These Views—The Outlook as Regards Individuality 91

vi

CONTENTS

CHAPTER X

MODERN COMMUNICATION: SUPERFICIALITY AND STRAIN

PAGE

Stimulating Effect of Modern Life—Superficiality—Strain—
Pathological Effects   98

PART III—THE DEMOCRATIC MIND

CHAPTER XI

THE ENLARGEMENT OF CONSCIOUSNESS

Narrowness of Consciousness in Tribal Society—Importance of
Face-to-Face Assembly—Individuality—Subconscious Char-
acter of Wider Relations—Enlargement of Consciousness—
Irregularity in Growth—Breadth of Modern Consciousness
—Democracy   107

CHAPTER XII

THE THEORY OF PUBLIC OPINION

Public Opinion as Organization—Agreement Not Essential—
Public Opinion *versus* Popular Impression—Public Thought
Not an Average—A Group Is Capable of Expression through
Its Most Competent Members—General and Special Public
Opinion—The Sphere of the Former—Of the Latter—The
Two Are United in Personality—How Public Opinion Rules
—Effective Rule Based on Moral Unity   121

CHAPTER XIII

WHAT THE MASSES CONTRIBUTE

The Masses the Initiators of Sentiment—They Live in the Cen-
tral Current of Experience—Distinction or Privilege Apt to
Cause Isolation—Institutional Character of Upper Classes
—The Masses Shrewd Judges of Persons—This the Main
Ground for Expecting that the People Will Be Right in the
Long Run—Democracy Always Representative—Con-
clusion   135

CONTENTS

CHAPTER XIV

DEMOCRACY AND CROWD EXCITEMENT

PAGE

The Crowd-Theory of Modern Life—The Psychology of Crowds
—Modern Conditions Favor Psychological Contagion—Democracy a Training in Self-Control—The Crowd Not Always
in the Wrong—Conclusion; the Case of France   149

CHAPTER XV

DEMOCRACY AND DISTINCTION

The Problem—Democracy Should Be Distinguished from
Transition—The Dead-Level Theory of Democracy—Confusion and Its Effects—"Individualism" May Not Be Favorable to Distinguished Individuality—Contemporary Uniformity—Relative Advantages of America and Europe—
Haste, Superficiality, Strain—Spiritual Economy of a Settled Order—Commercialism—Zeal for Diffusion—Conclusion   157

CHAPTER XVI

THE TREND OF SENTIMENT

Meaning and General Trend of Sentiment—Attenuation—Refinement—Sense of Justice—Truth as Justice—As Realism
As Expediency—As Economy of Attention—Hopefulness   177

CHAPTER XVII

THE TREND OF SENTIMENT—(CONTINUED)

Nature of the Sentiment of Brotherhood—Favored by Communication and Settled Principles—How Far Contemporary
Life Fosters It—How Far Uncongenial to It—General Outcome in this Regard—The Spirit of Service—The Trend of
Manners—Brotherhood in Relation to Conflict—Blame—
Democracy and Christianity   189

CONTENTS

PART IV—SOCIAL CLASSES

CHAPTER XVIII

THE HEREDITARY OR CASTE PRINCIPLE

Nature and Use of Classes—Inheritance and Competition the
Two Principles upon which Classes Are Based—Conditions
in Human Nature Making for Hereditary Classes—Caste
Spirit   209

CHAPTER XIX

CONDITIONS FAVORING OR OPPOSING THE GROWTH OF CASTE

Three Conditions Affecting the Increase or Diminution of Caste
—Race-Caste—Immigration and Conquest—Gradual Differentiation of Functions; Mediæval Caste; India—Influence of Settled Conditions—Influence of the State of
Communication and Enlightenment—Conclusion   217

CHAPTER XX

THE OUTLOOK REGARDING CASTE

The Question—How Far the Inheritance Principle Actually
Prevails—Influences Favoring Its Growth—Those Antagonizing It—The Principles of Inheritance and Equal Opportunity as Affecting Social Efficiency—Conclusion   229

CHAPTER XXI

OPEN CLASSES

The Nature of Open Classes—Whether Class-Consciousness Is
Desirable—Fellowship and Coöperation Deficient in Our
Society—Class Organization in Relation to Freedom   239

CHAPTER XXII

HOW FAR WEALTH IS THE BASIS OF OPEN CLASSES

Impersonal Character of Open Classes—Various Classifications—
Classes, as Commonly Understood, Based on Obvious Dis-

ix

CONTENTS

PAGE

tinctions—Wealth as Generalized Power—Economic Betterment as an Ideal of the Ill-Paid Classes—Conclusion   248

CHAPTER XXIII

ON THE ASCENDENCY OF A CAPITALIST CLASS

The Capitalist Class—Its Lack of Caste Sentiment—In What
Sense "the Fittest"—Moral Traits—How Far Based on Ser-
vice—Autocratic and Democratic Principles in the Control
of Industry—Reasons for Expecting an Increase of the
Democratic Principle—Social Power in General—Organizing
Capacity—Nature and Sources of Capitalist Power—Power
over the Press and over Public Sentiment—Upper Class
Atmosphere   256

CHAPTER XXIV

ON THE ASCENDENCY OF A CAPITALIST CLASS—(CONTINUED)

The Influence of Ambitious Young Men—Security of the Dominant Class in an Open System—Is There Danger of Anarchy
and Spoliation?—Whether the Sway of Riches Is Greater
Now than Formerly—Whether Greater in America than in
England   273

CHAPTER XXV

THE ORGANIZATION OF THE ILL-PAID CLASSES

The Need of Class Organization—Uses and Dangers of Unions
—General Disposition of the Hand-Working Classes   284

CHAPTER XXVI

POVERTY

The Meaning of Poverty—Personal and General Causes—Pov-
erty in a Prosperous Society Due Chiefly to Maladjustment
—Are the Poor the "Unfit"?—Who Is to Blame for Poverty?
—Attitude of Society toward the Poor—Fundamental
Remedies   290

x

CONTENTS

CHAPTER XXVII

HOSTILE FEELING BETWEEN CLASSES

PAGE

Conditions Producing Class Animosity—The Spirit of Service
Allays Bitterness—Possible Decrease of the Prestige of
Wealth—Probability of a More Communal Spirit in the
Use of Wealth—Influence of Settled Rules for Social Oppo-
sition—Importance of Face-to-Face Discussion   301

PART V—INSTITUTIONS

CHAPTER XXVIII

INSTITUTIONS AND THE INDIVIDUAL

The Nature of Institutions—Hereditary and Social Factors—
The Child and the World—Society and Personality—Person-
ality *versus* the Institution—The Institution as a Basis of
Personality—The Moral Aspect—Choice *versus* Mechanism
—Personality the Life of Institutions—Institutions Becom-
ing Freer in Structure   313

CHAPTER XXIX

INSTITUTIONS AND THE INDIVIDUAL—(CONTINUED)

Innovation as a Personal Tendency—Innovation and Conserva-
tism as Public Habit—Solidarity—French and Anglo-Saxon
Solidarity—Tradition and Convention—Not so Opposite as
They Appear—Real Difference, in this Regard, between
Modern and Mediæval Society—Traditionalism and Con-
ventionalism in Modern Life   327

CHAPTER XXX

FORMALISM AND DISORGANIZATION

The Nature of Formalism—Its Effect upon Personality—Form-
alism in Modern Life—Disorganization, "Individualism"
—How it Affects the Individual—Relation to Formalism—
"Individualism" Implies Defective Sympathy—Contem-
porary "Individualism"—Restlessness under Discomfort—
The Better Aspect of Disorganization   342

CONTENTS

CHAPTER XXXI

DISORGANIZATION: THE FAMILY

PAGE

Old and New Régimes in the Family—The Declining Birth-Rate
—"Spoiled" Children—The Opening of New Careers to
Women—European and American Points of View—Personal
Factors in Divorce—Institutional Factors—Conclusion   356

CHAPTER XXXII

DISORGANIZATION: THE CHURCH

The Psychological View of Religion—The Need of Social
Structure—Creeds—Why Symbols Tend to Become Formal
—Traits of a Good System of Symbols—Contemporary
Need of Religion—Newer Tendencies in the Church   372

CHAPTER XXXIII

DISORGANIZATION: OTHER TRADITIONS

Disorder in the Economic System—In Education—In Higher
Culture—In the Fine Arts   383

PART VI—PUBLIC WILL

CHAPTER XXXIV

THE FUNCTION OF PUBLIC WILL

Public and Private Will—The Lack of Public Will—Social
Wrongs Commonly Not Willed at All   395

CHAPTER XXXV

GOVERNMENT AS PUBLIC WILL

Government Not the Only Agent of Public Will—The Relative
Point of View; Advantages of Government as an Agent—
Mechanical Tendency of Government—Characteristics Fa-
vorable to Government Activity—Municipal Socialism—Self-
Expression the Fundamental Demand of the People—Actual
Extension of State Functions   402

CONTENTS

CHAPTER XXXVI

SOME PHASES OF THE LARGER WILL

PAGE

Growing Efficiency of the Intellectual Processes—Organic Idealism—The Larger Morality—Indirect Service—Increasing Simplicity and Flexibility in Social Structure—Public Will Saves Part of the Cost of Change—Human Nature the Guiding Force behind Public Will   411

Index   420

INTRODUCTION BY PHILIP RIEFF

> Individualism is a mature and calm feeling, which disposes each member of the community to sever himself from the mass of his fellow-creatures; and to draw apart with his family and friends; so that after he has thus formed a little circle of his own, he willingly leaves society at large to itself. . . . Amongst democratic nations . . . the interest of man is confined to those in close propinquity to himself. . . . Aristocracy had made a chain of all the members of the community, from the peasant to the king; democracy breaks that chain, and severs every link of it. . . . Thus not only does democracy make every man forget his ancestors, but it hides his descendants, and separates his contemporaries, from him; it throws him back forever upon himself alone, and threatens in the end to confine him entirely within the solitude of his own heart.
>
> TOCQUEVILLE, *Democracy in America*

CHARLES Horton Cooley's reputation is established, high and secure: in *Social Organization* (as before in *Human Nature and the Social Order*) he produced a classic text of American sociology—classic because it continues to give its readers something permanently important about which to think and, at the same time, adds to their intellectual equipment. My aim, in this introductory essay, is to exhibit one major aspect of Cooley's subtle response to the problems American culture presented not merely to him but also to the sociology that has followed after him. For, despite occasional rebellions against its inevitable subject, American sociology continues to cope with the moral quality of American life, and in ways for which Cooley set a superior standard. He came to a series

xv

of understandings with his subject that make him a representative American sociologist.

Cooley lived between the years 1864–1929, just that time during which, except for the Wilsonian interlude, Americans settled into the attitude Tocqueville first noted. In this time, sympathetic critics of the national attitude appeared, trying to lure the American out beyond the safe limit of his self-concern. Of these philosophical doctors, pacifying the American ego in order to retrain it, Cooley remains one of the most adroit, taking up sociology as once men took up theology or socialism: in order to resolve the perennial issue of whether men can live well for themselves and their intimates alone.

In America, where theology was, there, in the latter third of the nineteenth century, sociology appeared, to argue the perennial issue in a new and revealing way, often against the officially religious preachers, mainly of Calvinist persuasion, who had transformed their God into a likeness of themselves—rugged individualists, without the slightest sense of responsibility to the community. With the exception of William Graham Sumner, all the American converts to sociology—Ward, Small, Cooley and their company—made cases against the prevailing individualism. There was something unintentionally subversive about that first generation, in the very choice of sociology. The nature of the discipline itself dictated a struggle against what Small once called "the preposterous initial fact of the individual"—in sum, against the American's most reverent conception of himself. Cooley was attracted to sociology from economics, in which he had taken his doctorate, and from government service, in which he had been bored for the brief time he spent away from his place of birth and breeding, the campus of the University of Michigan, at Ann Arbor. But Cooley was attracted to sociology less by the size of its achievement than by the size of its target, as he came to see it, that false antinomy between self and society by which men improved themselves at the expense of others. "We must improve as a whole"—Cooley jotted down the subversive notion in his diaries. *Social Organization* makes the prior point that each exists only as a member of all. It is at once a book of analysis and recommendation, as sociology at its best must always be.

Unlike some among his successors in the discipline, Cooley never worried whether, as a sociologist, he would look acceptably scientific to his academic neighbors. But then, Cooley worked before the period when envy of the scientist's power to actually transform his subject matter had eaten the heart out of sociology. He did not choose to caricature the scientist by imitation, but to respect science the more by cultivating the necessary artist in himself, as his discipline required. The conditions of his science, Cooley believed, were irremediably different from those relating to the material world. Statistics might be used, in an ancillary way. But, as in all sciences, in sociology interpretation is all. A science may be loaded down with too many facts, its vision blurred by peering too intently at the machinery for collecting them. The selected facts can be brought to life, as the statisticians themselves agree, only by a compelling vision of their meaning. Untouched by the magic of a sufficiently powerful and trained imagination, data play dead. No exactitude will bring them to life. Nor are

xvii

statistics the sole language of precision. For his special purposes, Cooley practiced sociology with an old, but precise and difficult weapon: *le mot juste*.

There is, moreover, the question of who is to be compelled. Cooley wrote for an audience larger, and more important, than his own profession, while the audience of the physical scientist is usually his own profession. The function of the sociologist is both scientific and pedagogic; dealing with moral problems, he must teach moral lessons—otherwise, his sociology fails to be social enough. On the other hand, since Leibnitz, it has been the ambition of the scientific community to divorce itself from all others—national, cultural, political. The special language of the physical scientist enunciates an act of emancipation that, when imitated too strenuously by the social scientist, deprives the latter of his proper audience. Jargon is a curse; it permits professional groups to turn in upon themselves, thus helping them evade their pedagogic responsibility. Cooley remained readable because he knew that, given his subject matter, he was obliged to communicate like an artist, intimately, by the personal force of his vision.

Yet, although inherently pedagogic, sociology is not itself bound to any doctrine but can transform them all —Marxist, Freudian, Thomist, Durkheimian, Platonist, Weberian, Lucretian, any—into cues for prompting into presence and voice the otherwise silent and invisible actors of social reality. Sociologists may try on New Yorkers perspectives first applied to Samoans, so long as they remember that they are thus experimenting with angles of vision that may, in time, significantly alter what is seen. No more than the physical sciences can

xviii

sociology evade responsibility for transforming its subject matter. Even the most complex analytic perspectives may develop into ideology. More important, sociological analysis always carries with it a polemical implication. Who are scientists, that they should be, in their peculiar work, without passion, for and against their subject? Indeed, the analytic perspective may have been trained, in the first place, by a reaction against some established doctrine, which once itself may have been a polemically useful analytic perspective. Cooley judged that "behaviorism reflects mysticism." It is a new style of mystification, suitable for those who hated the old religious mystifications with such passion that they needed new ones to set against the old. Much "scientific animus," Cooley observed, is in this way "subservient to theology."

Only by multiplying analytic perspectives, shifting from one to another with a permanent tentativeness, can sociology avoid slipping over into ideology. That a unified sociological theory now may be emerging, from the varied and often conflicting analytic perspectives available, does not alter the case: this unity is unlikely to be more than a systematic presentation of multiple perspectives. And for such systematic presentation, a canon is necessary, from which students can expand and deepen their analytic competence. Cooley's *Social Organization* has canonical status; it has helped the discipline grow to its present strength.

Cooley was even harder on the polemicists than on the data-mongers. "Conspicuous radicals," he thought, are "likely to be contradictors," incapable of balancing their analyses, giving it that symmetry of yes and no which is a similitude of truth. In the Cooley tradition, a sociologist would learn to be generous to the beautiful, complex ugliness of things as they are.

Himself a theorist, yet Cooley was hostile to theoretical system-builders. It seemed to him that they made gratuitously hard reading; they are "seldom worth the trouble," he concluded, in a rare ungenerous mood. More important, systematic theory departed too far from the jurisdiction of common sense. "An enduring philosophy must appeal to everyday, human modes of thinking." But precisely modern scientific theory ignores—and may even contradict—everyday modes of thinking. Common sense has no place in modern science, no more than in modern art. By placing a limit on the abstract and systematic character of theorizing, Cooley too closely fused pedagogic appeal and analytic value. He thought those writers appealed most and saw most deeply who were "not very systematic." Thus Cooley rationalized a certain disconnectedness in his own style. At the same time, by his discursive manner, Cooley knew exactly what he was trying to achieve: he aimed to shift perspectives regularly. "From every new point of view, new forms are revealed." I would take this as a usable motto for a statement about sociological method. For a sociologist must, I think, wield multiple analytic perspectives across actions and ideas that are themselves thus rendered multiple, and perhaps even contradictory, in meaning. Without this intellectual-aesthetic capacity, which includes quantitative procedures as one tool of vision among others, the sociologist cannot deal, as Cooley put it, "with life in its fullness." Instead, as has happened, the discipline is broken up into many little sciences of detail, never to be brought together into a larger art of interpretation. It is only from confrontations of diverse theories, supported by obedient armies of fact, that the social sciences can hope to achieve something like unity. Perhaps that unity can only exist in the capacity of the social scientist himself to use multiple analytic perspectives, and not in an apparently more substantial unity—which is merely another name for doctrine.

In the absence of a unifying doctrine, the social scientist needs to experiment permanently with multiple perspectives. For this experimental skill, he needs training in the history of abandoned doctrines and current methodologies—the latter being styles of analytic address in which the doctrinal motive has been repressed. More important, the social scientist, doctrinally uncommitted, needs the aesthetic gift, without which his analytic powers remain trivial. Cooley has the aesthetic gift. What he understands is beautifully understood, because for him "visible society is, indeed, literally a work of art . . . of inexhaustible beauty and fascination." Yet, throughout *Social Organization*, Cooley's intellectual-aesthetic capacity strains against his pedagogic intention. On the one hand, he communicates the complex and contradictory nature of his subject matter; on the other hand, he tries to use his gift to compel the reader to share in his uniting and serene vision of the self lying peacefully in the maternal bed of society. The picture is too pious for contemporary taste. There is too much warmth and security, not enough cold and desolation, precisely because it was Cooley's intention to bring his reader in out of the solitude Tocqueville described. Thus Cooley's projection of the concept of the "primary group" swiftly takes on a doctrinal cast. As an American sociologist, he could scarcely avoid constructing some mode of analysis that would substitute for beliefs that had once regulated conduct but now could not organize the basic human need to choose. It was Cooley's business to teach his readers that, in one important respect, they did not have a choice. In the old theology, God chooses man, no matter how man hides. In the new sociology, Society creates the self in its own image, however autonomous the self believes itself. The primary group is Cooley's God-term, at once the principle of analysis and that which is the object of analysis. As a work of doctrine, *Social Organization* is an effort to overcome the "discontinuous life" that had broken the connective tissue of community in urban, industrial America. Cooley was himself a village intellectual, trying to save city civilization from an historic incapacity to generate emotional warmth.

In the concept of the primary group, Cooley created another of those formal symbols in which American sociology abounds, at once the vehicle of address and that which is being addressed. By thus identifying social reality with its own analytic devices, sociology does what it can to alleviate the shortage of symbols that has impoverished American culture since the passing of the age of doctrine. Symbolic impoverishment, in the midst of material plenty, characterizes all post-religious cultures. Or, put differently, the symbols must grow more and more concrete, with specific powers assigned to them, as in primitive cultures. In modern culture, power has again passed into things; the world is again a pantheon of weapons, with science where animistic belief used to be. Against these idolatrous practices, sociology, like psychiatry, has succeeded to the preaching function.

Books such as "The Lonely Crowd," "The Affluent Society," "The Power Elite" communicate warnings against this technological primitivism: as works of social analysis, they are at the same time modes of moral chastisement.

Cooley is a more sanguine writer. His primary group is an image of hope rather than of foreboding; it is thus an authentic God-term, the symbol from which his entire analysis derives, which may itself be symbolized but cannot be displaced by a superior unit of analysis. Sociology is a collection of such analytic symbols. They help unify and enrich a symbolically impoverished world, enabling the secular to become the shadow of what once the sacred was. The subtle functional *oughts* of societies replaced the simple *isness* of gods. Salvations give way to controls. An ounce of prevention is worth a pound of redemption. Thus sociology "tends to cure pessimism," not in the old messianic way, "by promising a bright future," but in the new pan-social way, "by showing each one's life as member of a great process."

The great process is industrialization. Cooley insists that a culture on wheels, talking perpetually on the telephone, might bring together the selves set wandering by the whirring machine of an industrial civilization. He could still hope that the radio, and the automobile (and all that has followed since his time), would reestablish local culture on a national scale—as if television were the opportunity for a gigantic town meeting. Nothing of the sort has happened. On the contrary, Tolstoy's fear that a Genghis Khan would learn to use the telephone seems more realistic than Cooley's hope that many Thomas Jeffersons would be trained through the use of it. Cooley indulges in the paradoxical hope that precisely the spread of "mechanical conditions" into everyday life would create the "organic society." It seems more reasonable than ever, now, to assume that mechanical conditions tend to create mechanical societies. Television in the bedroom helps the members of even that sticky primary group ignore each other.

Furthermore, in a free society, the delicate capacity for making free and rational choices among the plentitudes is not trained when the alternatives are so much alike as "Laramie" and "Cheyenne." Nor are genuinely different alternatives themselves enough. Plenty of great books and good thoughts are available. But a corrupt audience can corrupt even the finest work of art. Being a democrat, Cooley never considered the problem of how to train a public to accept the authority of the good, true, or beautiful.

People draw together, not to see the show, really, but because they prefer any company to being alone. In the concept of the primary group, into which all men are born and which they always seek, Cooley proposed the eternal and unchanging form that would save the American individualist from demoralizing belief in himself alone. Togetherness, it seemed to Cooley, rendered the content of the getting together quite secondary, a mere occasion for the chance to exercise the primary ideals, the chief of which is togetherness itself.* The social

* Simmel expresses the notion of the intractable sociability of individuals in the following passage: "above and beyond their [specific] content, all . . . associations are accompanied by a feeling for, by a satisfaction in, the very fact that one is associated with others and that the solitariness of the individual is resolved into togetherness, a union of others." (See Georg Simmel, "The Sociology of Sociability", trans. Everett C. Hughes, *American Journal of Sociology,* LV, No. 3. November, 1949, pp. 254–61.)

good follows from sociability. "The improvement of society does not call for any essential change in human nature, but, chiefly, for a larger and higher application of its familiar impulses"—that is, the ideals of truth-telling, kindness and loyalty bred in the primary group. A larger togetherness is now possible, thanks to the mass media. Indeed, according to Cooley, if only the mass media would be reasonable and truthful, thus confirming the native moral sense, a good society might at last be created, quite without any special creed. He assumed that it would be sufficient to present the best abundantly and well. His trust in the mass media reflected a deeper disinclination to take into account the demonic in man. Cooley's sociology was a variety of the religion of culture to which the cultured resort after all other religions fail them.

Cooley found in the modern potential of social organization that "differentiated unity of mental and social life" which, to him, defines the good society. Indeed, social organization is the very form of love, giving to human nature its specific quality of humanity. The entire first part of this book concentrates on demonstrating the classical proposition that man is a social animal, against the profound American sentiment that opposes self and society. The primary group is thus an analytic symbol forwarding a case as old as Aristotle. Man owes the form of his individuality not to his own creative ego but to the creative collectivity. The self is the creative act of others. "I imagine your mind, and especially what your mind thinks of my mind, and what your mind thinks about what my mind thinks about your mind. I dress my mind before yours and expect that you will dress yours before mine." From this tight erotic weave of reciprocal imagining, both self and society achieve their unity; without this reciprocity, both self and society disintegrate internally, lacking the sense of obligation that makes life worth living. Yet the ethic of responsibility that Cooley derives from the mingling of self and other has no special content. There is no criterion of judgment beyond the group. Cooley's worry about this problem can be expressed in a quotation he once asked himself: "The group disciplines its membership, but who will discipline the group?" It is the question of a man who still hankers after some authority larger than his own group writ small. Rarely does Cooley resort to the exhausted rhetoric of conscience; he was too fine a social psychologist for that.

In the second part of *Social Organization*, Cooley tries to show the ways in which the symbolic form of everyday life is diffused and complicated in order to meet the exigencies of less intimate contacts among selves. It is the point at which all selves can be analyzed as others that the task of the sociologist begins. Cooley tried, by the personal force of his analytic understanding, to help extend the "primary ideals" (i.e., the sentiments generated by primary group living) into areas of society where they cannot be carried directly by primary groups themselves. Cooley's essential conservatism—and, indeed, the essential conservatism of sociology—is most evident here. Implicit in all his intellectual work is the purpose of preserving the ideal values of small, pre-industrial communities in the period of massive, industrial societies. Cooley defended the old values of his idealized America, no less than Orwell defended the values of his imagined old England.

In the third part of this book, titled "Social Disorganization," Cooley tried to cope with the breakup of the basic form, and also with its inherent deficiencies. He is aware that the primary group does not appear cohesive enough to sustain its ideals even for itself. Yet he has nothing to offer as a substitute for the primary group, as Marx did, for example, in the symbolic form resting upon his mystique of class struggle. In consequence, the third is by far the weakest part of this book. The liberal sociologist, hoping for the extension of truth-telling, kindness and loyalty through the remote psychological space of the great society, depended entirely on his esteem for democracy as a self-correcting convergence of private sentiments into a reasoned and socially concerned public opinion. Cooley's belief in social democracy—in a culture effectively improving itself despite the absence of an authoritative set of moral standard-bearers—no longer elicits quite the same response of confident agreement as it did in 1909, when his book first appeared. The "enlightened public" appears now, more certainly than ever before, a figment of Cooley's sociological imagination, his edifying mass media pathetic reminders of what might have been. *Social Organization* is a book full of such beautiful hallucinations. All the fragments of the American dream are there arranged in a way that was perhaps, in Cooley's time, still a possible truth. The dream has become a futile wish, protecting the ugliness of the American reality. From the warmth of Cooley's Primary Group there is a sinister short way to the stifling creed of Togetherness.

No more than individuals can societies live without

love. Having been trained in this true belief, Americans have taken on, as their second job, the search for love. Searching thus, self-consciously, they have found sex, personality, and other similar creeds which render them incapable of loving. Yet Cooley's fundamental point, in his sociological version of the truth that societies cannot live without love, is that the usefulness of creeds has long passed. In the future, as Cooley envisioned it, American unity would consist not in agreement, or creed, but in "organization." The very form of our private experience, if judiciously diffused, would supply us with our sense of unity. In the form Cooley gave to it, love is an anti-doctrine, opposing all relations of power, an enactment that needs no symbolism. The most ordinary life is always and everywhere the most extraordinary demonstration of love. All social action expresses devotion.

Perhaps the final weakness in Cooley's argument can be located in his assumption that men perfect themselves in acts of devotion—whatever the varieties of purpose to which they may be devoted. But this describes the action of only one among many possible personality types, once dominant in western culture: the ascetic. Cooley's entire sociology depends upon the persistence of the ascetic, as the dominant personality type. Early in the book, he assures his readers that "the fullest self-realization will belong to the one who embraces in a passionate self-feeling the aims of the fellowship, and spends his life in fighting for their attainment." Here is a straightforward sociological reading of the Christian injunction that he who loses himself in God will find himself.

Cooley's conception of love remains the ascetic one of sacrificial action. "One is never more human, and as a rule never happier," Cooley asserts, in the traditional way, "than when he is sacrificing his narrow and merely private interest to the higher call of the congenial group." The primary group offers the individual an introductory course in self-sacrifice, without which he can never advance to full participation in the city-state, the Germanic *comitatis*, the New Jerusalem, the working class movement, American democracy. "It is a poor sort of individual that does not feel the need to devote himself to the larger purposes of the group." Yet, just that poor sort has learned, the hard way, to suspect all larger purposes and higher calls. More precisely, the American individualist demands of all higher calls that are not merely conscriptions that they demonstrate their usefulness to his personal sense of well-being.

There are other, easier points of criticism that might be directed against Cooley. His faith in the binding quality of face-to-face relations is difficult to sustain, once the ambivalence of personal experience becomes as clear as Freud has made it. And, of course, "larger purposes" can be made to look rather ugly by reviewing them too close up. Nevertheless, knowing all this, Cooley refused to contribute to the immense and popular literature of disappointment, both in the self for continuing to make sacrifices and in society for continuing to demand them. Cooley had the rare insight that in a democratic culture the self could live only through a series of sacrifices. To the dominant, individualistic view this is a doctrine of "anti-life", as D. H. Lawrence once called it. But then, significantly enough, Lawrence was no democrat. So, to Lawrence, for example, "the greatest democrats, like Abraham Lincoln, had always a sacrificial, self-murdering note in their voices. American Democracy was a form of self-murder, always." *Social Organization* is a book seeking to protect the life of American democracy against its members. No more gently resolute argument for the superiority of what Lawrence called "self-murder" has been made by an American writer. Conservative and democratic, advocating the moral bind in a fresh and subtle way, Cooley is a very American sociologist. His successors have been more energetic collectors of empirical data, but none are more clever advocates of the search for community built into the analysis of society.

PREFACE

Our life is all one human whole, and if we are to have any real knowledge of it we must see it as such. If we cut it up it dies in the process: and so I conceive that the various branches of research that deal with this whole are properly distinguished by change in the point of sight rather than by any division in the thing that is seen. Accordingly, in a former book (Human Nature and Social Order), I tried to see society as it exists in the social nature of man and to display that in its main outlines. In this one the eye is focussed on the enlargement and diversification of intercourse which I have called Social Organization, the individual, though visible, remaining slightly in the background.

It will be seen from my title and all my treatment that I apprehend the subject on the mental rather than the material side. I by no means, however, overlook or wish to depreciate the latter, to which I am willing to ascribe all the importance that any one can require for it. Our task as students of society is a large one, and each of us, I suppose, may undertake any part of it to which he feels at all competent.

Ann Arbor, Mich., *February*, 1909.

PART I
PRIMARY ASPECTS OF ORGANIZATION

SOCIAL ORGANIZATION

CHAPTER I

SOCIAL AND INDIVIDUAL ASPECTS OF MIND

MIND AN ORGANIC WHOLE—CONSCIOUS AND UNCONSCIOUS RELA-
TIONS—DOES SELF-CONSCIOUSNESS COME FIRST? COGITO, ERGO
SUM—THE LARGER INTROSPECTION—SELF-CONSCIOUSNESS IN
CHILDREN—PUBLIC CONSCIOUSNESS.

MIND is an organic whole made up of coöperating
individualities, in somewhat the same way that the music
of an orchestra is made up of divergent but related sounds.
No one would think it necessary or reasonable to divide
the music into two kinds, that made by the whole and that
of particular instruments, and no more are there two kinds
of mind, the social mind and the individual mind. When
we study the social mind we merely fix our attention on
larger aspects and relations rather than on the narrower
ones of ordinary psychology.

The view that all mind acts together in a vital whole
from which the individual is never really separate flows
naturally from our growing knowledge of heredity and
suggestion, which makes it increasingly clear that every
thought we have is linked with the thought of our ancestors and associates, and through them with that of
society at large. It is also the only view consistent with

3

the general standpoint of modern science, which admits nothing isolate in nature.

The unity of the social mind consists not in agreement but in organization, in the fact of reciprocal influence or causation among its parts, by virtue of which everything that takes place in it is connected with everything else, and so is an outcome of the whole. Whether, like the orchestra, it gives forth harmony may be a matter of dispute, but that its sound, pleasing or otherwise, is the expression of a vital coöperation, cannot well be denied. Certainly everything that I say or think is influenced by what others have said or thought, and, in one way or another, sends out an influence of its own in turn.

This differentiated unity of mental or social life, present in the simplest intercourse but capable of infinite growth and adaptation, is what I mean in this work by social organization. It would be useless, I think, to attempt a more elaborate definition. We have only to open our eyes to *see* organization; and if we cannot do that no definition will help us.

In the social mind we may distinguish—very roughly of course—conscious and unconscious relations, the unconscious being those of which we are not aware, which for some reason escape our notice. A great part of the influences at work upon us are of this character: our language, our mechanical arts, our government and other institutions, we derive chiefly from people to whom we are but indirectly and unconsciously related. The larger movements of society—the progress and decadence of nations, institutions and races—have seldom been a

4

matter of consciousness until they were past. And although the growth of social consciousness is perhaps the greatest fact of history, it has still but a narrow and fallible grasp of human life.

Social consciousness, or awareness of society, is inseparable from self-consciousness, because we can hardly think of ourselves excepting with reference to a social group of some sort, or of the group except with reference to ourselves. The two things go together, and what we are really aware of is a more or less complex personal or social whole, of which now the particular, now the general, aspect is emphasized.

In general, then, most of our reflective consciousness, of our wide-awake state of mind, is social consciousness, because a sense of our relation to other persons, or of other persons to one another, can hardly fail to be a part of it. Self and society are twin-born, we know one as immediately as we know the other, and the notion of a separate and independent ego is an illusion.

This view, which seems to me quite simple and in accord with common-sense, is not the one most commonly held, for psychologists and even sociologists are still much infected with the idea that self-consciousness is in some way primary, and antecedent to social consciousness, which must be derived by some recondite process of combination or elimination. I venture, therefore, to give some further exposition of it, based in part on first-hand observation of the growth of social ideas in children.

Descartes is, I suppose, the best-known exponent of the traditional view regarding the primacy of self-consciousness. Seeking an unquestionable basis for philosophy, he thought that he found it in the proposition "I think, therefore I am" (*cogito, ergo sum*). This seemed to him inevitable, though all else might be illusion. "I observed," he says, "that, whilst I thus wished to think that all was false, it was absolutely necessary that I, who thus thought, should be somewhat; and as I observed that this truth, *I think, hence I am*, was so certain and of such evidence that no ground of doubt, however extravagant, could be alleged by the sceptics capable of shaking it, I concluded that I might, without scruple, accept it as the first principle of the philosophy of which I was in search."*

From our point of view this reasoning is unsatisfactory in two essential respects. In the first place it seems to imply that "I"-consciousness is a part of all consciousness, when, in fact, it belongs only to a rather advanced stage of development. In the second it is one-sided or "individualistic" in asserting the personal or "I" aspect to the exclusion of the social or "we" aspect, which is equally original with it.

Introspection is essential to psychological or social insight, but the introspection of Descartes was, in this instance, a limited, almost abnormal, sort of introspection —that of a self-absorbed philosopher doing his best to isolate himself from other people and from all simple and natural conditions of life. The mind into which he looked was in a highly technical state, not likely to give him a just view of human consciousness in general.

* Discourse on Method, part iv.

Introspection is of a larger sort in our day. There is a world of things in the mind worth looking at, and the modern psychologist, instead of fixing his attention wholly on an extreme form of speculative self-consciousness, puts his mind through an infinite variety of experiences, intellectual and emotional, simple and complex, normal and abnormal, sociable and private, recording in each case what he sees in it. He does this by subjecting it to suggestions or incitements of various kinds, which awaken the activities he desires to study.

In particular he does it largely by what may be called *sympathetic introspection*, putting himself into intimate contact with various sorts of persons and allowing them to awake in himself a life similar to their own, which he afterwards, to the best of his ability, recalls and describes. In this way he is more or less able to understand—always by introspection—children, idiots, criminals, rich and poor, conservative and radical—any phase of human nature not wholly alien to his own.

This I conceive to be the principal method of the social psychologist.

One thing which this broader introspection reveals is that the "I"-consciousness does not explicitly appear until the child is, say, about two years old, and that when it does appear it comes in inseparable conjunction with the consciousness of other persons and of those relations which make up a social group. It is in fact simply one phase of a body of personal thought which is self-consciousness in one aspect and social consciousness in another.

7

The mental experience of a new-born child is probably a mere stream of impressions, which may be regarded as being individual, in being differentiated from any other stream, or as social, in being an undoubted product of inheritance and suggestion from human life at large; but is not aware either of itself or of society.

Very soon, however, the mind begins to discriminate personal impressions and to become both naïvely self-conscious and naïvely conscious of society; that is, the child is aware, in an unreflective way, of a group and of his own special relation to it. He does not say "I" nor does he name his mother, his sister or his nurse, but he has images and feelings out of which these ideas will grow. Later comes the more reflective consciousness which names both himself and other people, and brings a fuller perception of the relations which constitute the unity of this small world.*

And so on to the most elaborate phases of self-consciousness and social consciousness, to the metaphysician pondering the Ego, or the sociologist meditating on the Social Organism. Self and society go together, as phases

* There is much interest and significance in the matter of children's first learning the use of "I" and other self-words—just how they learn them and what they mean by them. Some discussion of the matter, based on observation of two children, will be found in Human Nature and the Social Order; and more recently I have published a paper in the Psychological Review (November, 1908) called A Study of the Early Use of Self-Words by a Child. "I" seems to mean primarily the assertion of will in a social medium of which the child is conscious and of which his "I" is an inseparable part. It is thus a social idea and, as stated in the text, arises by differentiation of a vague body of personal thought which is self-consciousness in one phase and social consciousness in another. It has no necessary reference to the body.

of a common whole. I am aware of the social groups in which I live as immediately and authentically as I am aware of myself; and Descartes might have said "We think," *cogitamus*, on as good grounds as he said *cogito*.

But, it may be said, this very consciousness that you are considering is after all located in a particular person, and so are all similar consciousnesses, so that what we see, if we take an objective view of the matter, is merely an aggregate of individuals, however social those individuals may be. Common-sense, most people think, assures us that the separate person is the primary fact of life.

If so, is it not because common-sense has been trained by custom to look at one aspect of things and not another? Common-sense, moderately informed, assures us that the individual has his being only as part of a whole. What does not come by heredity comes by communication and intercourse; and the more closely we look the more apparent it is that separateness is an illusion of the eye and community the inner truth. "Social organism," using the term in no abstruse sense but merely to mean a vital unity in human life, is a fact as obvious to enlightened common-sense as individuality.

I do not question that the individual is a differentiated centre of psychical life, having a world of his own into which no other individual can fully enter; living in a stream of thought in which there is nothing quite like that in any other stream, neither his "I," nor his "you," nor his "we," nor even any material object; all, probably, as they exist for him, have something unique about them. But this uniqueness is no more apparent and verifiable than the fact—not at all inconsistent with it—that he is

9

in the fullest sense member of a whole, appearing such not only to scientific observation but also to his own un-trained consciousness.

There is then no mystery about social consciousness. The view that there is something recondite about it and that it must be dug for with metaphysics and drawn forth from the depths of speculation, springs from a failure to grasp adequately the social nature of all higher conscious-ness. What we need in this connection is only a better seeing and understanding of rather ordinary and familiar facts.

We may view social consciousness either in a particular mind or as a coöperative activity of many minds. The social ideas that I have are closely connected with those that other people have, and act and react upon them to form a whole. This gives us public consciousness, or to use a more familiar term, public opinion, in the broad sense of a group state of mind which is more or less distinctly aware of itself. By this last phrase I mean such a mutual understanding of one another's points of view on the part of the individuals or groups concerned as naturally results from discussion. There are all degrees of this awareness in the various individuals. Generally speaking, it never embraces the whole in all its complexity, but almost al-ways some of the relations that enter into the whole. The more intimate the communication of a group the more complete, the more thoroughly knit together into a living whole, is its public consciousness.

In a congenial family life, for example, there may be a public consciousness which brings all the important thoughts and feelings of the members into such a living and coöperative whole. In the mind of each member, also, this same thing exists as a social consciousness embracing a vivid sense of the personal traits and modes of thought and feeling of the other members. And, finally, quite inseparable from all this, is each one's consciousness of himself, which is largely a direct reflection of the ideas about himself he attributes to the others, and is directly or indirectly altogether a product of social life. Thus all consciousness hangs together, and the distinctions are chiefly based on point of view.

The unity of public opinion, like all vital unity, is one not of agreement but of organization, of interaction and mutual influence. It is true that a certain underlying likeness of nature is necessary in order that minds may influence one another and so coöperate in forming a vital whole, but identity, even in the simplest process, is unnecessary and probably impossible. The consciousness of the American House of Representatives, for example, is by no means limited to the common views, if there are any, shared by its members, but embraces the whole consciousness of every member so far as this deals with the activity of the House. It would be a poor conception of the whole which left out the opposition, or even one dissentient individual. That all minds are different is a condition, not an obstacle, to the unity that consists in a differentiated and coöperative life.

Here is another illustration of what is meant by individual and collective aspects of social consciousness. Some of us possess a good many books relating to social questions of the day. Each of these books, considered by

11

itself, is the expression of a particular social consciousness; the author has cleared up his ideas as well as he can and printed them. But a library of such books expresses social consciousness in a larger sense; it speaks for the epoch. And certainly no one who reads the books will doubt that they form a whole, whatever their differences. The radical and the reactionist are clearly part of the same general situation.

There are, then, at least three aspects of consciousness which we may usefully distinguish: self-consciousness, or what I think of myself; social consciousness (in its individual aspect), or what I think of other people; and public consciousness, or a collective view of the foregoing as organized in a communicating group. And all three are phases of a single whole.

CHAPTER II

SOCIAL AND INDIVIDUAL ASPECTS OF MIND—*Continued.*

Moral Aspect of the Organic View—It Implies that Reform
Should Be Based on Sympathy—Uses of Praise and Blame
—Responsibility Broadened but not Lost—Moral Value
of a Larger View—Organic Morality Calls for Knowledge
—Nature of Social Organization.

So far as the moral aspect is concerned, it should be
the result of this organic view of mind to make the whole
teaching and practice of righteousness more rational and
effectual by bringing it closer to fact. A moral view
which does not see the individual in living unity with social
wholes is unreal and apt to lead to impractical results.

Have not the moral philosophies of the past missed
their mark, in great part, by setting before the individual
absolute standards of behavior, without affording him an
explanation for his backwardness or a programme for his
gradual advance? And did not this spring from not dis-
cerning clearly that the moral life was a social organism,
in which every individual or group of individuals had its
own special possibilities and limitations? In general
such systems, pagan and Christian, have said, "All of
us ought to be so and so, but since very few of us are, this
is evidently a bad world." And they have had no large,
well-organized, slow-but-sure plan for making it better.
Impracticable standards have the same ill effect as unen-
forcible law; they accustom us to separate theory from
practice and make a chasm between the individual and
the moral ideal.

13

The present way of thinking tends to close up this chasm and bring both persons and ideals into more intelligible relations to real life. The sins or virtues of the individual, it seems, are never fortuitous or disconnected; they have always a history and collateral support, and are in fact more or less pleasing phases of a struggling, aspiring whole. The ideals are also parts of the whole; states of being, achieved momentarily by those in front and treasured for the animation and solace of all. And the method of righteousness is to understand as well as may be the working of this whole and of all its parts, and to form and pursue practicable ideals based on this understanding. It is always to be taken for granted that there is no real break with history and environment. Each individual may be required to put forth a steadfast endeavor to make himself and his surroundings better, but not to achieve a standard unconnected with his actual state. And the same principle applies to special groups of all sorts, including nations, races, and religions; their progress must be along a natural line of improvement suggested by what they are. We are thus coming under the sway of that relative spirit, of which, says Walter Pater, "the ethical result is a delicate and tender justice in the criticism of human life."*

According to this, real reform must be sympathetic; that is, it must begin, not with denunciation—though that may have its uses—but with an intimate appreciation of things as they are, and should proceed in a spirit opposite to that in which we have commonly attacked such ques-

* See his essay on Coleridge.

14

tions as the suppression of intemperance and the conversion of the heathen.

Human nature, it appears, is very much the same in those we reckon sinners as in ourselves. Good and evil are always intimately bound up together; no sort of men are chiefly given over to conscious badness; and to abuse men or groups in the large is unjust and generally futile. As a rule the practical method is to study closely and kindly the actual situation, with the people involved in it; then gradually and carefully to work out the evil from the mixture by substituting good for it. No matter how mean or hideous a man's life is, the first thing is to understand him; to make out just how it is that our common human nature has come to work out in this way. This method calls for patience, insight, firmness, and confidence in men, leaving little room for the denunciatory egotism of a certain kind of reformers. It is more and more coming to be used in dealing with intemperance, crime, greed, and in fact all those matters in which we try to make ourselves and our neighbors better. I notice that the most effectual leaders of philanthropy have almost ceased from denunciation. Tacitly assuming that there are excuses for everything, they "shun the negative side" and spend their energy in building up the affirmative.

This sort of morality does not, however, dispense with praise and blame, which are based on the necessity of upholding higher ideals by example, and discrediting lower ones. All such distinctions get their meaning from their relation to an upward-striving general life, wherein conspicuous men serve as symbols through which the higher structure may be either supported or undermined. We must have heroes, and perhaps villains (though it is better not to think much about the latter), even though their performances, when closely viewed, appear to be an equally natural product of history and environment. In short it makes a difference whether we judge a man with reference to his special history and "lights," or to the larger life of the world; and it is right to assign exemplary praise or blame on the latter ground which would be unwarranted on the former. There is certainly a special right for every man; but the right of most men is partial, important chiefly to themselves and their immediate sphere; while there are some whose right is representative, like that of Jesus, fit to guide the moral thought of mankind; and we cherish and revere these latter because they corroborate the ideals we wish to hold before us.

It matters little for these larger purposes whether the sins or virtues of conspicuous persons are conscious or not; our concern is with what they stand for in the general mind. In fact conscious wickedness is comparatively unimportant, because it implies that the individual is divided in his own mind, and therefore weak. The most effective ill-doers believe in themselves and have a quiet conscience. And, in the same way, goodness is most effectual when it takes itself as a matter of course and feels no self-complacency.

Blame and punishment, then, are essentially symbolic, their function being to define and enforce the public will, and in no way imply that the offenders are of a different nature from the rest of us. We feel it to be true that with a little different training and surroundings we might have

16

committed almost any crime for which men are sent to prison, and can readily understand that criminals should not commonly feel that they are worse than others. The same principle applies to those malefactors, more dangerous perhaps, who keep within the law, and yet are terribly punished from time to time by public opinion.

Perhaps it would be well if both those who suffer punishment and those who inflict it were more distinctly aware of its symbolic character and function. The former might find their sense of justice appeased by perceiving that though what they did was natural and perhaps not consciously wrong, it may still need to be discredited and atoned for. The culprit is not separated from society by his punishment, but restored to it. It is his way of service; and if he takes it in the right spirit he is better off than those who do wrong but are not punished.

The rest of us, on the other hand, might realize that those in the pillory are our representatives, who suffer, in a real sense, for us. This would disincline us to spend in a cheap abuse of conspicuous offenders that moral ardor whose proper function is the correction of our own life. The spectacle of punishment is not for us to gloat over, but to remind us of our sins, which, as springing from the same nature and society, are sure to be much the same as that of the one punished. It is precisely because he is like us that he is punished. If he were radically different he would belong in an insane asylum, and punishment would be mere cruelty.

Under the larger view of mind responsibility is broadened, because we recognize a broader reach of causation, but

17

by no means lost in an abstract "society." It goes with power and increases rapidly in proportion as the evil comes nearer the sphere of the individual's voluntary action, so that each of us is peculiarly responsible for the moral state of his own trade, family, or social connection. Contrary to a prevalent impression, it is in these familiar relations that the individual is least of all justified in being no better than his environment.

Every act of the will, especially where the will is most at home, should be affirmative and constructive; it being the function and meaning of individuality that each one should be, in the direction of his chief activities, something other and better than his surroundings. Once admit the plea "I may do what other people do," and the basis of righteousness is gone; perhaps there is no moral fallacy so widespread and so pernicious as this. It is these no-worse-than-other-people decisions that paralyze the moral life in the one and in the whole, involving a sort of moral *panmixia*, as the biologists say, which, lacking any progressive impulse, must result in deterioration. In the end it will justify anything, since there are always bad examples to fall back upon.

It is commonly futile, however, to require any sharp break with the past; we must be content with an upward endeavor and tendency. It is quite true that we are all involved in a net of questionable practices from which we can only escape a little at a time and in coöperation with our associates.

It is an error to imagine that the doctrine of individual responsibility is always the expedient and edifying one in matters of conduct.   There is a sort of people who grow indignant whenever general causes are insisted upon, apparently convinced that whether these are real or not it is immoral to believe in them.   But it is not invariably a good thing to urge the will, since this, if overstimulated, becomes fagged, stale, and discouraged.   Often it is better that one should let himself go, and trust himself to the involuntary forces, to the nature of things, to God.   The nervous or strained person only harasses and weakens his will by fixing attention upon it: it will work on more effectually if he looks away from it, calming himself by a view of the larger whole;   and not without reason Spinoza counts among the advantages of determinism "the attainment of happiness by man through realizing his intimate union with the whole nature of things; the distinction between things in our power and things not in our power; the avoidance of all disturbing passions, and the performance of social duties from rational desire for the common good."*

An obvious moral defect of the unbalanced doctrine of responsibility is that it permits the successful to despise the unfortunate, in the belief that the latter "have only themselves to blame," a belief not countenanced by the larger view of fact.   We may pardon this doctrine when it makes one too hard on himself or on successful wrong-doers, but as a rod with which to beat those already down it is despicable.

The annals of religion show that the moral life has always these two aspects, the particular and the general, as in the doctrines of freedom and predestination, or in

* Pollock's Spinoza, 2d ed., 195.

19

the wrestlings with sin followed by self-abandonment that we find in the literature of conversion.* Perhaps we may say that the deterministic attitude is morally good in at least two classes of cases: First, for nervous, conscientious individuals, like Spinoza, whose wills need rather calming than stimulating, also for any one who may be even temporarily in a state of mental strain; second, in dealing on a large scale with social or moral questions whose causes must be treated dispassionately and in a mass.

These questions of free-will *versus* law, and the like, are but little, if at all, questions of fact—when we get down to definite facts bearing upon the matter we find little or no disagreement—but of point of view and emphasis. If you fix attention on the individual phase of things and see life as a theatre of personal action, then the corresponding ideas of private will, responsibility, praise, and blame rise before you; if you regard its total aspect you see tendency, evolution, law and impersonal grandeur. Each of these is a half truth needing to be completed by the other; the larger truth, including both, being that life is an organic whole, presenting itself with equal reality in individual and general aspects. Argument upon such questions is without limit—since there is really nothing

* Amply expounded, with due stress on the moral value of letting-go, by William James, in his Varieties of Religious Experience: "This abandonment of self-responsibility seems to be the fundamental act in specifically religious, as distinguished from moral practice. It antedates theologies and is independent of philosophies . . . it is capable of entering into closest marriage with every speculative creed." Page 289.

at issue—and in that sense the problem of freedom *versus* law is insoluble.

Above all, the organic view of mind calls for· social knowledge as the basis of morality. We live in a system, and to achieve right ends, or any rational ends whatever, we must learn to understand that system. The public mind must emerge somewhat from its subconscious condition and know and guide its own processes.

Both consciously and unconsciously the larger mind is continually building itself up into wholes—fashions, traditions, institutions, tendencies, and the like—which spread and diversify like the branches of a tree, and so generate an ever higher and more various structure of differentiated thought and symbols. The immediate motor and guide of this growth is interest, and wherever that points social structure comes into being, as a picture grows where the artist moves his pencil. Visible society is, indeed, literally, a work of art, slow and mostly subconscious in its production—as great art often is—full of grotesque and wayward traits, but yet of inexhaustible beauty and fascination. It is this we find in the history of old civilizations, getting from it the completed work of the artist without that strain and confusion of production which defaces the present. We get it, especially, not from the history of the theorist or the statistician, but from the actual, naïve, human record to be found in memoirs, in popular literature, in architecture, painting, sculpture, and music, in the industrial arts, in every unforced product of the mind. Social organization is nothing less than this variega-

21

tion of life, taken in the widest sense possible. It should not be conceived as the product merely of definite and utilitarian purpose, but as the total expression of conscious and subconscious tendency, the slow crystallization in many forms and colors of the life of the human spirit.

Any fairly distinct and durable detail of this structure may be called a social type; this being a convenient term to use when we wish to break up the whole into parts, for analysis or description. Thus there are types of personality, of political structure, of religion, of classes, of the family, of art, of language; also of processes, like communication, coöperation, and competition; and so on. The whole is so various that from every new point of view new forms are revealed. Social types are analogous to the genera, species, and varieties of the animal world, in being parts of one living whole and yet having a relative continuity and distinctness which is susceptible of detailed study. Like biological types, also, they exist in related systems and orders, are subject to variation, compete with one another, flourish and decay, may be flexible or rigid, and may or may not form prolific crosses with one another.

Without forgetting to see life as individuals, we must learn to see it also as types, processes, organization, the latter being just as real as the former. And especially, in order to see the matter truly, should we be able to interpret individuals by wholes, and *vice versa*.

CHAPTER III

PRIMARY GROUPS

MEANING OF PRIMARY GROUPS—FAMILY, PLAYGROUND, AND NEIGH-
BORHOOD—HOW FAR INFLUENCED BY LARGER SOCIETY—MEAN-
ING AND PERMANENCE OF "HUMAN NATURE"—PRIMARY
GROUPS THE NURSERY OF HUMAN NATURE.

By primary groups I mean those characterized by intimate face-to-face association and coöperation. They are
primary in several senses, but chiefly in that they are
fundamental in forming the social nature and ideals of
the individual. The result of intimate association, psychologically, is a certain fusion of individualities in a common
whole, so that one's very self, for many purposes at least,
is the common life and purpose of the group. Perhaps the
simplest way of describing this wholeness is by saying that
it is a "we"; it involves the sort of sympathy and mutual
identification for which "we" is the natural expression.
One lives in the feeling of the whole and finds the chief
aims of his will in that feeling.

It is not to be supposed that the unity of the primary
group is one of mere harmony and love. It is always a
differentiated and usually a competitive unity, admitting of
self-assertion and various appropriative passions; but
these passions are socialized by sympathy, and come, or
tend to come, under the discipline of a common spirit.
The individual will be ambitious, but the chief object of

23

his ambition will be some desired place in the thought of the others, and he will feel allegiance to common standards of service and fair play. So the boy will dispute with his fellows a place on the team, but above such disputes will place the common glory of his class and school.

The most important spheres of this intimate association and coöperation—though by no means the only ones—are the family, the play-group of children, and the neighborhood or community group of elders. These are practically universal, belonging to all times and all stages of development; and are accordingly a chief basis of what is universal in human nature and human ideals. The best comparative studies of the family, such as those of Westermarck* or Howard,† show it to us as not only a universal institution, but as more alike the world over than the exaggeration of exceptional customs by an earlier school had led us to suppose. Nor can any one doubt the general prevalence of play-groups among children or of informal assemblies of various kinds among their elders. Such association is clearly the nursery of human nature in the world about us, and there is no apparent reason to suppose that the case has anywhere or at any time been essentially different.

As regards play, I might, were it not a matter of common observation, multiply illustrations of the universality and spontaneity of the group discussion and coöperation to which it gives rise. The general fact is that children, especially boys after about their twelfth year, live in fellow-

* The History of Human Marriage.
† A History of Matrimonial Institutions.

EX LIBRIS
James H. Mahon

ships in which their sympathy, ambition and honor are engaged even more, often, than they are in the family. Most of us can recall examples of the endurance by boys of injustice and even cruelty, rather than appeal from their fellows to parents or teachers—as, for instance, in the hazing so prevalent at schools, and so difficult, for this very reason, to repress. And how elaborate the discussion, how cogent the public opinion, how hot the ambitions in these fellowships.

Nor is this facility of juvenile association, as is sometimes supposed, a trait peculiar to English and American boys; since experience among our immigrant population seems to show that the offspring of the more restrictive civilizations of the continent of Europe form self-governing play-groups with almost equal readiness. Thus Miss Jane Addams, after pointing out that the "gang" is almost universal, speaks of the interminable discussion which every detail of the gang's activity receives, remarking that "in these social folk-motes, so to speak, the young citizen learns to act upon his own determination."*

Of the neighborhood group it may be said, in general, that from the time men formed permanent settlements upon the land, down, at least, to the rise of modern industrial cities, it has played a main part in the primary, heart-to-heart life of the people. Among our Teutonic forefathers the village community was apparently the chief sphere of sympathy and mutual aid for the commons all through the "dark" and middle ages, and for many purposes it remains so in rural districts at the present day. In some countries we still find it with all its ancient vi-

* Newer Ideals of Peace, 177.

25

tality, notably in Russia, where the mir, or self-governing village group, is the main theatre of life, along with the family, for perhaps fifty millions of peasants.

In our own life the intimacy of the neighborhood has been broken up by the growth of an intricate mesh of wider contacts which leaves us strangers to people who live in the same house. And even in the country the same principle is at work, though less obviously, diminishing our economic and spiritual community with our neighbors. How far this change is a healthy development, and how far a disease, is perhaps still uncertain.

Besides these almost universal kinds of primary association, there are many others whose form depends upon the particular state of civilization; the only essential thing, as I have said, being a certain intimacy and fusion of personalities. In our own society, being little bound by place, people easily form clubs, fraternal societies and the like, based on congeniality, which may give rise to real intimacy. Many such relations are formed at school and college, and among men and women brought together in the first instance by their occupations—as workmen in the same trade, or the like. Where there is a little common interest and activity, kindness grows like weeds by the roadside.

But the fact that the family and neighborhood groups are ascendant in the open and plastic time of childhood makes them even now incomparably more influential than all the rest.

Primary groups are primary in the sense that they give the individual his earliest and completest experience

26

of social unity, and also in the sense that they do not change in the same degree as more elaborate relations, but form a comparatively permanent source out of which the latter are ever springing. Of course they are not independent of the larger society, but to some extent reflect its spirit; as the German family and the German school bear somewhat distinctly the print of German militarism. But this, after all, is like the tide setting back into creeks, and does not commonly go very far. Among the German, and still more among the Russian, peasantry are found habits of free coöperation and discussion almost uninfluenced by the character of the state; and it is a familiar and well-supported view that the village commune, self-governing as regards local affairs and habituated to discussion, is a very widespread institution in settled communities, and the continuator of a similar autonomy previously existing in the clan. "It is man who makes monarchies and establishes republics, but the commune seems to come directly from the hand of God."*

In our own cities the crowded tenements and the general economic and social confusion have sorely wounded the family and the neighborhood, but it is remarkable, in view of these conditions, what vitality they show; and there is nothing upon which the conscience of the time is more determined than upon restoring them to health.

These groups, then, are springs of life, not only for the individual but for social institutions. They are only in part moulded by special traditions, and, in larger degree, express a universal nature. The religion or government of other civilizations may seem alien to us, but the chil-

* De Tocqueville, Democracy in America, vol. i, chap. 5.

dren or the family group wear the common life, and with them we can always make ourselves at home.

By human nature, I suppose, we may understand those sentiments and impulses that are human in being superior to those of lower animals, and also in the sense that they belong to mankind at large, and not to any particular race or time. It means, particularly, sympathy and the innumerable sentiments into which sympathy enters, such as love, resentment, ambition, vanity, hero-worship, and the feeling of social right and wrong.*

Human nature in this sense is justly regarded as a comparatively permanent element in society. Always and everywhere men seek honor and dread ridicule, defer to public opinion, cherish their goods and their children, and admire courage, generosity, and success. It is always safe to assume that people are and have been human.

It is true, no doubt, that there are differences of race capacity, so great that a large part of mankind are possibly incapable of any high kind of social organization. But these differences, like those among individuals of the same race, are subtle, depending upon some obscure intellectual deficiency, some want of vigor, or slackness of moral fibre, and do not involve unlikeness in the generic impulses of human nature. In these all races are very much alike. The more insight one gets into the life of savages, even those that are reckoned the lowest, the more human, the more like ourselves, they appear. Take for instance the natives of Central Australia, as described

* These matters are expounded at some length in the writer's Human Nature and the Social Order.

28

by Spencer and Gillen,* tribes having no definite government or worship and scarcely able to count to five. They are generous to one another, emulous of virtue as they understand it, kind to their children and to the aged, and by no means harsh to women. Their faces as shown in the photographs are wholly human and many of them attractive.

And when we come to a comparison between different stages in the development of the same race, between ourselves, for instance, and the Teutonic tribes of the time of Cæsar, the difference is neither in human nature nor in capacity, but in organization, in the range and complexity of relations, in the diverse expression of powers and passions essentially much the same.

There is no better proof of this generic likeness of human nature than in the ease and joy with which the modern man makes himself at home in literature depicting the most remote and varied phases of life—in Homer, in the Nibelung tales, in the Hebrew Scriptures, in the legends of the American Indians, in stories of frontier life, of soldiers and sailors, of criminals and tramps, and so on. The more penetratingly any phase of human life is studied the more an essential likeness to ourselves is revealed.

To return to primary groups: the view here maintained is that human nature is not something existing separately in the individual, but a *group-nature or primary phase of society*, a relatively simple and general condition

* The Native Tribes of Central Australia. Compare also Darwin's views and examples given in chap. 7 of his Descent of Man.

of the social mind. It is something more, on the one hand, than the mere instinct that is born in us—though that enters into it—and something less, on the other, than the more elaborate development of ideas and sentiments that makes up institutions. It is the nature which is developed and expressed in those simple, face-to-face groups that are somewhat alike in all societies; groups of the family, the playground, and the neighborhood. In the essential similarity of these is to be found the basis, in experience, for similar ideas and sentiments in the human mind. In these, everywhere, human nature comes into existence. Man does not have it at birth; he cannot acquire it except through fellowship, and it decays in isolation.

If this view does not recommend itself to common-sense I do not know that elaboration will be of much avail. It simply means the application at this point of the idea that society and individuals are inseparable phases of a common whole, so that wherever we find an individual fact we may look for a social fact to go with it. If there is a universal nature in persons there must be something universal in association to correspond to it.

What else can human nature be than a trait of primary groups? Surely not an attribute of the separate individual—supposing there were any such thing—since its typical characteristics, such as affection, ambition, vanity, and resentment, are inconceivable apart from society. If it belongs, then, to man in association, what kind or degree of association is required to develop it? Evidently nothing elaborate, because elaborate phases of society are transient and diverse, while human nature is compara-

30

tively stable and universal.   In short the family and neighborhood life is essential to its genesis and nothing more is.

Here as everywhere in the study of society we must learn to see mankind in psychical wholes, rather than in artificial separation.   We must see and feel the communal life of family and local groups as immediate facts, not as combinations of something else.   And perhaps we shall do this best by recalling our own experience and extending it through sympathetic observation.   What, in our life, is the family and the fellowship; what do we know of the we-feeling?   Thought of this kind may help us to get a concrete perception of that primary group-nature of which everything social is the outgrowth.

CHAPTER IV

PRIMARY IDEALS

NATURE OF PRIMARY IDEALISM—THE IDEAL OF A "WE" OR MORAL
UNITY—IT DOES NOT EXCLUDE SELF-ASSERTION—IDEALS
SPRINGING FROM HOSTILITY—LOYALTY, TRUTH, SERVICE—
KINDNESS—LAWFULNESS—FREEDOM—THE DOCTRINE OF NAT-
URAL RIGHT—BEARING OF PRIMARY IDEALISM UPON EDUCATION
AND PHILANTHROPY.

LIFE in the primary groups gives rise to social ideals
which, as they spring from similar experiences, have much
in common throughout the human race.   And these naturally become the motive and test of social progress.   Under
all systems men strive, however blindly, to realize objects
suggested by the familiar experience of primary association.

Where do we get our notions of love, freedom, justice,
and the like which we are ever applying to social institutions?   Not from abstract philosophy, surely, but from
the actual life of simple and widespread forms of society,
like the family or the play-group.   In these relations
mankind realizes itself, gratifies its primary needs, in a
fairly satisfactory manner, and from the experience forms
standards of what it is to expect from more elaborate
association.   Since groups of this sort are never obliterated
from human experience, but flourish more or less under
all kinds of institutions, they remain an enduring criterion
by which the latter are ultimately judged.

Of course these simpler relations are not uniform for

32

all societies, but vary considerably with race, with the general state of civilization, and with the particular sort of institutions that may prevail. The primary groups themselves are subject to improvement and decay, and need to be watched and cherished with a very special care.

Neither is it claimed that, at the best, they realize ideal conditions; only that they approach them more nearly than anything else in general experience, and so form the practical basis on which higher imaginations are built. They are not always pleasant or righteous, but they almost always contain elements from which ideals of pleasantness and righteousness may be formed.

The ideal that grows up in familiar association may be said to be a part of human nature itself. In its most general form it is that of a moral whole or community wherein individual minds are merged and the higher capacities of the members find total and adequate expression. And it grows up because familiar association fills our minds with imaginations of the thought and feeling of other members of the group, and of the group as a whole, so that, for many purposes, we really make them a part of ourselves and identify our self-feeling with them.

Children and savages do not formulate any such ideal, but they have it nevertheless; they see it; they see themselves and their fellows as an indivisible, though various, "we," and they desire this "we" to be harmonious, happy, and successful. How heartily one may merge himself in the family and in the fellowships of youth is perhaps within the experience of all of us; and we come to feel that the same spirit should extend to our country,

33

our race, our world. "All the abuses which are the objects of reform . . . are unconsciously amended in the intercourse of friends." *

A congenial family life is the immemorial type of moral unity, and source of many of the terms—such as brotherhood, kindness, and the like—which describe it. The members become merged by intimate association into a whole wherein each age and sex participates in its own way. Each lives in imaginative contact with the minds of the others, and finds in them the dwelling-place of his social self, of his affections, ambitions, resentments, and standards of right and wrong. Without uniformity, there is yet unity, a free, pleasant, wholesome, fruitful, common life.

As to the playground, Mr. Joseph Lee, in an excellent paper on Play as a School of the Citizen, gives the following account of the merging of the one in the whole that may be learned from sport. The boy, he says,

"is deeply participating in a common purpose. The team and the plays that it executes are present in a very vivid manner to his consciousness. His conscious individuality is more thoroughly lost in the sense of membership than perhaps it ever becomes in any other way. So that the sheer experience of citizenship in its simplest and essential form—of the sharing in a public consciousness, of having the social organization present as a controlling ideal in your heart—is very intense. . .

Along with the sense of the team as a mechanical instrument, and unseparated from it in the boy's mind, is the consciousness of it as the embodiment of a common purpose. There is in team play a very intimate experience of the ways in which such a purpose is built up and made effective. You feel, though without analysis, the subtle ways in which a single strong character breaks out the road ahead

* Thoreau, A Week on the Concord and Merrimack Rivers, 283.

and gives confidence to the rest to follow; how the creative power of one ardent imagination, bravely sustained, makes possible the putting through of the play as he conceives it. You feel to the marrow of your bones how each loyal member contributes to the salvation of all the others by holding the conception of the whole play so firmly in his mind as to enable them to hold it, and to participate in his single-minded determination to see it carried out. You have intimate experience of the ways in which individual members contribute to the team and of how the team, in turn, builds up their spiritual nature . . .

And the team is not only an extension of the player's consciousness; it is a part of his personality. His participation has deepened from coöperation to membership. Not only is he now a part of the team, but the team is a part of him."*

Moral unity, as this illustration implies, admits and rewards strenuous ambition; but this ambition must either be for the success of the group, or at least not inconsistent with that. The fullest self-realization will belong to the one who embraces in a passionate self-feeling the aims of the fellowship, and spends his life in fighting for their attainment.

The ideal of moral unity I take to be the mother, as it were, of all social ideals.

It is, then, not my aim to depreciate the self-assertive passions. I believe that they are fierce, inextinguishable, indispensable. Competition and the survival of the fittest are as righteous as kindness and coöperation, and not necessarily opposed to them: an adequate view will embrace and harmonize these diverse aspects. The point I wish particularly to bring out in this chapter is that the normal self is moulded in primary groups to be a social

* Charities and the Commons, Aug. 3, 1907.

self whose ambitions are formed by the common thought of the group.

In their crudest form such passions as lust, greed, revenge, the pride of power and the like are not, distinctively, *human* nature at all, but animal nature, and so far as we rise into the spirit of family or neighborhood association we control and subordinate them. They are rendered human only so far as they are brought under the discipline of sympathy, and refined into sentiments, such as love, resentment, and ambition. And in so far as they are thus humanized they become capable of useful function.

Take the greed of gain, for example, the ancient sin of avarice, the old wolf, as Dante says, that gets more prey than all the other beasts.* The desire of possession is in itself a good thing, a phase of self-realization and a cause of social improvement. It is immoral or greedy only when it is without adequate control from sympathy, when the self realized is a narrow self. In that case it is a vice of isolation or weak social consciousness, and indicates a state of mind intermediate between the brutal and the fully human or moral, when desire is directed toward social objects—wealth or power—but is not social in its attitude toward others who desire the same objects. Intimate association has the power to allay greed. One will hardly be greedy as against his family or close friends, though very decent people will be so as against almost any one else. Every one must have noticed that after

* Antica lupa,
Che piu che tutte l'altre bestie hai preda.
Purgatorio, xx, 10.

36

frank association, even of a transient character, with another person, one usually has a sense of kindred with him which makes one ashamed to act greedily at his expense.

Those who dwell preponderantly upon the selfish aspect of human nature and flout as sentimentalism the "altruistic" conception of it, make their chief error in failing to see that our self itself is altruistic, that the object of our higher greed is some desired place in the minds of other men, and that through this it is possible to enlist ordinary human nature in the service of ideal aims. The improvement of society does not call for any essential change in human nature, but, chiefly, for a larger and higher application of its familiar impulses.

I know, also, that the most truculent behavior may be exalted into an ideal, like the ferocity of Samuel, when he hewed Agag to pieces before the Lord,* or of the orthodox Christian of a former age in the destruction of heretics. In general there is always a morality of opposition, springing from the need of the sympathetic group to assert itself in the struggle for existence. Even at the present day this more or less idealizes destructiveness and deceit in the conflicts of war, if not of commerce.

But such precepts are secondary, not ideals in the same primary and enduring sense that loyalty and kindness are. They shine by reflected light, and get their force mainly from the belief that they express the requirements of the "we" group in combating its enemies. Flourishing at certain stages of development because they are requisite

* 1 Samuel, 15 : 33.

37

under the prevailing conditions of destructive conflict, they are slowly abandoned or transformed when these conditions change. Mankind at large has no love of them for their own sake, though individuals, classes, or even nations may acquire them as a habit. With the advance of civilization conflict itself is brought more and more under the control of those principles that prevail in primary groups, and, so far as this is the case, conduct which violates such principles ceases to have any ideal value.

To break up the ideal of a moral whole into particular ideals is an artificial process which every thinker would probably carry out in his own way. Perhaps, however, the most salient principles are loyalty, lawfulness, and freedom.

In so far as one identifies himself with a whole, loyalty to that whole is loyalty to himself; it is self-realization, something in which one cannot fail without losing self-respect. Moreover this is a larger self, leading out into a wider and richer life, and appealing, therefore, to enthusiasm and the need of quickening ideals. One is never more human, and as a rule never happier, than when he is sacrificing his narrow and merely private interest to the higher call of the congenial group. And without doubt the natural genesis of this sentiment is in the intimacy of face-to-face coöperation. It is rather the rule than the exception in the family, and grows up among children and youth so fast as they learn to think and act to common ends. The team feeling described above illustrates it as well as anything.

Among the ideals inseparable from loyalty are those of

truth, service, and kindness, always conceived as due to the intimate group rather than to the world at large.

Truth or good faith toward other members of a fellow-ship is, so far as I know, a universal human ideal. It does not involve any abstract love of veracity, and is quite consistent with deception toward the outside world, being essentially "truth of intercourse" or fair dealing among intimates. There are few, even among those reckoned lawless, who will not keep faith with one who has the gift of getting near to them in spirit and making them feel that he is one of themselves. Thus Judge Lindsey of Denver has worked a revolution among the neglected boys of his city, by no other method than that of entering into the same moral whole, becoming part of a "we" with them. He awakens their sense of honor, trusts it, and is almost never disappointed. When he wishes to send a boy to the reform school the latter promises to repair to the institution at a given time and invariably does so. Among tramps a similar sentiment prevails. "It will be found," said a young man who had spent the summer among vagrants, "that if they are treated square they will do the same."

The ideal of service likewise goes with the sense of unity. If there is a vital whole the right aim of individual activity can be no other than to serve that whole. And this is not so much a theory as a feeling that will exist wherever the whole is felt. It is a poor sort of an individual that does not feel the need to devote himself to the larger purposes of the group. In our society many feel this need in youth and express it on the playground who never succeed in realizing it among the less intimate relations of business or professional life.

All mankind acknowledges kindness as the law of right intercourse within a social group. By communion minds are fused into a sympathetic whole, each part of which tends to share the life of all the rest, so that kindness is a common joy, and harshness a common pain. It is the simplest, most attractive, and most diffused of human ideals. The golden rule springs directly from human nature.

Accordingly this ideal has been bound up with association in all past times and among all peoples: it was a matter of course that when men acted together in war, industry, devotion, sport, or what not, they formed a brotherhood or friendship. It is perhaps only in modern days, along with the great and sudden differentiation of activities, that feeling has failed to keep up, and the idea of coöperation without friendship has become familiar.

Mr. Westermarck, than whom there is no better authority on a question of this sort, has filled several chapters of his work on the Origin and Development of Moral Ideas with evidence of the universality of kindness and the kindly ideal. After showing at length that uncivilized people recognize the duty of kindness and support from mother to child, father to child, child to parent, and among brethren and kinsmen, he goes on to say:* "But the duty of helping the needy and protecting those in danger goes beyond the limits of the family and the *gens*. Uncivilized peoples are, as a rule, described as kind toward members

* Vol. i, 540 *ff*.

of their own community or tribe. Between themselves charity is enjoined as a duty and generosity is praised as a virtue. Indeed their customs regarding mutual aid are often much more stringent than our own. And this applies even to the lowest savages."

Beginning with the Australians, he quotes the statement of Spencer and Gillen that their treatment of one another "is marked on the whole by considerable kindness, that is, of course, in the case of members of friendly groups, with every now and then the perpetration of acts of cruelty." Concerning the North American Indians he cites many writers. Catlin says "to their friends there are no people on earth that are more kind." Adair that "they are very kind and liberal to every one of their own tribe, even to the last morsel of food they enjoy"; also that Nature's school "teaches them the plain, easy rule, Do to others as you would be done by." Morgan reports that "among the Iroquois kindness to the orphan, hospitality to all, and a common brotherhood were among the doctrines held up for acceptance by their religious instructors." An Iroquois "would surrender his dinner to feed the hungry, vacate his bed to refresh the weary, and give up his apparel to clothe the naked."

And so Westermarck goes on, in the exhaustive way familiar to readers of his works, to show that like sentiments prevail the world over. Kropotkin has collected similar evidence in his Mutual Aid a Factor in Civilization. The popular notion of savages as lacking in the gentler feelings is an error springing from the external, usually hostile, nature of our contact with them. Indeed, a state of things, such as is found in our own cities, where want

41

and plenty exist side by side without the latter feeling
any compulsion to relieve the former, is shocking and in-
comprehensible to many savages.

Ordinarily the ideal of kindness, in savage and civilized
societies alike, applies only to those within the sympathetic
group; the main difference between civilization and sav-
agery, in this regard, being that under the former the
group tends to enlarge. One reason for the restriction
is that kindness is aroused by sympathy, and can have
little life except as our imaginations are opened to the
lives of others and they are made part of ourselves. Even
the Christian church, as history shows, has for the most
part inculcated kindness only to those within its own pale,
or within a particular sect; and the modern ideal of a
kindness embracing all humanity (modern at least so
far as western nations are concerned) is connected with
a growing understanding of the unity of the race.

Every intimate group, like every individual, experiences
conflicting impulses within itself, and as the individual
feels the need of definite principles to shape his conduct
and give him peace, so the group needs law or rule for the
same purpose. It is not merely that the over-strong or
the insubordinate must be restrained, but that all alike
may have some definite criterion of what the good member ought to do. It is a mere fact of psychology that where
a social whole exists it may be as painful to do wrong as
to suffer it—because one's own spirit is divided—and the
common need is for harmony through a law, framed in
the total interest, which every one can and must obey.

This need of rules to align differentiated impulse with

the good of the whole is nowhere more apparent than on the playground. Miss Buck, the author of an instructive work on Boys' Self-Governing Clubs, suggests that the elementary form of equity is "taking turns," as at swings and the like; and any one who has shared in a boys' camp will recall the constant demand, by the boys themselves, for rules of this nature. There must be a fair distribution of privileges as to boats, games, and so on, and an equal distribution of food. And we learn from Robert Woods that gangs of boys on the streets of cities generally have a "judge" to whom all disputes are referred if no agreement is otherwise reached.*

No doubt every one remembers how the idea of justice is developed in children's games. There is always something to be done, in which various parts are to be taken, success depending upon their efficient distribution. All see this and draw from experience the idea that there is a higher principle that ought to control the undisciplined ambition of individuals. "Rough games," says Miss Buck, "in many respects present in miniature the conditions of a society where an ideal state of justice, freedom and equality prevails."† Mr. Joseph Lee, in the paper quoted above, expounds the matter at more length and with much insight.

You may be very intent to beat the other man in the race, but after experience of many contests the fair promise of whose morning has been clouded over by the long and many-worded dispute terminating in a general row, with indecisive and unsatisfying result, you begin dimly to perceive that you and the other fellows and the rest of the crowd, for the very reason that you are contestants and prospective

* The City Wilderness, 116.
† Boys' Self-Governing Clubs, 4, 5.

contestants, have interests in common—interests in the establishment and maintenance of those necessary rules and regulations without which satisfactory contests cannot be carried on. . . . The child's need of conflict is from a desire not to exterminate his competitor, but to overcome him and to have his own superiority acknowledged. The boy desires to be somebody; but being somebody is to him a social achievement. And though there is temptation to pervert justice, to try to get the decision when you have not really furnished the proof, there is also a motive against such procedure. The person whom you really and finally want to convince is yourself. Your deepest desire is to beat the other boy, not merely to seem to beat him. By playing unfairly and forcing decisions in your own favor, you may possibly cheat the others, but you cannot cheat yourself.

But the decisions in most of the disputes have behind them the further, more obviously social, motive of carrying on a successful game. The sense of common interest has been stretched so as to take the competitive impulse itself into camp, domesticate it, and make it a part of the social system. The acutely realized fact that a society of chronic kickers can never play a game or anything else, comes to be seen against the background of a possible orderly arrangement of which one has had occasional experience, and with which one has come at last to sympathize; there comes to be to some extent an identification of one's own interests and purposes with the interests and purposes of the whole. Certainly the decisions of the group as to whether Jimmy was out at first, as to who came out last, and whether Mary Ann was really caught, are felt as community and not as individual decisions.*

No doubt American boys have more of the spirit and practice of this sort of organization than those of any other country, except possibly England: they have the constant spectacle of self-government among their elders, and also, perhaps, some advantage in natural aptitude to help them on. But it is doubtful if there is any great difference among the white peoples in the latter regard. American children of German and Irish descent are not

* Charities and the Commons, Aug. 3, 1907, abridged.

inferior to the Anglo-Saxons, and among the newer immigrants the Jewish children, at least, show a marked aptitude for organization. The question might profitably be investigated in our great cities.

Of course the ideals derived from juvenile experience are carried over into the wider life, and men always find it easy to conceive righteousness in terms of fair play. "The Social Question," says a penetrative writer, "is forever an attack upon what, in some form, is thought to be unfair privilege."*

The law or rule that human nature demands has a democratic principle latent in it, because it must be one congenial to general sentiment. Explicit democracy, however—deciding by popular vote and the like—is not primary and general like the need of law, but is rather a mechanism for deciding what the rule is to be, and no more natural than the appeal to authority. Indeed, there seems to be, among children as among primitive peoples, a certain reluctance to ascribe laws to the mere human choice of themselves and their fellows. They wish to assign them to a higher source and to think of them as having an unquestionable sanction. So far as my own observation goes, even American boys prefer to receive rules from tradition or from their elders, when they can. Nothing is easier than for a parent, or mentor of any kind, to be a lawgiver to children, if only he has their confidence, and if the laws themselves prove workable. But the test of law is social and popular; it must suit the general mind. If, for instance, a man takes a group of boys camping, and has their confidence, they will gladly receive

* John Graham Brooks, The Social Unrest, 135.

45

rules from him, expecting, of course, that they will be good rules. But if they prove to be unreasonable and troublesome, they will soon cease to work.

Freedom is that phase of the social ideal which emphasizes individuality. The whole to which we belong is made up of diverse energies which enkindle one another by friction; and its vigor requires that these have play. Thus the fierce impulses of ambition and pride may be as organic as anything else—provided they are sufficiently humanized as to their objects—and are to be interfered with only when they become destructive or oppressive. Moreover, we must not be required to prove to others the beneficence of our peculiarity, but should be allowed, if we wish, to "write *whim* on the lintels of the door-post." Our desires and purposes, though social in their ultimate nature, are apt to be unacceptable on first appearance, and the more so in proportion to their value. Thus we feel a need to be let alone, and sympathize with a similar need in others.

This is so familiar a principle, especially among English and Americans, to whose temperament and traditions it is peculiarly congenial, that I need not discuss it at length. It is a phase of idealism that comes most vividly to consciousness when formal and antiquated systems of control need to be broken up, as in the eighteenth century. It then represented the appeal to human nature as against outworn mechanism. Our whole social and political philosophy still echoes that conflict.

The bearing of this view of human nature may perhaps be made clearer by considering its relation to the familiar but now somewhat discredited doctrine of Natural Right. This is traced from the speculations of Greek philosophers down through Roman jurisprudence to Hobbes, Locke, Rousseau, and others, who gave it its modern forms and through whose works it became a factor in modern history. It was familiar to our forefathers and is set forth in the Declaration of Independence. According to it society is made up, primarily, of free individuals, who must be held to create government and other institutions by a sort of implied contract, yielding up a part of their natural right in order to enjoy the benefits of organization. But if the organization does not confer these benefits, then, as most writers held, it is wrong and void, and the individuals may properly reclaim their natural freedom.

Now in form this doctrine is wholly at variance with evolutionary thought. To the latter, society is an organic growth; there is no individual apart from society, no freedom apart from organization, no social contract of the sort taught by these philosophers. In its practical applications, however, the teaching of natural right is not so absurd and obsolete as is sometimes imagined. If it is true that human nature is developed in primary groups which are everywhere much the same, and that there also springs from these a common idealism which institutions strive to express, we have a ground for somewhat the same conclusions as come from the theory of a natural freedom modified by contract. Natural freedom would correspond roughly to the ideals generated and partly realized in primary association, the social contract to the limitations these ideals encounter in seeking a larger expression.

47

Indeed, is it not true that the natural rights of this philosophy—the right to personal freedom, the right to labor, the right to property, the right to open competition —are ideals which in reality sprang then as they do now largely from what the philosophers knew of the activities of men in small, face-to-face groups?

The reluctance to give up ideals like those of the Declaration of Independence, without something equally simple and human to take their place, is healthy and need not look far for theoretical justification.

The idea of the germinal character of primary association is one that is fast making its way in education and philanthropy. As we learn that man is altogether social and never seen truly except in connection with his fellows, we fix our attention more and more on group conditions as the source, for better or worse, of personal character, and come to feel that we must work on the individual through the web of relations in which he actually lives.

The school, for instance, must form a whole with the rest of life, using the ideas generated by the latter as the starting-point of its training. The public opinion and traditions of the scholars must be respected and made an ally of discipline. Children's associations should be fostered and good objects suggested for their activity.

In philanthropy it is essential that the unity of the family be regarded and its natural bonds not weakened for the sake of transient benefit to the individual. Children, especially, must be protected from the destructive kindness which inculcates irresponsibility in the parent. In general the heart of reform is in control of the conditions

48

which act upon the family and neighborhood. When the housing, for example, is of such a character as to make a healthy home life impossible, the boys and girls are driven to the streets, the men into saloons, and thus society is diseased at its source.

Without healthy play, especially group play, human nature cannot rightly develop, and to preserve this, in the midst of the crowding and aggressive commercialism of our cities, is coming to be seen as a special need of the time. Democracy, it is now held, must recognize as one of its essential functions the provision of ample spaces and apparatus for this purpose, with enough judicious supervision to ensure the ascendency of good play traditions. And with this must go the suppression of child labor and other inhumane conditions.

Fruitful attention is being given to boys' fellowships or "gangs." It appears—as any one who recalls his own boyhood might have anticipated—that nearly all the juvenile population belong to such fellowships, and put an ardent, though often misdirected, idealism into them. "Almost every boy in the tenement-house quarters of the district," says Robert A. Woods, speaking of Boston, "is a member of a gang. The boy who does not belong is not only the exception but the very rare exception."* In crowded neighborhoods, where there are no playgrounds and street sports are unlawful, the human nature of these gangs must take a semi-criminal direction; but with better opportunities and guidance it turns quite as naturally to wholesome sport and social service. Accordingly social settlements and similar agencies are converting gangs into

* The City Wilderness, 113.

clubs, with the best results; and there is also coming to be a regular organization of voluntary clubs in affiliation with the public schools.

It is much the same in the country. In every village and township in the land, I suppose, there are one or more groups of predatory boys and hoydenish girls whose mischief is only the result of ill-directed energy. If each of these could receive a little sympathetic attention from kindred but wiser spirits, at least half of the crime and vice of the next generation would almost certainly be done away with.

CHAPTER V

THE EXTENSION OF PRIMARY IDEALS

PRIMARY IDEALS UNDERLIE DEMOCRACY AND CHRISTIANITY—WHY
THEY ARE NOT ACHIEVED ON A LARGER SCALE—WHAT THEY
REQUIRE FROM PERSONALITY—FROM SOCIAL MECHANISM—
THE PRINCIPLE OF COMPENSATION.

IT will be found that those systems of larger idealism
which are most human and so of most enduring value,
are based upon the ideals of primary groups. Take,
for instance, the two systems that have most vitality at
the present time—democracy and Christianity.

The aspirations of ideal democracy—including, of
course, socialism, and whatever else may go by a special
name—are those naturally springing from the playground
or the local community; embracing equal opportunity,
fair play, the loyal service of all in the common good, free
discussion, and kindness to the weak. These are renewed
every day in the hearts of the people because they spring
from and are corroborated by familiar and homely experience. Moreover, modern democracy as a historical
current is apparently traceable back to the village community life of the Teutonic tribes of northern Europe,
from which it descends through English constitutional
liberty and the American and French revolutions to its
broad and deep channels of the nineteenth and twentieth
centuries.

51

And Christianity, as a social system, is based upon the family, its ideals being traceable to the domestic circle of a Judaean carpenter. God is a kind father; men and women are brothers and sisters; we are all members one of another, doing as we would be done by and referring all things to the rule of love. In so far as the church has departed from these principles it has proved transient; these endure because they are human.

But why is it that human nature is not more successful in achieving these primary aims? They appear to be simple and reasonable, and one asks why they are so little realized, why we are not, in fact, a moral whole, a happy family.

It is not because we do not wish it. There can be no doubt, I should say, that, leaving aside a comparatively few abnormal individuals, whose influence is small, men in general have a natural allegiance to the community ideal, and would gladly see it carried out on a large as well as a small scale. And nearly all imaginative and aspiring persons view it with enthusiasm, and would devote themselves to it with some ardor and sacrifice if they saw clearly how they could do so with effect. It is easy to imagine types of pure malignity in people of whom we have little knowledge, but who ever came to know any one intimately without finding that he had somewhere in him the impulses of a man and a brother?

The failure to realize these impulses in practice is, of course, due in part to moral weakness of a personal character, to the fact that our higher nature has but an imperfect and transient mastery of our lower, so that we never

52

live up to our ideals.   But going beyond this and looking at the matter from the standpoint of the larger mind, the cause of failure is seen to be the difficulty of organization. Even if our intentions were always good, we should not succeed, because, to make good intentions effective, they must be extended into a system.   In attempting to do this our constructive power is used up and our ideals confused and discouraged.   We are even led to create a kind of institutions which, though good in certain aspects, may brutalize or ossify the individual, so that primary idealism in him is almost obliterated.   The creation of a moral order on an ever-growing scale is the great historical task of mankind, and the magnitude of it explains all short-comings.

From personality the building of a moral order re-quires not only good impulses but character and capacity. The ideal must be worked out with steadfastness, self-control, and intelligence.   Even families and fellowships, though usually on a higher level than more elaborate structures, often break down, and commonly from lack of character in their members.   But if it is insufficient here, how much less will it suffice for a righteous state.   Our new order of life, with its great extension of structure and its principle of freedom, is an ever severer test of the po-litical and moral fibre of mankind, of its power to hold itself together in vast, efficient, plastic wholes.   Whatever races or social systems fail to produce this fibre must yield ascendency to those which succeed.

This stronger personality depends also upon training; and whatever peoples succeed in being righteous on a

53

great scale will do so only by adding to natural capacity an education suited to the growing demands of the situation—one at the same time broad and special, technical and humane. There can be no moral order that does not live in the mind of the individual.

Besides personality—or rather correlative with it—there must be an adequate mechanism of communication and organization. In small groups the requirements of structure are so simple as to make little trouble, but in proportion as the web of relations extends and diversifies, they become more and more difficult to meet without sacrificing human nature; so that, other things equal, the freedom and real unity of the system are likely to vary inversely with its extent. It is only because other things have not remained equal, because the mechanism has been improved, that it has become possible, in a measure, to reconcile freedom with extent.

Communication must be full and quick in order to give that promptness in the give-and-take of suggestions upon which moral unity depends. Gesture and speech ensure this in the face-to-face group; but only the recent marvellous improvement of communicative machinery makes a free mind on a great scale even conceivable. If there is no means of working thought and sentiment into a whole by reciprocation, the unity of the group cannot be other than inert and unhuman. This cause alone would account for the lack of extended freedom previous to the nineteenth century.

There must also be forms and customs of rational organization, through which human nature may express itself

54

in an orderly and effective manner. Even children learn the need of regular discussion and decision, while all bodies of adults meeting for deliberation find that they can think organically only by observance of the rules which have been worked out for such occasions. And if we are to have great and stable nations, it is easy to see that these rules of order must become a body of law and custom including most, if not all, of the familiar institutions of society. These are a product of progressive invention, trial, and survival as much as the railroad or the factory, and they have in the long run the same purpose, that of the fuller expression of human nature in a social system.

As might be expected from these conditions, there is a principle of compensation at work in the growth of the larger mind. The more betterment there is, the more of vital force, of human reason, feeling, and choice, goes into it; and, as these are limited, improvement in one respect is apt to be offset, at least in part or temporarily, by delay or retrogression in others.

Thus a rapid improvement in the means of communication, as we see in our own time, supplies the basis for a larger and freer society, and yet it may, by disordering settled relations, and by fixing attention too much upon mechanical phases of progress, bring in conditions of confusion and injustice that are the opposite of free.

A very general fact of early political history is deterioration by growth. The small state cannot escape its destiny as part of a larger world, but must expand or perish. It grows in size, power, and diversity by the necessities of its struggle for existence—as did Rome, Athens, and a hundred other states—but in so doing sacrifices human nature to military expediency and develops a mechanical or despotic structure. This, in the long run, produces weakness, decay, and conquest, or perhaps revolt and revolution. The requirements of human nature—both direct, as expressed in social idealism, and indirect, as felt in the ultimate weakness and failure of systems which disregard them—are irrepressible. Gradually, therefore, through improvement and through the survival of higher types in conflict, a type of larger structure is developed which less sacrifices these requirements.

Much of what is unfree and unhuman in our modern life comes from mere inadequacy of mental and moral energy to meet the accumulating demands upon it. In many quarters attention and effort must be lacking, and where this is the case social relations fall to a low plane— just as a teacher who has too much to do necessarily adopts a mechanical style of instruction. So what we call "red tape" prevails in great clerical offices because much business is done by persons of small ability, who can work only under rule. And great bureaucratic systems, like the Russian Empire, are of much the same nature.

In general the wrongs of the social system come much more from inadequacy than from ill intention. It is indeed not to be expected that all relations should be fully rational and sympathetic; we have to be content with infusing reason and sympathy into what is most vital.

Society, then, as a moral organism, is a progressive creation, tentatively wrought out through experiment, struggle, and survival. Not only individuals but ideas, institutions, nations, and races do their work upon it and perish. Its ideals, though simple in spirit, are achieved through endless elaboration of means.

It will be my further endeavor to throw some light upon this striving whole by considering certain phases of its organization, such as Communication, Public Opinion, Sentiment, Classes, and Institutions; always trying to see the whole in the part, the part in the whole, and human nature in both.

PART II
COMMUNICATION

CHAPTER VI

THE SIGNIFICANCE OF COMMUNICATION

MEANING OF COMMUNICATION—ITS RELATION TO HUMAN NATURE
—TO SOCIETY AT LARGE.

BY Communication is here meant the mechanism through which human relations exist and develop—all the symbols of the mind, together with the means of conveying them through space and preserving them in time. It includes the expression of the face, attitude and gesture, the tones of the voice, words, writing, printing, railways, telegraphs, telephones, and whatever else may be the latest achievement in the conquest of space and time. All these taken together, in the intricacy of their actual combination, make up an organic whole corresponding to the organic whole of human thought; and everything in the way of mental growth has an external existence therein. The more closely we consider this mechanism the more intimate will appear its relation to the inner life of mankind, and nothing will more help us to understand the latter than such consideration.

There is no sharp line between the means of communication and the rest of the external world. In a sense all objects and actions are symbols of the mind, and nearly anything may be used as a sign—as I may signify the moon or a squirrel to a child by merely pointing at it, or

61

by imitating with the voice the chatter of the one or drawing an outline of the other. But there is also, almost from the first, a conventional development of communication, springing out of spontaneous signs but soon losing evident connection with them, a system of standard symbols existing for the mere purpose of conveying thought; and it is this we have chiefly to consider.

Without communication the mind does not develop a true human nature, but remains in an abnormal and nondescript state neither human nor properly brutal. This is movingly illustrated by the case of Helen Keller, who, as all the world knows, was cut off at eighteen months from the cheerful ways of men by the loss of sight and hearing; and did not renew the connection until she was nearly seven years old. Although her mind was not wholly isolated during this period, since she retained the use of a considerable number of signs learned during infancy, yet her impulses were crude and uncontrolled, and her thought so unconnected that she afterward remembered almost nothing that occurred before the awakening which took place toward the close of her seventh year.

The story of that awakening, as told by her teacher, gives as vivid a picture as we need have of the significance to the individual mind of the general fact and idea of communication. For weeks Miss Sullivan had been spelling words into her hand which Helen had repeated and associated with objects; but she had not yet grasped the idea of language in general, the fact that everything had a name, and that through names she could share her own experiences with others, and learn theirs—the idea that there is *fellowship in thought*. This came quite suddenly.

"This morning," writes her teacher, "while she was washing, she wanted to know the name for water. . . . I spelled w-a-t-e-r and thought no more about it until after breakfast. Then it occurred to me that with the help of this new word I might succeed in straightening out the mug-milk difficulty [a confusion of ideas previously discussed]. We went out into the pump-house and I made Helen hold her mug under the pump while I pumped. As the cold water gushed forth filling the mug I spelled w-a-t-e-r in Helen's free hand. The word coming so close upon the sensation of cold water rushing over her hand seemed to startle her. She dropped the mug and stood as one transfixed. A new light came into her face. She spelled water several times. Then she dropped on the ground and asked for its name, and pointed to the pump and the trellis, and suddenly turning round she asked for my name. I spelled 'teacher.' Just then the nurse brought Helen's little sister into the pump-house, and Helen spelled 'baby' and pointed to the nurse. All the way back to the house she was highly excited, and learned the name of every object she touched, so that in a few hours she had added thirty new words to her vocabulary."

The following day Miss Sullivan writes, "Helen got up this morning like a radiant fairy. She has flitted from object to object, asking the name of everything and kissing me for very gladness." And four days later, "Everything must have a name now. . . . She drops the signs and pantomime she used before, so soon as she has words to supply their place, and the acquirement of a new word affords her the liveliest pleasure. And we notice that her face grows more expressive each day." *

This experience is a type of what happens more gradually to all of us: it is through communication that we get our higher development. The faces and conversation of our associates; books, letters, travel, arts, and the like,

* The Story of My Life, 316, 317.

by awakening thought and feeling and guiding them in certain channels, supply the stimulus and framework for all our growth.

In the same way, if we take a larger view and consider the life of a social group, we see that communication, including its organization into literature, art, and institutions, is truly the outside or visible structure of thought, as much cause as effect of the inside or conscious life of men. All is one growth: the symbols, the traditions, the institutions are projected from the mind, to be sure, but in the very instant of their projection, and thereafter, they react upon it, and in a sense control it, stimulating, developing, and fixing certain thoughts at the expense of others to which no awakening suggestion comes. By the aid of this structure the individual is a member not only of a family, a class, and a state, but of a larger whole reaching back to prehistoric men whose thought has gone to build it up. In this whole he lives as in an element, drawing from it the materials of his growth and adding to it whatever constructive thought he may express.

Thus the system of communication is a tool, a progressive invention, whose improvements react upon mankind and alter the life of every individual and institution. A study of these improvements is one of the best ways by which to approach an understanding of the mental and social changes that are bound up with them; because it gives a tangible framework for our ideas—just as one who wished to grasp the organic character of industry and commerce might well begin with a study of the railway system and of the amount and kind of commodities it carries, proceeding thence to the more abstract transactions of finance.

And when we come to the modern era, especially, we can understand nothing rightly unless we perceive the manner in which the revolution in communication has made a new world for us. So in the pages that follow I shall aim to show what the growth of intercourse implies in the way of social development, inquiring particularly into the effect of recent changes.

CHAPTER VII

THE GROWTH OF COMMUNICATION

PRE-VERBAL COMMUNICATION—THE RISE OF SPEECH—ITS MENTAL AND SOCIAL FUNCTION—THE FUNCTION OF WRITING—PRINTING AND THE MODERN WORLD—THE NON-VERBAL ARTS.

THE chief means of what we may call pre-verbal communication are the expression of the face—especially of the mobile portions about the eyes and mouth—the pitch, inflection, and emotional tone of the voice; and the gestures of the head and limbs. All of these begin in involuntary movements but are capable of becoming voluntary, and all are eagerly practised and interpreted by children long before they learn to speak. They are immediately joined to action and emotion: the inflections of the voice, for instance, play upon the child's feelings as directly as music, and are interpreted partly by an instinctive sensibility. I have heard a child seventeen months old using her voice so expressively, though inarticulately, that it sounded, a little way off, as if she were carrying on an animated conversation. And gesture, such as reaching out the hand, bending forward, turning away the head, and the like, springs directly from the ideas and feelings it represents.

The human face, "the shape and color of a mind and life," is a kind of epitome of society, and if one could only read all that is written in the countenances of men as they pass he might find a great deal of sociology in them. Hereditary bias, family nurture, the print of the school, current opinion, contemporary institutions, all are there, drawn with a very fine pencil. If one wishes to get a real human insight into the times of Henry the Eighth, for example, he can hardly do better than to study the portrait drawings of Holbein; and so of other periods, including our own, whose traits would appear conspicuously in a collection of portraits. Many people can discriminate particular classes, as, for instance, clergymen, by their expression, and not a few will tell with much accuracy what church the latter belong to and whether they are of the lower rank or in authority. Again there is a difference, indescribable, perhaps, yet apparent, between the look of American and of English youths—still more of girls—which reflects the differing social systems.

This sort of communication is, of course, involuntary. An artificial mechanism of communication originates when man begins purposely to reproduce his own instinctive motions and cries, or the sounds, forms, and movements of the world about him, in order to recall the ideas associated with them. All kinds of conventional communication are believed to be rooted in these primitive imitations, which, by a process not hard to imagine, extend and differentiate into gesture, speech, writing, and the special symbols of the arts and sciences; so that the whole exterior organization of thought refers back to these beginnings.

We can only conjecture the life of man, or of his humanizing progenitor, before speech was achieved; but we may suppose that facial expression, inarticulate cries and songs,*

* On the probability that song preceded speech, see Darwin, Descent of Man, chap. 19.

67

and a variety of imitative sounds and actions aroused sympathy, permitted the simpler kinds of general ideas to be formed, and were the medium through which tradition and convention had their earliest development. It is probable that artificial gesture language was well organized before speech had made much headway. Even without words life may have been an active and continuous mental whole, not dependent for its unity upon mere heredity, but bound together by some conscious community in the simpler sorts of thought and feeling, and by the transmission and accumulation of these through tradition. There was presumably coöperation and instruction of a crude sort in which was the germ of future institutions.

No one who has observed children will have any difficulty in conjecturing the beginnings of speech, since nearly every child starts in to invent a language for himself, and only desists when he finds that there is one all ready-made for him. There are as many natural words (if we may call them so) as there are familiar sounds with definite associations, whether coming from human beings, from animals, or from inanimate nature. These the child instinctively loves to reproduce and communicate, at first in mere sport and sociability, then, as occasion arises, with more definite meaning. This meaning is easily extended by various sorts of association of ideas; the sounds themselves are altered and combined in usage; and thus speech is well begun.

Many humble inventors contribute to its growth, every man, possibly, altering the heritage in proportion as he puts his individuality into his speech. Variations of idea are preserved in words or other symbols, and so stored up in a continuing whole, constantly growing in bulk and diversity, which is, as we have seen, nothing less than the outside or sensible embodiment of human thought, in which every particular mind lives and grows, drawing from it the material of its own life, and contributing to it whatever higher product it may make out of that material.

A word is a vehicle, a boat floating down from the past, laden with the thought of men we never saw; and in coming to understand it we enter not only into the minds of our contemporaries, but into the general mind of humanity continuous through time. The popular notion of learning to speak is that the child first has the idea and then gets from others a sound to use in communicating it; but a closer study shows that this is hardly true even of the simplest ideas, and is nearly the reverse of truth as regards developed thought. In that the word usually goes before, leading and kindling the idea—we should not have the latter if we did not have the word first. "This way," says the word, "is an interesting thought: come and find it." And so we are led on to rediscover old knowledge. Such words, for instance, as *good, right, truth, love, home, justice, beauty, freedom;* are powerful makers of what they stand for.

A mind without words would make only such feeble and uncertain progress as a traveller set down in the midst of a wilderness where there were no paths or conveyances and without even a compass. A mind with them is like the same traveller in the midst of civilization, with beaten roads and rapid vehicles ready to take him in any direction where men have been before. As the traveller must pass over the ground in either case, so the mind must pass through experience, but if it has language it finds its experience foreseen, mapped out and interpreted by all the wisdom of the past, so that it has not only its own experience but that of the race—just as the modern traveller sees not only the original country but the cities and plantations of men.

The principle that applies to words applies also to all structures that are built of words, to literature and the manifold traditions that it conveys. As the lines of Dante are "foot-paths for the thought of Italy," so the successful efforts of the mind in every field are preserved in their symbols and become foot-paths by which other minds reach the same point. And this includes feeling as well as definite idea. It is almost the most wonderful thing about language that by something intangible in its order and movement and in the selection and collocation of words, it can transmit the very soul of a man, making his page live when his definite ideas have ceased to have value. In this way one gets from Sir Thomas Browne, let us say, not his conceits and credulities, but his high and religious spirit, hovering, as it were, over the page.

The achievement of speech is commonly and properly regarded as the distinctive trait of man, as the gate by which he emerged from his pre-human state. It means that, like Helen Keller, he has learned that everything has, or may have, a name, and so has entered upon a life of conscious fellowship in thought. It not only permitted the rise of a more rational and human kind of thinking and feeling, but was also the basis of the earliest definite

70

institutions. A wider and fuller unity of thought took place in every group where it appeared. Ideas regarding the chief interests of primitive life—hunting, warfare, marriage, feasting and the like—were defined, communicated and extended. Public opinion no doubt began to arise within the tribe, and crystallized into current sayings which served as rules of thought and conduct; the festal chants, if they existed before, became articulate and historical. And when any thought of special value was achieved in the group, it did not perish, but was handed on by tradition and made the basis of new gains. In this way primitive wisdom and rule were perpetuated, enlarged and improved until, in connection with ceremonial and other symbols, they became such institutions, of government, marriage, religion and property as are found in every savage tribe.

Nor must we forget that this state of things reacted upon the natural capacities of man, perhaps by the direct inheritance of acquired social habits and aptitudes, certainly by the survival of those who, having these, were more fitted than others to thrive in a social life. In this way man, if he was human when speech began to be used, rapidly became more so, and went on accumulating a social heritage.

So the study of speech reveals a truth which we may also reach in many other ways, namely, that the growth of the individual mind is not a separate growth, but rather a differentiation within the general mind. Our personal life, so far as we can make out, has its sources partly in congenital tendency, and partly in the stream of communication, both of which flow from the corporate life of the race. The individual has no better ground for thinking of himself as separate from humanity than he has for thinking of the self he is to-day as separate from the self he was yesterday; the continuity being no more certain in the one case than in the other. If it be said that he is separate because he feels separate, it may be answered that to the infant each moment is separate, and that we know our personal life to be a whole only through the growth of thought and memory. In the same way the sense of a larger or social wholeness is perhaps merely a question of our growing into more vivid and intelligent consciousness of a unity which is already clear enough to reflective observation.

It is the social function of writing, by giving ideas a lasting record, to make possible a more certain, continuous and diversified growth of the human mind. It does for the race very much what it does for the individual. When the student has a good thought he writes it down, so that it may be recalled at will and made the starting-point for a better thought in the same direction; and so mankind at large records and cherishes its insights.

Until writing is achieved the accumulation of ideas depends upon oral tradition, the capacity of which is measured by the interest and memory of the people who transmit it. It must, therefore, confine itself chiefly to ideas and sentiments for which there is a somewhat general and constant demand, such as popular stories—like the Homeric legends—chants, proverbs, maxims and the like. It is true that tradition becomes more or less specialized in families and castes—as we see, for instance, in the widespread existence of a hereditary priesthood—but this specialization cannot be very elaborate or very secure in its continuance. There can hardly be, without writing, any science or any diversified literature. These require a means by which important ideas can be passed on unimpaired to men distant in time and space from their authors. We may safely pronounce, with Gibbon, that "without some species of writing no people has ever preserved the faithful annals of their history, ever made any considerable progress in the abstract sciences, or ever possessed, in any tolerable degree of perfection, the useful and agreeable arts of life."*

Nor can stable and extended government be organized without it, for such government requires a constitution of some sort, a definite and permanent body of law and custom, embracing the wisdom of the past regarding the maintenance of social order.

It is quite the same with religious systems. The historical religions are based upon Scriptures, the essential part of which is the recorded teaching of the founder and his immediate disciples, and without such a record Christianity, Buddhism or Mohammedanism could never have been more than a small and transient sect. There may well have been men of religious genius among our illiterate forefathers, but it was impossible that they should found enduring systems.

The whole structure and progress of modern life evidently rests upon the preservation, in writing, of the achievements of the antique mind, upon the records, especially, of Judea, Greece and Rome. To inquire what

* Decline and Fall, Milman-Smith edition, i, 354.

73

we should have been without these would be like asking what we should have been if our parents had not existed. Writing made history possible, and the man of history with his complex institutions. It enabled a rapid and secure enlargement of that human nature which had previously been confined within small and unstable groups.

If writing, by giving thought permanence, brought in the earlier civilization, printing, by giving it diffusion opened the doors of the modern world.

Before its advent access to the records of the race was limited to a learned class, who thus held a kind of monopoly of the traditions upon which the social system rested. Throughout the earlier Middle Ages, for example, the clergy, or that small portion of the clergy who were educated, occupied this position in Europe, and their system was the one animate and wide-reaching mental organization of the period. For many centuries it was rare for a layman, of whatever rank, to know how to sign his name. Through the Latin language, written and spoken, which would apparently have perished had it not been for the Church, the larger continuity and coöperation of the human mind was maintained. Those who could read it had a common literature and a vague sense of unity and brotherhood. Roman ideas were preserved, however imperfectly, and an ideal Rome lived in the Papacy and the Empire. Education, naturally, was controlled by the clergy, who were also intrusted with political correspondence and the framing of laws. As is well known they somewhat recast the traditions in their own interest, and were aided by their control of the communicating medium in becoming the dominant power in Europe.

Printing means democracy, because it brings knowledge within the reach of the common people; and knowledge, in the long run, is sure to make good its claim to power. It brings to the individual whatever part in the heritage of ideas he is fit to receive. The world of thought, and eventually the world of action, comes gradually under the rule of a true aristocracy of intelligence and character, in place of an artificial one created by exclusive opportunity.

Everywhere the spread of printing was followed by a general awakening due to the unsettling suggestions which it scattered abroad. Political and religious agitation, by no means unknown before, was immensely stimulated, and has continued unabated to the present time. "The whole of this movement," says Mr. H. C. Lea, speaking of the liberal agitations of the early sixteenth century, "had been rendered possible by the invention of printing, which facilitated so enormously the diffusion of intelligence, which enabled public opinion to form and express itself, and which, by bringing into communication minds of similar ways of thinking, afforded opportunity for combined action." "When, therefore, on October 31, 1517, Luther's fateful theses were hung on the church door at Wittenberg, they were, as he tells us, known in a fortnight throughout Germany; and in a month they had reached Rome and were being read in every school and convent in Europe—a result manifestly impossible without the aid of the printing press."*

* The Cambridge Modern History, i, 684, 685.

The printed page is also the door by which the individual, in our own time, enters the larger rooms of life. A good book, "the precious life blood of a master spirit stored upon purpose to a life beyond life,"* is almost always the channel through which uncommon minds get incitement and aid to lift themselves into the higher thought that other uncommon minds have created. "In study we hold converse with the wise, in action usually with the foolish."† While the mass of mankind about us is ever commonplace, there is always, in our day, a more select society not far away for one who craves it, and a man like Abraham Lincoln, whose birth would have meant hopeless serfdom a few centuries ago, may get from half a dozen books aspirations which lead him out to authority and beneficence.

While spoken language, along with the writing and printing by which it is preserved and disseminated, is the main current of communication, there are from the start many side channels.

Thus among savage or barbarous peoples we everywhere find, beside gesture language, the use of a multitude of other symbols, such as the red arrow for war, the pipe of peace, signal fires, notched sticks, knotted cords, totems, and, among nations more advanced in culture, coats-of-arms, flags and an infinite diversity of symbolic ritual. There is, indeed, a world of signs outside of language, most of which, however, we may pass by, since its general nature is obvious enough.

* Milton, Areopagitica.
† Bacon, Antitheta on Studies.

THE GROWTH OF COMMUNICATION

The arts of painting, sculpture, music, and architecture. considered as communication, have two somewhat different functions: First, as mere picture or image writing, conveying ideas that could also be conveyed (though with a difference) in words; and, second, as the vehicle of peculiar phases of sentiment incommunicable in any other way. These two were often, indeed usually, combined in the art of the past. In modern times the former, because of the diffusion of literacy, has become of secondary importance.

Of the picture-writing function the mosaics, in colors on a gold ground, that cover the inner walls of St. Mark's at Venice are a familiar instance. They set forth in somewhat rude figures, helped out by symbols, the whole system of Christian theology as it was then understood. They were thus an illuminated book of sacred learning through which the people entered into the religious tradition. The same tradition is illustrated in the sculpture of the cathedrals of Chartres and Rheims, together with much other matter—secular history, typified by figures of the kings of France; moral philosophy, with virtues and vices, rewards and punishments; and emblems of husbandry and handicraft. Along with these sculptures went the pictured windows, the sacred relics—which, as Gibbon says, "fixed and inflamed the devotion of the faithful"*—the music, and the elaborate pageants and ritual; all working together as one rich sign, in which was incarnated the ideal life of the times.

A subtler function of the non-verbal arts is to communicate matter that could not go by any other road,

* Decline and Fall, Milman-Smith edition, iii, 428.

77

especially certain sorts of sentiment which are thus perpetuated and diffused.

One of the simplest and most fruitful examples of this is the depiction of human forms and faces which embody, as if by living presence, the nobler feelings and aspirations of the time. Such works, in painting or sculpture, remain as symbols by the aid of which like sentiments grow up in the minds of whomsoever become familiar with them. Sentiment is cumulative in human history in the same manner as thought, though less definitely and surely, and Christian feeling, as it grew and flourished in the Middle Ages, was fostered by painting as much, perhaps, as by the Scriptures. And so Greek sculpture, from the time of the humanists down through Winckelmann and Goethe to the present day, has been a channel by which Greek sentiment has flowed into modern life.

This record of human feeling in expressive forms and faces, as in the madonnas and saints of Raphael, is called by some critics "illustration"; and they distinguish it from "decoration," which includes all those elements in a work of art which exist not to transmit something else but for their own more immediate value, such as beauty of color, form, composition and suggested movement. This latter is communication also, appealing to vivid but otherwise inarticulate phases of human instinct. Each art can convey a unique kind of sentiment and has "its own peculiar and incommunicable sensuous charm, its own special mode of reaching the imagination." In a picture the most characteristic thing is "that true pictorial quality . . . the inventive or creative handling of pure line and color, which, as almost always in Dutch painting, as

78

often also in the works of Titian or Veronese, is quite independent of anything definitely poetical in the subject it accompanies." in music "the musical charm—that essential music, which presents no words, no matter of sentiment or thought, separable from the special form in which it is conveyed to us."* And so with architecture, an art peculiarly close to social organization, so that in many cases—as in the Place of Venice—the spirit of a social system has been visibly raised up in stone.

It needs no argument, I suppose, to show that these arts are no less essential to the growth of the human spirit than literature or government.

* Walter Pater, Essay on the School of Giorgione.

CHAPTER VIII

MODERN COMMUNICATION: ENLARGEMENT AND ANIMATION

CHARACTER OF RECENT CHANGES—THEIR GENERAL EFFECT—THE CHANGE IN THE UNITED STATES—ORGANIZED GOSSIP—PUBLIC OPINION, DEMOCRACY, INTERNATIONALISM—THE VALUE OF DIFFUSION—ENLARGEMENT OF FEELING—CONCLUSION.

THE changes that have taken place since the beginning of the nineteenth century are such as to constitute a new epoch in communication, and in the whole system of society. They deserve, therefore, careful consideration, not so much in their mechanical aspect, which is familiar to every one, as in their operation upon the larger mind.

If one were to analyze the mechanism of intercourse, he might, perhaps, distinguish four factors that mainly contribute to its efficiency, namely:

Expressiveness, or the range of ideas and feelings it is competent to carry.

Permanence of record, or the overcoming of time.

Swiftness, or the overcoming of space.

Diffusion, or access to all classes of men.

Now while gains have no doubt been made in expressiveness, as in the enlargement of our vocabulary to embrace the ideas of modern science; and even in permanence of record, for scientific and other special purposes; yet certainly the long steps of recent times have been made in the direction of swiftness and diffusion. For most purposes our speech is no better than in the age of Elizabeth, if so good; but what facility we have gained in the application of it! The cheapening of printing, permitting an inundation of popular books, magazines and newspapers, has been supplemented by the rise of the modern postal system and the conquest of distance by railroads, telegraphs and telephones. And along with these extensions of the spoken or written word have come new arts of reproduction, such as photography, photo-engraving, phonography and the like—of greater social import than we realize—by which new kinds of impression from the visible or audible world may be fixed and disseminated.

It is not too much to say that these changes are the basis, from a mechanical standpoint, of nearly everything that is characteristic in the psychology of modern life. In a general way they mean the expansion of human nature, that is to say, of its power to express itself in social wholes. They make it possible for society to be organized more and more on the higher faculties of man, on intelligence and sympathy, rather than on authority, caste, and routine. They mean freedom, outlook, indefinite possibility. The public consciousness, instead of being confined as regards its more active phases to local groups, extends by even steps with that give-and-take of suggestions that the new intercourse makes possible, until wide nations, and finally the world itself, may be included in one lively mental whole.

The general character of this change is well expressed

81

by the two words *enlargement* and *animation*. Social contacts are extended in space and quickened in time, and in the same degree the mental unity they imply becomes wider and more alert. The individual is broadened by coming into relation with a larger and more various life, and he is kept stirred up, sometimes to excess, by the multitude of changing suggestions which this life brings to him.

From whatever point of view we study modern society to compare it with the past or to forecast the future, we ought to keep at least a subconsciousness of this radical change in mechanism, without allowing for which nothing else can be understood.

In the United States, for instance, at the close of the eighteenth century, public consciousness of any active kind was confined to small localities. Travel was slow, uncomfortable and costly, and people undertaking a considerable journey often made their wills beforehand. The newspapers, appearing weekly in the larger towns, were entirely lacking in what we should call news; and the number of letters sent during a year in all the thirteen states was much less than that now handled by the New York office in a single day. People are far more alive to-day to what is going on in China, if it happens to interest them, than they were then to events a hundred miles away. The isolation of even large towns from the rest of the world, and the consequent introversion of men's minds upon local concerns, was something we can hardly conceive. In the country "the environment of the farm was the neighborhood; the environment of the village was the encircling farms and the local tradition; . . . few conventions assembled for discussion and common action; educational centres did not radiate the shock of a new intellectual life to every hamlet; federations and unions did not bind men, near and remote, into that fellowship that makes one composite type of many human sorts. It was an age of sects, intolerant from lack of acquaintance."*

The change to the present régime of railroads, telegraphs, daily papers, telephones and the rest has involved a revolution in every phase of life; in commerce, in politics, in education, even in mere sociability and gossip—this revolution always consisting in an enlargement and quickening of the kind of life in question.

Probably there is nothing in this new mechanism quite so pervasive and characteristic as the daily newspaper, which is as vehemently praised as it is abused, and in both cases with good reason. What a strange practice it is, when you think of it, that a man should sit down to his breakfast table and, instead of conversing with his wife, and children, hold before his face a sort of screen on which is inscribed a world-wide gossip!

The essential function of the newspaper is, of course, to serve as a bulletin of important news and a medium for the interchange of ideas, through the printing of interviews, letters, speeches and editorial comment. In this way it is indispensable to the organization of the public mind.

The bulk of its matter, however, is best described by

* W. L. Anderson, The Country Town, 209, 210.

the phrase organized gossip. The sort of intercourse that people formerly carried on at cross-road stores or over the back fence, has now attained the dignity of print and an imposing system. That we absorb a flood of this does not necessarily mean that our minds are degenerate, but merely that we are gratifying an old appetite in a new way. Henry James speaks with a severity natural to literary sensibility of "the ubiquitous newspaper face, with its mere monstrosity and deformity of feature, and the vast open mouth, adjusted as to the chatter of Bedlam, that flings the flood-gates of vulgarity farther back [in America] than anywhere else on earth."* But after all is it any more vulgar than the older kind of gossip? No doubt it seems worse for venturing to share with literature the use of the printed word.

That the bulk of the contents of the newspaper is of the nature of gossip may be seen by noting three traits which together seem to make a fair definition of that word. It is copious, designed to occupy, without exerting, the mind. It consists mostly of personalities and appeals to superficial emotion. It is untrustworthy—except upon a few matters of moment which the public are likely to follow up and verify. These traits any one who is curious may substantiate by a study of his own morning journal.

There is a better and a worse side to this enlargement of gossip. On the former we may reckon the fact that it promotes a widespread sociability and sense of community; we know that people all over the country are laughing at the same jokes or thrilling with the same mild excitement over the foot-ball game, and we absorb a conviction

* The Manners of American Women, Harper's Bazar, May, 1907.

84

that they are good fellows much like ourselves. It also tends powerfully, through the fear of publicity, to enforce a popular, somewhat vulgar, but sound and human standard of morality. On the other hand it fosters superficiality and commonplace in every sphere of thought and feeling, and is, of course, the antithesis of literature and of all high or fine spiritual achievement. It stands for diffusion as opposed to distinction.

In politics communication makes possible public opinion, which, when organized, is democracy. The whole growth of this, and of the popular education and enlightenment that go with it, is immediately dependent upon the telegraph, the newspaper and the fast mail, for there can be no popular mind upon questions of the day, over wide areas, except as the people are promptly informed of such questions and are enabled to exchange views regarding them.

Our government, under the Constitution, was not originally a democracy, and was not intended to be so by the men that framed it. It was expected to be a representative republic, the people choosing men of character and wisdom, who would proceed to the capital, inform themselves there upon current questions, and deliberate and decide regarding them. That the people might think and act more directly was not foreseen. The Constitution is not democratic in spirit, and, as Mr. Bryce has noted,* might under different conditions have become the basis of an aristocratic system.

That any system could have held even the original

* The American Commonwealth, chap. 26.

thirteen states in firm union without the advent of modern communication is very doubtful. Political philosophy, from Plato to Montesquieu, had taught that free states must be small, and Frederick the Great is said to have ridiculed the idea of one extending from Maine to Georgia. "A large empire," says Montesquieu, "supposes a despotic authority in the person who governs. It is necessary that the quickness of the prince's resolutions should supply the distance of the places they are sent to."*

Democracy has arisen here, as it seems to be arising everywhere in the civilized world, not, chiefly, because of changes in the formal constitution, but as the outcome of conditions which make it natural for the people to have and to express a consciousness regarding questions of the day. It is said by those who know China that while that country was at war with Japan the majority of the Chinese were unaware that a war was in progress. Such ignorance makes the sway of public opinion impossible; and, conversely, it seems likely that no state, having a vigorous people, can long escape that sway except by repressing the interchange of thought. When the people have information and discussion they will have a will, and this must sooner or later get hold of the institutions of society.

One is often impressed with the thought that there ought to be some wider name for the modern movement than democracy, some name which should more distinctly suggest the enlargement and quickening of the general mind, of which the formal rule of the people is only one among many manifestations. The current of new life that is sweeping with augmenting force through the older

* The Spirit of Laws, book viii, chap. 19.

structures of society, now carrying them away, now leaving them outwardly undisturbed, has no adequate name.

Popular education is an inseparable part of all this: the individual must have at least those arts of reading and writing without which he can hardly be a vital member of the new organism. And that further development of education, rapidly becoming a conscious aim of modern society, which strives to give to every person a special training in preparation for whatever function he may have aptitude for, is also a phase of the freer and more flexible organization of mental energy. The same enlargement runs through all life, including fashion and other trivial or fugitive kinds of intercourse. And the widest phase of all, upon whose momentousness I need not dwell, is that rise of an international consciousness, in literature, in science and, finally, in politics, which holds out a trustworthy promise of the indefinite enlargement of justice and amity.

This unification of life by a freer course of thought is not only contemporaneous, overcoming space, but also historical, bringing the past into the present, and making every notable achievement of the race a possible factor in its current life—as when, by skilful reproduction the work of a mediæval painter is brought home to people dwelling five hundred years later on the other side of the globe. Our time is one of "large discourse, looking before and after."

There are remarkable possibilities in this diffusive vigor. Never, certainly, were great masses of men so rapidly rising to higher levels as now. There are the same facilities for disseminating improvement in mind and manners as in material devices; and the new communication has spread like morning light over the world, awakening, enlightening, enlarging, and filling with expectation. Human nature desires the good, when it once perceives it, and in all that is easily understood and imitated great headway is making.

Nor is there, as I shall try to show later, any good reason to think that the conditions are permanently unfavorable to the rise of special and select types of excellence. The same facility of communication which animates millions with the emulation of common models, also makes it easy for more discriminating minds to unite in small groups. The general fact is that human nature is set free; in time it will no doubt justify its freedom.

The enlargement affects not only thought but feeling, favoring the growth of a sense of common humanity, of moral unity, between nations, races and classes. Among members of a communicating whole feeling may not always be friendly, but it must be, in a sense, sympathetic, involving some consciousness of the other's point of view. Even the animosities of modern nations are of a human and imaginative sort, not the blind animal hostility of a more primitive age. They are resentments, and resentment, as Charles Lamb says, is of the family of love.

The relations between persons or communities that are without mutual understanding are necessarily on a low plane. There may be indifference, or a blind anger due to interference, or there may be a good-natured tolerance; but there is no consciousness of a common nature to warm up the kindly sentiments. A really human fellow-feeling was anciently confined within the tribe, men outside not being felt as members of a common whole. The alien was commonly treated as a more or less useful or dangerous animal—destroyed, despoiled or enslaved. Even in these days we care little about people whose life is not brought home to us by some kind of sympathetic contact. We may read statistics of the miserable life of the Italians and Jews in New York and Chicago; of bad housing, sweatshops and tuberculosis; but we care little more about them than we do about the sufferers from the Black Death, unless their life is realized to us in some human way, either by personal contact, or by pictures and imaginative description.

And we are getting this at the present time. The resources of modern communication are used in stimulating and gratifying our interest in every phase of human life. Russians, Japanese, Filipinos, fishermen, miners, millionaires, criminals, tramps and opium-eaters are brought home to us. The press well understands that nothing human is alien to us if it is only made comprehensible.

With a mind enlarged and suppled by such training, the man of to-day inclines to look for a common nature everywhere, and to demand that the whole world shall be brought under the sway of common principles of kindness and justice. He wants to see international strife allayed— in such a way, however, as not to prevent the expansion of capable races and the survival of better types; he wishes the friction of classes reduced and each interest fairly treated—but without checking individuality and enterprise. There was never so general an eagerness that

89

righteousness should prevail; the chief matter of dispute is upon the principles under which it may be established.

The work of communication in enlarging human nature is partly immediate, through facilitating contact, but even more it is indirect, through favoring the increase of intelligence, the decline of mechanical and arbitrary forms of organization, and the rise of a more humane type of society. History may be regarded as a record of the struggle of man to realize his aspirations through organization; and the new communication is an efficient tool for this purpose. Assuming that the human heart and conscience, restricted only by the difficulties of organization, is the arbiter of what institutions are to become, we may expect the facility of intercourse to be the starting-point of an era of moral progress.

CHAPTER IX

MODERN COMMUNICATION: INDIVIDUALITY

THE QUESTION—WHY COMMUNICATION SHOULD FOSTER INDIVIDU-
ALITY—THE CONTRARY OR DEAD-LEVEL THEORY—RECONCILI-
ATION OF THESE VIEWS—THE OUTLOOK AS REGARDS INDIVIDU-
ALITY.

IT is a question of utmost interest whether these changes
do or do not contribute to the independence and productivity of the individual mind. Do they foster a self-
reliant personality, capable at need of pursuing high and
rare aims, or have they rather a levelling tendency, repressive of what is original and characteristic? There
are in fact opposite opinions regarding this matter, in
support of either of which numerous expressions by writers
of some weight might be collected.

From one point of view it would appear that the new
communication ought to encourage individuality of all
kinds; it makes it easier to get away from a given environment and to find support in one more congenial. The
world has grown more various and at the same time more
accessible, so that one having a natural bent should be
the more able to find influences to nourish it. If he has
a turn, say, for entomology, he can readily, through
journals, correspondence and meetings, get in touch with
a group of men similarly inclined, and with a congenial

91

tradition. And so with any sect of religion, or politics, or art, or what not; if there are in the civilized world a few like-minded people it is comparatively easy for them to get together in spirit and encourage one another in their peculiarity.

It is a simple and recognized principle of development that an enlarged life in the organism commonly involves greater differentiation in its parts. That the social enlargement of recent times has in general this character seems plain, and has been set forth in much detail by some writers, notably by Herbert Spencer. Many, indeed, find the characteristic evil of the new era in an extreme individuality, a somewhat anarchic differentiation and working at cross purposes. "Probably there was never any time," says Professor Mackenzie, "in which men tended to be so unintelligible to each other as they are now, on account of the diversity of the objects with which they are engaged, and of the points of view at which they stand."*

On the other hand we have what we may call the dead level theory, of which De Tocqueville, in his Democracy in America, was apparently the chief author. Modern conditions, according to this, break down all limits to the spread of ideas and customs. Great populations are brought into one mental whole, through which movements of thought run by a contagion like that of the mob; and instead of the individuality which was fostered by former obstacles, we have a universal assimilation. Each locality, it is pointed out, had formerly its peculiar accent

* Introduction to Social Philosophy, 110.

and mode of dress; while now dialects are disappearing, and almost the same fashions prevail throughout the civilized world. This uniformity in externals is held to be only the outward and visible sign of a corresponding levelling of ideas. People, it is said, have a passion to be alike, which modern appliances enable them to gratify. Already in the eighteenth century Dr. Johnson complained that "commerce has left the people no singularities," and in our day many hold with John Burroughs that, "Constant intercommunication, the friction of travel, of streets, of books, of newspapers, make us all alike; we are, as it were, all pebbles upon the same shore, washed by the same waves."*

The key to this matter, in my judgment, is to perceive that there are two kinds of individuality, one of isolation and one of choice, and that modern conditions foster the latter while they efface the former. They tend to make life rational and free instead of local and accidental. They enlarge indefinitely the competition of ideas, and whatever has owed its persistence merely to lack of comparison is likely to go, while that which is really congenial to the choosing mind will be all the more cherished and increased. Human nature is enfranchised, and works on a larger scale as regards both its conformities and its non-conformities.

Something of this may be seen in the contrast between town and country, the latter having more of the individuality of isolation, the former of choice. "The rural environment," says Mr. R. L. Hartt, speaking of country

* Nature's Way, Harper's Magazine, July, 1904.

villages in New England, "is psychically extravagant. It tends to extremes. A man carries himself out to his logical conclusions; he becomes a concentrated essence of himself."* I travelled some years ago among the mountains of North Carolina, at that time wholly unreached by modern industry and communication, and noticed that not only was the dialect of the region as a whole distinct from that of neighboring parts of the country, but that even adjoining valleys often showed marked differences. Evidently this sort of local individuality, characteristic of an illiterate people living on their own corn, pork and neighborhood traditions, can hardly survive the new communication.

It must be said, however, that rural life has other conditions that foster individuality in a more wholesome way than mere isolation, and are a real advantage in the growth of character. Among these are control over the immediate environment, the habit of face-to-face struggle with nature, and comparative security of economic position. All these contribute to the self-reliance upon which the farming people justly pride themselves.

In the city we find an individuality less picturesque but perhaps more functional. There is more facility for the formation of specialized groups, and so for the fostering of special capacities. Notwithstanding the din of communication and trade, the cities are, for this reason, the chief seats of productive originality in art, science and letters.

The difference is analogous to that between the development of natural species on islands or other isolated areas,

* A New England Hill Town. The Atlantic Monthly, April, 1899.

and on a wide and traversable continent. The former produces many quaint species, like the kangaroos, which disappear when brought into contact with more capable types; but the continent by no means brings about uniformity. It engenders, rather, a complex organism of related species and varieties, each of which is comparatively perfect in its special way; and has become so through the very fact of a wider struggle for existence.

So, easy communication of ideas favors differentiation of a rational and functional sort, as distinguished from the random variations fostered by isolation. And it must be remembered that any sort is rational and functional that really commends itself to the human spirit. Even revolt from an ascendant type is easier now than formerly, because the rebel can fortify himself with the triumphant records of the non-conformers of the past.

It is, then, probable that local peculiarity of speech and manner, and other curious and involuntary sorts of individuality, will diminish. And certainly a great deal is thus lost in the way of local color and atmosphere, of the racy flavor of isolated personalities and unconscious picturesqueness of social types. The diversities of dress, language and culture, which were developed in Europe during the Middle Ages, when each little barony was the channel of peculiar traditions, can hardly reappear. Nor can we expect, in modern cities, the sort of architectural individuality we find in those of Italy, built when each village was a distinct political and social unit. Heine, speaking of Scott, long ago referred to "the great pain caused by the loss of national characteristics in consequence of the spread of the newer culture—a pain which now quivers in the heart of all peoples."

But the more vital individuality, the cultivation by special groups of peculiar phases of knowledge, art or conduct, of anything under the heavens in fact that a few people may agree to pursue, will apparently be increased. Since uniformity is cheap and convenient, we may expect it in all matters wherein men do not specially care to assert themselves. We have it in dress and domestic architecture, for instance, just so far as we are willing to take these things ready-made; but when we begin to put ourselves into them we produce something distinctive.

Even languages and national characteristics, if the people really care about them, can be, and in fact are, preserved in spite of political absorption and the assimilating power of communication. There is nothing more notable in recent history than the persistence of nationality, even when, as in Poland, it has lost its political expression; and, as to languages, it is said that many, such as Roumanian, Bulgarian, Servian, Finnish, Norsk and Flemish, have revived and come into literary and popular use during the nineteenth century. Mr. Lecky, in his "Democracy and Liberty"* declared that "there has been in many forms a marked tendency to accentuate distinct national and local types."

To assume that a free concourse of ideas will produce uniformity is to beg the whole question. If it be true that men have a natural diversity of gifts, free intercourse should favor its development, especially when we consider that strong instinct which causes man to take pleasure in

* I, 501.

96

distinguishing himself, and to abhor to be lost in the crowd. And, as regards the actual tendency of modern life, only an obstinate *a priori* reasoner will maintain with any confidence the decline of individuality. Those who charge that we possess it in extravagant excess have at least an equal show of reason.

Nor, from the standpoint of sentiment, does the modern expansion of feeling and larger sense of unity tend necessarily to a loss of individuality. There is no prospect that self-feeling and ambition will be "lost in love's great unity."* On the contrary these sentiments are fostered by freedom, and are rather guided than repressed by sympathy.

In a truly organic life the individual is self-conscious and devoted to his own work, but feels himself and that work as part of a large and joyous whole. He is self-assertive, just because he is conscious of being a thread in the great web of events, of serving effectually as a member of a family, a state, of humanity, and of whatever greater whole his faith may picture. If we have not yet an organic society in this sense, we have at least the mechanical conditions that must underly it.

* The concluding line of E. W. Sill's poem, Dare You?

CHAPTER X

MODERN COMMUNICATION: SUPERFICIALITY AND STRAIN

STIMULATING EFFECT OF MODERN LIFE—SUPERFICIALITY—STRAIN
—PATHOLOGICAL EFFECTS.

THE action of the new communication is essentially stimulating, and so may, in some of its phases, be injurious. It costs the individual more in the way of mental function to take a normal part in the new order of things than it did in the old. Not only is his outlook broader, so that he is incited to think and feel about a wider range of matters, but he is required to be a more thorough-going specialist in the mastery of his particular function; both extension and intension have grown. General culture and technical training are alike more exigent than they used to be, and their demands visibly increase from year to year, not only in the schools but in life at large. The man who does not meet them falls behind the procession, and becomes in some sense a failure: either unable to make a living, or narrow and out of touch with generous movements.

Fortunately, from this point of view, our mental functions are as a rule rather sluggish, so that the spur of modern intercourse is for the most part wholesome, awakening the mind, abating sensuality, and giving men idea and purpose. Such ill effect as may be ascribed to it

98

seems to fall chiefly under the two heads, superficiality and strain, which the reader will perceive to be another view of that enlargement and animation discussed in the last chapter but one.

There is a rather general agreement among observers that, outside of his specialty, the man of our somewhat hurried civilization is apt to have an impatient, touch-and-go habit of mind as regards both thought and feeling. We are trying to do many and various things, and are driven to versatility and short cuts at some expense to truth and depth. "The habit of inattention," said De Tocqueville about 1835, "must be considered as the greatest defect of the democratic character"*; and recently his judgment has been confirmed by Ostrogorski, who thinks that deliverance from the bonds of space and time has made the American a man of short views, wedded to the present, accustomed to getting quick returns, and with no deep root anywhere.† We have reduced *ennui* considerably; but a moderate *ennui* is justly reckoned by Comte and others as one of the springs of progress, and it is no unmixed good that we are too busy to be unhappy.

In this matter, as in so many others, we should discriminate, so far as we can, between permanent conditions of modern life and what is due merely to change, between democracy and confusion. There is nothing in the nature of democracy to prevent its attaining, when transition has somewhat abated, a diverse and stable organization of its

* Democracy in America, vol. ii, book iii, chap. 15.
† Democracy and the Organization of Political Parties, ii, 579–588.

own sort, with great advantage to our spiritual composure and productivity.

In the meanwhile it is beyond doubt that the constant and varied stimulus of a confused time makes sustained attention difficult. Certainly our popular literature is written for those who run as they read, and carries the principle of economy of attention beyond anything previously imagined. And in feeling it seems to be true that we tend toward a somewhat superficial kindliness and adaptability, rather than sustained passion of any kind. Generally speaking, mind is spread out very thin over our civilization; a good sort of mind, no doubt, but quite thin.

All this may be counteracted in various ways, especially by thoroughness in education, and is perhaps to be regarded as lack of maturity rather than as incurable defect.

Mental strain, in spite of the alarming opinions sometimes expressed, is by no means a general condition in modern society, nor likely to become so; it is confined to a relatively small number, in whom individual weakness, or unusual stress, or both, has rendered life too much for the spirit. Yet this number includes a great part of those who perform the more exacting intellectual functions in business and the professions, as well as peculiarly weak, or sensitive, or unfortunate individuals in all walks of life. In general there is an increase of self-consciousness and choice; there is more opportunity, more responsibility, more complexity, a greater burden upon intelligence, will and character. The individual not only can but must deal with a flood of urgent suggestions, or be swamped by them. "This age that blots out life with question marks"* forces us to think and choose whether we are ready or not.

Worse, probably, than anything in the way of work—though that is often destructive—is the anxious insecurity in which our changing life keeps a large part of the population, the well-to-do as well as the poor. And an educated and imaginative people feels such anxieties more than one deadened by ignorance. "In America," said De Tocqueville, "I saw the freest and most enlightened men placed in the happiest circumstances which the world affords; it seemed to me as if a cloud habitually hung upon their brows, and I thought them serious and almost sad, even in their pleasures."†

Not long ago Mr. H. D. Sedgwick contributed to a magazine a study of what he called "The New American Type,"‡ based on an exhibition of English and American portraits, some recent, some a century old. He found that the more recent were conspicuously marked by the signs of unrest and strain. Speaking of Mr. Sargent's subjects he says, "The obvious qualities in his portraits are disquiet, lack of equilibrium, absence of principle, . . . a mind unoccupied by the rightful heirs, as if the home of principle and dogma had been transformed into an inn for wayfarers. Sargent's women are more marked than his men; women, as physically more delicate, are the first to reveal the strain of physical and psychical maladjustment. The thin spirit of life shivers pathetically in

---

* J. R. Lowell, The Cathedral.
† Democracy in America, vol. ii, book ii, chap. 13.
‡ Since published in a book having this title.

its 'fleshly dress'; in the intensity of its eagerness it is all unconscious of its spiritual fidgeting on finding itself astray —no path, no blazings, the old forgotten, the new not formed." The early Americans, he says, "were not limber minded men, not readily agnostic, not nicely sceptical; they were . . . eighteenth century Englishmen." Of Reynolds' women he observes, "These ladies led lives unvexed; natural affections, a few brief saws, a half-dozen principles, kept their brows smooth, their cheeks ripe, their lips most wooable." People had "a stable physique and a well-ordered, logical, dogmatic philosophy." The older portraits "chant a chorus of praise for national character, for class distinctions, for dogma and belief, for character, for good manners, for honor, for contemplation, for vision to look upon life as a whole, for appreciation that the world is to be enjoyed, for freedom from democracy, for capacity in lighter mood to treat existence as a comedy told by Goldoni."*

This may or may not be dispassionately just, but it sets forth one side of the case—a side the more pertinent for being unpopular—and suggests a very real though intangible difference between the people of our time and those of a century ago—one which all students must have felt. It is what we feel in literature when we compare the people of Jane Austen with those, let us say, of the author of The House of Mirth.

I do not propose to inquire how far the effects of strain may be seen in an increase of certain distinctly pathological phenomena, such as neurasthenia, the use of drugs,

* The Atlantic Monthly, April, 1904.

insanity and suicide. That it has an important working in this way—difficult, however, to separate from that of other factors—is generally conceded. In the growth of suicide we seem to have a statistical demonstration of the destructive effect of social stress at its worst; and of general paralysis, which is rapidly increasing and has been called the disease of the century, we are told that "it is the disease of excess, of vice, of overwork, of prolonged worry; it is especially the disease of great urban centres, and its existence usually seems to show that the organism has entered upon a competitive race for which it is not fully equipped."

PART III

THE DEMOCRATIC MIND

PART II

THE DEMOCRATIC STATE

CHAPTER XI

THE ENLARGEMENT OF CONSCIOUSNESS

NARROWNESS OF CONSCIOUSNESS IN TRIBAL SOCIETY—IMPORTANCE OF FACE-TO-FACE ASSEMBLY—INDIVIDUALITY—SUBCONSCIOUS CHARACTER OF WIDER RELATIONS—ENLARGEMENT OF CONSCIOUSNESS—IRREGULARITY IN GROWTH—BREADTH OF MODERN CONSCIOUSNESS—DEMOCRACY.

IN a life like that of the Teutonic tribes before they took on Roman civilization, the social medium was small, limited for most purposes to the family, clan or village group. Within this narrow circle there was a vivid interchange of thought and feeling, a sphere of moral unity, of sympathy, loyalty, honor and congenial intercourse. Here precious traditions were cherished, and here also was the field for an active public opinion, for suggestion and discussion, for leading and following, for conformity and dissent. "In this kindly soil of the family," says Professor Gummere in his Germanic Origins, "flourished such growth of sentiment as that rough life brought forth. Peace, good-will, the sense of honor, loyalty to friend and kinsman, brotherly affection, all were plants that found in the Germanic home that congenial warmth they needed for their earliest stages of growth. . . . Originally the family or clan made a definite sphere or system of life; outside of it the homeless man felt indeed that chaos had come again."*

* Pages 169, 171.

When we say that public opinion is modern, we mean, of course, the wider and more elaborate forms of it. On a smaller scale it has always existed where people have had a chance to discuss and act upon matters of common interest. Among our American Indians, for example, "Opinion was a most potent factor in all tribes, and this would be largely directed by those having popularity and power. Officers, in fact all persons, became extremely well known in the small community of an Amerind tribe. Every peculiarity of temperament was understood, and the individual was respected or despised according to his predominating characteristics. Those who were bold and fierce and full of strategy were made war-chiefs, while those who possessed judgment and decision were made civil chiefs or governors."* The Germanic tribes were accustomed to assemble in those village moots to which the historian recurs with such reverence, where "the men from whom Englishmen were to spring learned the worth of public opinion, of public discussion, the worth of the agreement, the 'common-sense' to which discussion leads, as of the laws which derive their force from being expressions of that general conviction."†

Discussion and public opinion of this simple sort, as every one knows, takes place also among children wherever they mingle freely. Indeed, it springs so directly from human nature, and is so difficult to suppress even by the most inquisitorial methods, that we may assume it to exist locally in all forms of society and at all periods of history   It grows by looks and gestures where

* F. S. Dellenbaugh, The North Americans of Yesterday, 416.
† J. R. Green, History of the English People, i, 13.

speech is forbidden, so that even in a prison there is public opinion among the inmates. But in tribal life these local groups contained all the vivid and conscious society there was, the lack of means of record and of quick transmission making a wider unity impracticable.

In the absence of indirect communication people had to come into face-to-face contact in order to feel social excitement and rise to the higher phases of consciousness. Hence games, feasts and public assemblies of every sort meant more to the general life than they do in our day. They were the occasions of exaltation, the theatre for the display of eloquence—either in discussing questions of the moment or recounting deeds of the past—and for the practice of those rhythmic exercises that combined dancing, acting, poetry and music in one comprehensive and communal art. Such assemblies are possibly more ancient than human nature itself—since human nature implies a preceding evolution of group life—and in some primitive form of them speech itself is supposed by some to have been born. Just as children invent words in the eagerness of play, and slang arises among gangs of boys on the street, so the earliest men were perhaps incited to the invention of language by a certain ecstasy and self-forgetting audacity, like that of the poet, sprung from the excitement of festal meetings.*

Something of the spirit of these primitive assemblies is perhaps reproduced in the social exaltation of those festal evenings around the camp-fire which many of us can recall, with individual and group songs, chants, "stunts" and the

* J. Donovan, The Festal Origin of Human Speech. Mind, October, 1891.

like; when there were not wanting original, almost impromptu, compositions—celebrating notable deeds or satirizing conspicuous individuals—which the common excitement generated in the minds of one or more ingenious persons.

It is sometimes said that the individual counted for nothing in tribal life, that the family or the clan was the unit of society, in which all personalities were merged. From the standpoint of organization there is much truth in this; that is the group of kindred was for many purposes (political, economic, religious, etc.) a corporate unit, acting as a whole and responsible as a whole to the rest of society; so that punishment of wrong-doing, for example, would be exacted from the group rather than from the particular offender. But taken psychologically, to mean that there was a lack of self-assertion, the idea is without foundation. On the contrary, the barbaric mind exalts an aggressive and even extravagant individuality. Achilles is a fair sample of its heroes, mighty in valor and prowess, but vain, arrogant and resentful—what we should be apt to call an individualist.* The men of the Niebelungenlied, of Beowulf, of Norse and Irish tales and of our Indian legends are very much like him.

Consider, also, the personal initiative displayed in the formation of a war-party among the Omahas, as described by Dorsey, and note how little it differs from the way in which commercial and other enterprises are started at the present day.

* "Jura neget sibi nata, nihil non arroget armis."—Horace, Ars Poet., 122.

110

"It is generally a young man who decides to undertake an expedition against the enemy. Having formed his plan he speaks thus to his friend: 'My friend, as I wish to go on the war path, let us go. Let us boil the food as for a feast.' The friend having consented, the two are the leaders . . . if they can induce others to follow them. So they find two young men whom they send as messengers to invite those whom they name. . . . When all have assembled the planner of the expedition addresses the company. 'Ho! my friends, my friend and I have invited you to a feast, because we wish to go on the war path.' Then each one who is willing to go replies thus: 'Yes, my friend, I am willing.' But he who is unwilling replies, 'My friend, I do not wish to go, I am unwilling.' Sometimes the host says, 'Let us go by such a day. Prepare yourselves.'"*

The whole proceeding reminds one also of the way games are initiated among boys, the one who "gets it up" having the right to claim the best position. No doubt the structure of some tribal societies permitted of less initiative than others; but such differences exist at all stages of culture.

Self-feeling, self-assertion and the general relation of the individual to the group are much the same at all epochs, and there was never a time since man became human when, as we sometimes read, "personality emerged." Change has taken place chiefly in the extent and character of the group to which the individual appeals, and in the ways in which he tries to distinguish

* J. O. Dorsey, Omaha Sociology, 315, 316. A publication of the U. S. Bureau of Ethnology.

111

himself. The Germanic tribesman, the mediæval knight, the Renaissance artist or scholar and the modern captain of industry are alike ambitious: it is the object that differs. There has, indeed, been a development of personality in history, but it has been correlative with that of the general life, and has brought no essential change in the relation between the two.

In tribal life, then, since the conditions did not admit of wider unification, public consciousness could be only local in scope. Beyond its narrow range the cords which held life together were of a subconscious character— heredity, of course, with its freight of mental and social tendency; oral tradition, often vague and devious, and a mass of custom that was revered without being understood. These wider relations, not being surveyed and discussed, could not be the objects of deliberate thought and will, but were accepted as part of the necessary order of things, and usually ascribed to some divine source. In this way language, laws, religion, forms of government, social classes, traditional relations to other clans or tribes—all of which we know to have been built up by the cumulative workings of the human mind—were thought of as beyond the sphere of man's control.

The wider unity existed, then as now; human development was continuous in time and, after a blind fashion, coöperative among contemporaries. The tools of life were progressively invented and spread by imitation from tribe to tribe, the fittest always tending to survive; but only the immediate details of such changes were matters of consciousness: as processes they were beyond human cognizance. A man might adapt an ancient custom to a fresh emergency, but he would be unaware that he was shaping the growth of institutions.

There was even a tribal or national opinion, of a slow, subconscious sort; a growth and consensus of ideas upon matters of general and enduring interest, such as religion, marriage and government. And, under unusual pressure, some more conscious unity of spirit might be aroused, as among the Germans or Gauls confederated against Rome; but this was likely to be transient.

The central fact of history, from a psychological point of view, may be said to be the gradual enlargement of social consciousness and rational coöperation. The mind constantly, though perhaps not regularly, extends the sphere within which it makes its higher powers valid. Human nature, possessed of ideals moulded in the family and the commune, is ever striving, somewhat blindly for the most part, with those difficulties of communication and organization which obstruct their realization on a larger scale. Whether progress is general or not we need not now inquire; it is certain that great gains have been made by the more vigorous or fortunate races, and that these are regarded with emulation and hope by many of the others.

Throughout modern European history, at least, there has been an evident extension of the local areas within which communication and coöperation prevail, and, on the whole, an advance in the quality of coöperation as judged by an ideal moral unity. It has tended to become more

113

free and human, more adequately expressive of communal feeling.

Perhaps all apparent departures from this tendency may plausibly be explained as cases of irregular growth. If we find that vast systems of discipline, like the Roman Empire, have broken down, we find also that these systems were of a low type, psychologically, that the best features of them were after all preserved, and that the new systems that arose, though perhaps less in extent, were on the whole a higher and fuller expression of human nature.

In the later Empire, for example, it seems plain that social mechanism (in its proper kind and measure one of the conditions of freedom) had grown in such a way as to shackle the human mind. In order to achieve and maintain an imperial reach of control, the state had gradually been forced to take on a centralized bureaucratic structure, which left the individual and the local group no sphere of self-reliant development. Public spirit and political leadership were suppressed, and the habit of organized self-expression died out, leaving the people without group vitality and as helpless as children. They were not, in general, cowards or voluptuaries—it seems that the decline of courage and domestic morals has been exaggerated—but they had no trained and effective public capacity. Society, as Professor Dill says, had been elaborately and deliberately stereotyped.

The decline of vitality and initiative pervaded all spheres of life. There were no inventions and little industrial or agricultural progress of any kind. Literature de-

114

generated into rhetoric: "In the same manner," says
Longinus, "as some children always remain pigmies,
whose infant limbs have been too closely confined, thus
our tender minds, fettered by the prejudices and habits
of a just servitude, are unable to expand themselves, or
to attain that well-proportioned greatness which we admire in the ancients, who, living under a popular government, wrote with the same freedom as they acted."*

The growing states of the earlier world were confronted,
whether they knew it or not, with an irreconcilable opposition between freedom and expansion. They might
retain in small areas those simple and popular institutions which nearly all the great peoples started with, and
to which they owed their vigor; or they could organize
on a larger scale a more mechanical unity. In the first
case their careers were brief, because they lacked the
military force to ensure permanence in a hostile world.
In the latter they incurred, by the suppression of human
nature, that degeneracy which sooner or later overtook
every great state of antiquity.

In some such way as this we may, perhaps, dispose of
the innumerable instances which history shows of the
failure of free organization—as in the decay of ancient
and mediæval city republics. Not only was their freedom
of an imperfect nature at the best, but they were too small
to hold their own in a world that was necessarily, for the
most part, autocratic or customary. Freedom, though
in itself a principle of strength, was on too little a scale
to defend itself. "If a republic be small," said Montes-

* Quoted by Gibbon, Decline and Fall, Milman-Smith edition,
i, 194, 195.

quieu, "it is destroyed by a foreign force; if it be large it is ruined by internal imperfection."*

But how splendid, in literature, in art, and even in arms, were many of these failures. How well did Athens, Florence and a hundred other cities illustrate the intrinsic strength and fecundity of that free principle to which modern conditions permit an indefinite expansion.

The present epoch, then, brings with it a larger and, potentially at least, a higher and freer consciousness. In the individual aspect of life this means that each one of us has, as a rule, a wider grasp of situations, and is thus in a position to give a wider application to his intelligence, sympathy and conscience. In proportion as he does this he ceases to be a blind agent and becomes a rational member of the whole.

Because of this more conscious relation to the larger wholes—nations, institutions, tendencies—he takes a more vital and personal part in them. His self-feeling attaches itself, as its nature is, to the object of his free activity, and he tends to feel that "love of the maker for his work," that spiritual identification of the member with the whole, which is the ideal of organization.

De Tocqueville found that in the United States there was no proletariat. "That numerous and turbulent multitude does not exist, who regarding the law as their natural enemy look upon it with fear and distrust. It is impossible, on the contrary, not to perceive that all classes . . . are attached to it by a kind of parental affection."†

* The Spirit of Laws, book ix, chap. 1.
† Democracy in America, vol. i, chap. 24.

And, notwithstanding a deep and well-grounded "social unrest," this remains essentially true at the present day, and should be true of all real democracy. Where the state is directly and obviously founded upon the thought of the people it is impossible to get up much fundamental antagonism to it; the energies of discontent are absorbed by moderate agitation.

The extension of reach and choice favors, in the long run, not only political but every kind of opportunity and freedom. It opens to the individual a more vital, self-determined and energetic part in all phases of the whole.

At the same time, the limits of human faculty make it impossible that any one of us should actually occupy all the field of thought thus open to him. Although stimulated to greater activity than before, one must constantly select and renounce; and most of his life will still be on the plane of custom and mechanism. He is freer chiefly in that he can survey the larger whole and choose in what relations he will express himself.

Indeed, an ever-present danger of the new order is that one will not select and renounce enough, that he will swallow more than he can properly digest, and fail of the benefits of a thorough subconscious assimilation. The more one studies current life, the more he is inclined to look upon superficiality as its least tractable defect.

The new conditions demand also a thorough, yet diversified and adaptable, system of training for the individual who is to share in this freer and more exigent society. While democracy as a spirit is spontaneous, only the fullest development of personal faculty can make this spirit effectual on a great scale. Our confidence in our

117

instincts need not be shaken, but our application of them must be enlarged and enlightened. We must be taught to do some one thing well, and yet never allowed to lose our sense of the relation of that one thing to the general endeavor.

The general or public. phase of larger consciousness is what we call Democracy. I mean by this primarily the organized sway of public opinion. It works out also in a tendency to humanize the collective life, to make institutions express the higher impulses of human nature, instead of brutal or mechanical conditions. That which most inwardly distinguishes modern life from ancient or mediæval is the conscious power of the common people trying to effectuate their instincts. All systems rest, in a sense, upon public opinion; but the peculiarity of our time is that this opinion is more and more rational and self-determining. It is not, as in the past, a mere reflection of conditions believed to be inevitable, but seeks principles, finds these principles in human nature, and is determined to conform life to them or know why not. In this all earnest people, in their diverse ways, are taking part.

We find, of course, that but little can be carried out on the highest moral plane; the mind cannot attend to many things with that concentration which achieves adequate expression, and the principle of compensation is ever at work. If one thing is well done, others are overlooked, so that we are constantly being caught and ground in our own neglected mechanism.

On the whole, however, the larger mind involves a

118

democratic and humanistic trend in every phase of life. A right democracy is simply the application on a large scale of principles which are universally felt to be right as applied to a small group—principles of free coöperation motived by a common spirit which each serves according to his capacity. Most of what is characteristic of the time is evidently of this nature; as, for instance, our sentiment of fair play, our growing kindliness, our cult of womanhood, our respect for hand labor, and our endeavor to organize society economically or on "business principles." And it is perhaps equally evident that the ideas which these replace—of caste, of domination, of military glory, of "conspicuous leisure"* and the like—sprang from a secondary and artificial system, based on conditions which forbade a large realization of primary ideals.

May we not say, speaking largely, that there has always been a democratic tendency, whose advance has been conditioned by the possibility, under actual conditions, of organizing popular thought and will on a wide scale? Free coöperation is natural and human; it takes place spontaneously among children on the playground, among settlers in new countries, and among the most primitive sorts of men—everywhere, in short, where the secondary and artificial discipline has not supplanted it. The latter, including every sort of coercive or mechanical control is, of course, natural in the larger sense, and functional in human development; but there must ever be some resistance to it, which will tend to become effective when the control ceases to be maintained by the pressure of ex-

* One of many illuminating phrases introduced by T. V. Veblen in his work on The Theory of the Leisure Class.

pediency. Accordingly we see that throughout modern history, and especially during the past century, there has been a progressive humanism, a striving to clear away lower forms of coöperation no longer essential, and to substitute something congenial to natural impulse.

Discussion regarding the comparative merits of monarchy, aristocracy and democracy has come to be looked upon as scholastic. The world is clearly democratizing; it is only a question of how fast the movement can take place, and what, under various conditions, it really involves. Democracy, instead of being a single and definite political type, proves to be merely a principle of breadth in organization, naturally prevalent wherever men have learned how to work it, under which life will be at least as various in its forms as it was before.

It involves a change in the character of social discipline not confined to politics, but as much at home in one sphere as another. With facility of communication as its mechanical basis, it proceeds inevitably to discuss and experiment with freer modes of action in religion, industry, education, philanthropy and the family. The law of the survival of the fittest will prevail in regard to social institutions, as it has in the past, but the conditions of fitness have undergone a change the implications of which we can but dimly foresee.

CHAPTER XII

THE THEORY OF PUBLIC OPINION

PUBLIC OPINION AS ORGANIZATION—AGREEMENT NOT ESSENTIAL
—PUBLIC OPINION VERSUS POPULAR IMPRESSION—PUBLIC
THOUGHT NOT AN AVERAGE—A GROUP IS CAPABLE OF EX-
PRESSION THROUGH ITS MOST COMPETENT MEMBERS—GENERAL
AND SPECIAL PUBLIC OPINION—THE SPHERE OF THE FORMER
—OF THE LATTER—THE TWO ARE UNITED IN PERSONALITY—
HOW PUBLIC OPINION RULES—EFFECTIVE RULE BASED ON
MORAL UNITY.

PUBLIC opinion is no mere aggregate of separate individual judgments, but an organization, a coöperative
product of communication and reciprocal influence. It
may be as different from the sum of what the individuals
could have thought out in separation as a ship built by
a hundred men is from a hundred boats each built by
one man.

A group "makes up its mind" in very much the same
manner that the individual makes up his. The latter
must give time and attention to the question, search his
consciousness for pertinent ideas and sentiments, and
work them together into a whole, before he knows what
his real thought about it is. In the case of a nation the
same thing must take place, only on a larger scale. Each
individual must make up his mind as before, but in doing
so he has to deal not only with what was already in his
thought or memory, but with fresh ideas that flow in from

others whose minds are also aroused. Every one who has any fact, or thought, or feeling, which he thinks is unknown, or insufficiently regarded, tries to impart it; and thus not only one mind but all minds are searched for pertinent material, which is poured into the general stream of thought for each one to use as he can. In this manner the minds in a communicating group become a single organic whole. Their unity is not one of identity, but of life and action, a crystallization of diverse but related ideas.

It is not at all necessary that there should be agreement; the essential thing is a certain ripeness and stability of thought resulting from attention and discussion. There may be quite as much difference of opinion as there was before, but the differences now existing are comparatively intelligent and lasting. People know what they really think about the matter, and what other people think. Measures, platforms, candidates, creeds and other symbols have been produced which serve to express and assist coöperation and to define opposition. There has come to be a relatively complete organization of thought, to which each individual or group contributes in its own peculiar way.

Take, for instance, the state of opinion in the United States regarding slavery at the outbreak of the civil war. No general agreement had been reached; but the popular mind had become organized with reference to the matter, which had been turned over and regarded from all points of view, by all parts of the community, until a certain ripeness regarding it had been reached; revealing in this case a radical conflict of thought between the North and the South, and much local diversity in both sections.

One who would understand public opinion should distinguish clearly between a true or mature opinion and a popular impression. The former requires earnest attention and discussion for a considerable time, and when reached is significant, even if mistaken. It rarely exists regarding matters of temporary interest, and current talk or print is a most uncertain index of it. A popular impression, on the other hand, is facile, shallow, transient, with that fickleness and fatuity that used to be ascribed to the popular mind in general. It is analogous to the unconsidered views and utterances of an individual, and the more one studies it the less seriously he will take it. It may happen that ninety-nine men in a hundred hold opinions to-day contrary to those they will hold a month hence—partly because they have not yet searched their own minds, partly because the few who have really significant and well-grounded ideas have not had time to impress them upon the rest.

It is not unreasonable, then, to combine a very slight regard for most of what passes as public opinion with much confidence in the soundness of an aroused, mature, organic social judgment.

There is a widespread, but as I believe a fallacious, idea that the public thought or action must in some way express the working of an average or commonplace mind, must be some kind of a mean between the higher and lower intelligences making up the group. It would be

123

more correct to say that it is representative, meaning by this that the preponderant *feeling* of the group seeks definite and effectual expression through individuals specially competent to give it such expression. Take for instance the activities of one of our colleges in intercollegiate athletics or debates. What belongs to the group at large is a vague desire to participate and excel in such competitions; but in realizing itself this desire seeks as its agents the best athletes or debaters that are to be found. A little common-sense and observation will show that the expression of a group is nearly always superior, for the purpose in hand, to the average capacity of its members.

I do not mean morally superior, but simply more effective, in a direction determined by the prevalent feeling. If a mob is in question, the brutal nature, for the time-being ascendant, may act through the most brutal men in the group; and in like manner a money-making enterprise is apt to put forward the shrewdest agents it can find, without regard for any moral qualities except fidelity to itself.

But if the life of the group is deliberate and sympathetic, its expression may be morally high, on a level not merely of the average member, but of the most competent, of the best. The average theory as applied to public consciousness is wholly out of place. The public mind may be on a lower plane than that of the individual thinking in separation, or it may be on a higher, but is almost sure to be on a different plane; and no inkling of its probable character can be had by taking a mean. One mind in the right, whether on statesmanship, science, morals, or what not,

124

may raise all other minds to its own point of view—because of the general capacity for recognition and deference —just as through our aptitude for sudden rage or fear one mind in the wrong may debase all the rest.

This is the way in which right social judgments are reached in matters so beyond commonplace capacity as science, philosophy, and much of literature and art. All good critics tell us that the judgment of mankind, in the long run, is sure and sound. The world makes no mistake as to Plato, though, as Emerson said, there are never enough understanding readers alive to pay for an edition of his works. This, to be sure, is a judgment of the few; and so, in a sense, are all finer judgments. The point is that the many have the sense to adopt them.

And let us note that those collective judgments in literature, art and science which have exalted Plato and Dante and Leonardo and Michelangelo and Beethoven and Newton and Darwin, are democratic judgments, in the sense that every man has been free to take a part in proportion to his capacity, precisely as the citizen of a democracy is free to take a part in politics. Wealth and station have occasionally tried to dictate in these matters, but have failed.

It is natural for an organism to use its appropriate organ, and it would be as reasonable to say that the capacity of the body for seeing is found by taking an average of the visual power of the hand, nose, liver, etc., along with that of the eye, as that the capacity of a group for a special purpose is that of its average member. If a group does not function through its most competent instruments, it is simply because of imperfect organization.

125

It is strange that people who apply the average theory to democracy do not see that if it were sound it must apply to all the social phenomena of history, which is a record of the works of the collective mind. Since the main difference between democracy and ancient or mediæval systems is merely that the former is less restricted by time, space and caste, is essentially an appeal to free human power as against what is merely mechanical or conventional; by what magic is this appeal to deprive us of our ancient privilege of acting through our efficient individuals ?

One who ponders these things will see that the principles of collective expression are the same now as ever, and that the special difficulties of our time arise partly from confusion, due to the pace of change, and partly from the greater demands which a free system makes upon human capacity. The question is, whether, in practice, democracy is capable of the effective expression to which no very serious theoretical obstacle can be discerned. It is a matter of doing a rather simple thing on a vaster and more complicated scale than in the past.

Public opinion is no uniform thing, as we are apt to assume, but has its multifarious differentiations. We may roughly distinguish a general opinion, in which almost everybody in the community has a part, and an infinite diversity of special or class opinions—of the family, the club, the school-room, the party, the union, and so on.

And there is an equal diversity in the kind of thought with which the public mind may be concerned: the content may be of almost any sort. Thus there are group ideals, like the American ideal of indissoluble unity among

THE THEORY OF PUBLIC OPINION

the states, the French ideal of national glory, or the ideals
of honor and good-breeding cherished in many families;
and there are group beliefs, regarding religion, trade,
agriculture, marriage, education and the like. Upon all
matters in which the mind has, in the past, taken a lively
interest there are latent inclinations and prepossessions,
and when these are aroused and organized by discussion
they combine with other elements to form public opinion.
Mr. Higginson, recounting his experience in the Massa-
chusetts legislature, speaks of "certain vast and inscrutable undercurrents of prejudice . . . which could never
be comprehended by academic minds, or even city-bred
minds," but which were usually irresistible. They related to the rights of towns, the public school system, the
law of settlement, roads, navigable streams, breadth of
wheels, close time of fishing, etc. "Every good debater
in the House, and every one of its recognized legal authorities, might be on one side, and yet the smallest contest with one of these latent prejudices would land them
in a minority."*

This diversity merely reflects the complexity of organization, current opinion and discussion being a pervasive
activity, essential to growth, that takes place throughout
the system at large and in each particular member.
General opinion existing alone, without special types of
thought as in the various departments of science and art,
would indicate a low type of structure, more like a mob
than a rational society. It is upon these special types, and
the individuals that speak for them, that we rely for the

* On the Outskirts of Public Life, The Atlantic Monthly, Feb.,
1898.

127

guidance of general opinion (as, for instance, we rely upon economists to teach us what to think about the currency), and the absence of mature speciality involves weakness and flatness of general achievement. This fault is often charged to democracy, but it should rather be said that democracy is substituting a free type of speciality, based upon choice, for the old type based upon caste, and that whatever deficiency exists in this regard is due chiefly to the confused conditions that accompany transition.

General public opinion has less scope than is commonly imagined. It is true that with the new communication, the whole people, if they are enough interested, may form public judgments even upon transient questions. But it is not possible, nor indeed desirable, that they should be enough interested in many questions to form such judgments. A likeness of spirit and principle is essential to moral unity, but as regards details differentiation is and should be the rule. The work of the world is mostly of a special character, and it is quite as important that a man should mind his own business—that is, his own particular kind of general service—as that he should have public spirit. Perhaps we may say that the main thing is to mind his private business in a public spirit—always remembering that men who are in a position to do so should make it their private business to attend to public affairs. It is not indolence and routine, altogether, but also an inevitable conflict of claims, that makes men slow to exert their minds upon general questions, and underlies the political maxim that you cannot arouse public opinion

128

upon more than one matter at a time. It is better that the public, like the general-in-chief of an army, should be relieved of details and free to concentrate its thought on essential choices.

I have only a limited belief in the efficacy of the referendum and similar devices for increased participation of the people at large in the details of legislation. In so far as these facilitate the formation and expression of public will upon matters to which the public is prepared to give earnest and continuous attention, they are serviceable; but if many questions are submitted, or those of a technical character, the people become confused or indifferent, and the real power falls into the hands of the few who manage the machinery.

The questions which can profitably be decided by this direct and general judgment of the public are chiefly those of organic change or readjustment, such, for instance, as the contemporary question of what part the government is to take in relation to the consolidation of industries. These the people must decide, since no lesser power will be submitted to, but routine activities, in society as in individuals, are carried on without arousing a general consciousness. The people are also, as I shall shortly point out, peculiarly fit to make choice among conspicuous personalities.

Specialists of all sorts—masons, soldiers, chemists, lawyers, bankers, even statesmen and public officials—are ruled for the most part by the opinion of their special group, and have little immediate dependence upon the general public, which will not concern itself with them so

129

long as their work is not palpably inefficient or in some way distasteful.

Yet special phases of thought are not really independent, but are to be looked upon as the work of the public mind acting with a less general consciousness—partly automatic like the action of the legs in walking. They are still responsible to the general state of opinion; and it is usually a general need of the special product, as shoes, banks, education, medical aid and so on, that gives the special group its pecuniary support and social standing. Moreover, the general interest in a particular group is likely to become awakened and critical when the function is disturbed, as with the building trades or the coal-mine operators in case of a strike; or when it becomes peculiarly important, as with the army in time of war. Then is the day of reckoning when the specialist has to render an account of the talents entrusted to him.

The separateness of the special group is also limited by personality, by the fact that the men who perform the specialty do not in other matters think apart from the rest of the society, but, in so far as it is a moral whole, share its general spirit and are the same men who, all taken together, are the seat of public opinion. How far the different departments of a man's mind, corresponding to general and special opinion, may be ruled by different principles, is a matter of interest from the fact that every one of us is the theatre of a conflict of moral standards arising in this way. It is evident by general observation and confession that we usually accept without much criticism the principles we become accustomed to in each sphere of

130

activity, whether consistent with one another or not. Yet this is not rational, and there is and must ever be a striving of conscience to redress such conflicts, which are really divisions in society itself, and tend toward anarchy. It is an easy but weak defence of low principles of conduct, in business, in politics, in war, in paying taxes, to say that a special standard prevails in this sphere, and that our behavior is justified by custom. We cannot wholly escape from the customary, but conscience should require of ourselves and others an honest effort to raise its standard, even at much sacrifice of lower aims. Such efforts are the only source of betterment, and without them society must deteriorate.

In other words, it is the chief and perhaps the only method of moral and intellectual progress that the thought and sentiment pertaining to the various activities should mingle in the mind, and that whatever is higher or more rational in each should raise the standard of the others. If one finds that as a business man he tends to be greedy and narrow, he should call into that sphere his sentiments as a patriot, a member of a family and a student, and he may enrich these latter provinces by the system and shrewdness he learns in business. The keeping of closed compartments is a principle of stagnation and decay.

The rule of public opinion, then, means for the most part a latent authority which the public will exercise when sufficiently dissatisfied with the specialist who is in immediate charge of a particular function. It cannot extend to the immediate participation of the group as a whole in the details of public business.

131

This principle holds good in the conduct of government as well as elsewhere, experience showing that the politics of an intricate state is always a specialty, closer to the public interest, perhaps, than most specialties, but ordinarily controlled by those who, for whatever reason, put their main energy into it. Professional politicians, in this sense, are sure to win as against the amateur; and if politics is badly managed the chief remedy is to raise the level of the profession.

De Tocqueville says that "the people reign in the American political world as the Deity does in the universe. They are the cause and the aim of all things; everything comes from them and is absorbed by them."* And we may add that, also like the Deity, they do things through agents in whom the supposed attributes of their master are much obscured.

There are some who say we have no democracy, because much is done, in government as elsewhere, in neglect or defiance of general sentiment. But the same is true under any form of sovereignty; indeed, much more true under monarchy or oligarchy than under our form. The rule of the people is surely more real and pervasive than that of Louis XIV or Henry VIII. No sovereign possesses completely its instruments, but democracy perhaps does so more nearly than any other.

When an important function, such as government, or trade or education, is not performed to the satisfaction of watchful consciences, the remedy is somewhat as follows. A rather general moral sentiment regarding the matter must be aroused by publishing the facts and ex-

* Democracy in America, vol. i, chap. 4.

posing their inconsistency with underlying standards of right. This sentiment will effect little so long as it is merely general, but if vigorous it rapidly begets organs through which to work. It is the nature of such a sentiment to stimulate particular individuals or groups to organize and effectuate it. The press has a motive to exploit and increase it by vivid exposition of the state of affairs; enthusiasm, seeking for an outlet, finds it in this direction; ambition and even pecuniary interest are enlisted to gratify the demand. Effective leadership thus arises, and organization, which thrives in the warmth of public attention, is not long wanting. Civic leagues and the like —supposing that it is a matter of politics—unite with trusted leaders and the independent press to guide the voter in choosing between honesty and corruption. The moral standard of the professional group begins to rise: a few offenders are punished, many are alarmed, and things which every one has been doing or conniving at are felt as wrong. In a vigorous democracy like that of the United States, this process is ever going on, on a great scale and in innumerable minor groups: the public mind, like a careful farmer, moves about its domain, hoeing weeds, mending fences and otherwise setting things to rights, undeterred by the fact that the work will not stay done.

Such regeneration implies the existence of a real, though perhaps latent, moral unity in the group whose standards are thus revived and applied. It is, for instance, of untold advantage to all righteous movements in the United States, that the nation traditionally exists to the

133

ends of justice, freedom and humanity. This tradition means that there is already a noble and cherished ideal, no sincere appeal to which is vain; and we could as well dispense with the wisdom of the Constitution as with the sentiment of the Declaration of Independence.

On the same principle, it is a chief factor in the misgovernment of our cities that they are mostly too new and heterogeneous to have an established consciousness. As soon as the people feel their unity, we may hopefully look for civic virtue and devotion, because these things require a social medium in which to work. A man will not devote himself, ordinarily, where there is no distinct and human whole to devote himself to, no mind in which his devotion will be recognized and valued. But to a vital and enduring group devotion is natural, and we may expect that a self-conscious city, state, university or profession will prove to be a theatre of the magnanimous virtues.

CHAPTER XIII

WHAT THE MASSES CONTRIBUTE

The Masses the Initiators of Sentiment—They Live in the Central Current of Experience—Distinction or Privilege Apt to Cause Isolation—Institutional Character of Upper Classes—The Masses Shrewd Judges of Persons—This the Main Ground for Expecting that the People Will Be Right in the Long Run—Democracy Always Representative—Conclusion.

The function of leaders in defining and organizing the confused tendencies of the public mind is evident enough, but just what the masses themselves contribute is perhaps not so apparent.* The thought of the undistinguished many is, however, not less important, not necessarily less original, than that of the conspicuous few; the originality of the latter, just because it is more conspicuous, being easy to overestimate. Leadership is only salient initiative; and among the many there may well be increments of initiative which though not salient are yet momentous as a whole.

The originality of the masses is to be found not so much in formulated idea as in sentiment. In capacity to feel and to trust those sentiments which it is the proper aim of social development to express, they are, perhaps, commonly superior to the more distinguished or privileged classes. The reason is that their experience usually

* Some discussion of leadership will be found in Human Nature and the Social Order, chaps. 8 and 9.

135

keeps them closer to the springs of human nature, and so more under the control of its primary impulses.

Radical movements aiming to extend the application of higher sentiment have generally been pushed on by the common people, rather than by privileged orders, or by conspicuous leadership of any sort.* This seems to be true of Christianity in all ages, and of the many phases of modern democracy and enfranchisement. In American history, particularly, both the revolution which gave us independence and the civil war which abolished slavery and reunited the country, were more generally and steadfastly supported by the masses than by people of education or wealth. Mr. Higginson, writing on the Cowardice of Culture,† asserts that at the opening of the Revolution the men of wealth and standing who took the side of liberty were so few that they could be counted, and that "there was never a period in our history, since the American Nation was independent, when it would not have been a calamity to have it controlled by its highly educated men alone." And in England also it was the masses who upheld abolition in the colonies and sympathized with the North in the American struggle.

The common people, as a rule, live more in the central current of human experience than men of wealth or distinction. Domestic morality, religious sentiment, faith in man and God, loyalty to country and the like, are the fruit of the human heart growing in homely conditions,

* So Mr. Bryce, The American Commonwealth, chap. 76. Some emphasis should be given to the phrase "pushed on," as distinguished from "initiated."

† In the Atlantic Monthly, Oct., 1905.

and they easily wither when these conditions are lost. To be one among many, without individual pretension, is in one way a position of security and grandeur. One stands, as it were, with the human race at his back, sharing its claim on truth, justice and God. *Qui quærit habere privata amittit communia;* * the plain man has not conspicuously gained private things, and should be all the richer in things that are common, in faith and fellowship. Nothing, perhaps, is healthy that isolates us from the common destiny of men, that is merely appropriative and not functional, that is not such as all might rejoice in if they understood it.

Miss Jane Addams has advanced a theory,† far from absurd, that the confused and deprived masses of our cities, collected from all lands by immigration, are likely to be the initiators of new and higher ideals for our civilization. Since "ideals are born of situations," they are perhaps well situated for such a function by the almost complete destruction, so far as they are concerned, of old traditions and systems. In this promiscuous mingling of elements everything is cancelled but human nature, and they are thrown back upon that for a new start. They are an "unencumbered proletariat" notable for primary faith and kindness, "simple people who carry in their hearts a desire for mere goodness. They regularly deplete their scanty livelihood in response to a primitive pity, and, independent of the religions they have professed, of the wrongs they have suffered, and of the fixed morality they

* Who seeks to have private things loses common things. Thomas à Kempis, De Imitatione Christi, book iii, chap. 13, sec. 1.
† In her book, Newer Ideals of Peace.

137

have been taught, they have an unquenchable desire that charity and simple justice shall regulate men's relations."*

Some tendency to isolation and spiritual impoverishment is likely to go with any sort of distinction or privilege. Wealth, culture, reputation, bring special gratifications. These foster special tastes, and these in turn give rise to special ways of living and thinking which imperceptibly separate one from common sympathy and put him in a special class. If one has a good income, for instance, how natural it is to spend it, and how naturally, also, that expenditure withdraws one from familiar intercourse with people who have not a good income. Success means possessions, and possessions are apt to imprison the spirit.

It has always been held that worldly goods, which of course include reputation as well as wealth, make the highest life of the mind difficult if not impossible, devotional orders in nearly all religions requiring personal poverty and lowliness as the condition of edification. *Tantum homo impeditur et distrahitur, quantum sibi res attrahit.*† "Sloth or cowardice," says a psychologist, "creep in with every dollar or guinea we have to guard . . . lives based on having are less free than lives based on either doing or being."‡ "It is easier for a camel to pass through the eye of a needle." Not for nothing have men of insight agreed upon such propositions as these.

Distinction, also, is apt to go with an exaggerated self-consciousness little favorable to a natural and hearty

* Newer Ideals of Peace, chap. 1.
† De Imitatione Christi, book ii, chap. 1, sec. 7.
‡ William James, Varieties of Religious Experience, 319.

participation in the deeper currents of the general life. Ambition and the passion for difference are good in their way, but like most good things they are bought at a price, in this case a preoccupation with ideas that separate one from immediate fellowship. It is right to have high and unusual aims and activities, but hard to keep them free from pride, mistrust, gloom and other vices of isolation. Only a very sane mind can carry distinction and fellowship without spilling either.

In the social regard paid to wealth and standing we symbolize our vague sense of the value of personal faculty working in the service of the whole, but it requires an unusual purity and depth of social feeling for the possessor of faculty not to be demoralized by this regard, which is—perhaps necessarily—almost disassociated from definite and cogent responsibility. I mean that the eminent usually get the credit of virtue as it were *ex officio*, whether they really have it or not. We find therefore that power, instead of being simply higher service, is generally more or less corrupt or selfish, and those who are raised up are so much the more cast down. At the best they make some sacrifice of innocence to function; at the worst they destroy themselves and debauch society.

Even vulgarity (by etymology the vice of the crowd) if we take it to mean undisciplined selfishness and pretension, flourishes at least as much among the prosperous as among the handworking people. Wealth which is not dominated by noble tradition or by rare personal inspiration falls into vulgarity because it permits the inflation of those crude impulses which are much kept down in the poor by the discipline of hardship. Whatever is severely

139

necessary can never be vulgar, while only nobleness can prevent the superfluous from being so. And a superficial, functionless education and refinement is nearly as vulgar as uninspired wealth. So it has been remarked that when artists paint our contemporary life they are apt to choose it as humble as possible in order "to get down below the strata which vulgarity permeates."*

Moreover, conspicuous and successful persons are more likely than the commonalty to be institutionized, to have sacrificed human nature to speciality. To succeed in the hour one must be a man of the hour, and must ordinarily harness his very soul to some sort of contemporary activity which may after all be of no real worth. An upper class is institutional in its very essence, since it is control of institutions that makes it an upper class, and men can hardly keep this control except as they put their hearts into it. Successful business men, lawyers, politicians, clergymen, editors and the like are such through identifying their minds, for better or worse, with the present activities and ideals of commercial and other institutions. "Seldom does the new conscience, when it seeks a teacher to declare to men what is wrong, find him in the dignitaries of the church, the state, the culture, that is. The higher the rank the closer the tie that binds those to what is but ought not to be."†

The humbler classes are somewhat less entangled in spirit. It is better to have the hand subdued to what it works in than the soul; and the mechanic who sells to the

* P. G. Hamerton, Thoughts About Art, 222.
† Henry D. Lloyd, Man the Social Creator, 101.

times only his ten hours a day of muscular work is perhaps more free to think humanly the rest of the time than his employer. He can also more easily keep the habit of simple look and speech, since he does not have to learn to conceal his thoughts in the same degree that the lawyer, the merchant and the statesman do. Even among students I have observed, in the matter of openness of countenance, a marked difference, on the whole, between the graduates of an engineering school and those of a law school, very much in favor of the former.* Again, the hand laborer is used to reckoning his wages by the hour—so much time so much pay—and would feel dishonest if he did anything else. But in the professions, and still more in commerce and finance, there is, as a rule, no definite measure of service, and men insensibly come to base their charges on their view of what the other man will pay; thus perilously accustoming themselves to exploit the wealth or weakness of others.

The life of special institutions is often transient in proportion to its speciality, and it is only natural that commercial and professional activity should deal largely with evanescent interests of little dignity in themselves. The "demand" of the public which the merchant has to meet, is in great part a thing of vanity, if not of degradation, which it can hardly be edifying to supply. Indeed, many, if not most, business men play their occupation as a game, rather than in a spirit of service, and are widely infected by the fallacy that they are justified in selling anything

* I mean merely that the law graduates look sophisticated—not dishonest. They have learned to use voice and facial expression as weapons of controversy.

141

that the people will buy. Simple minds are revolted by
the lack of tangible human service in many of the higher-
paid occupations, and young men enter them for the pay
alone when their better impulses would lead them to prefer hand labor.

The sentiment of the people is most readily and successfully exercised in their judgment of persons. Montesquieu, in discussing republican government, advocated
on this ground an almost universal manhood suffrage in
the choosing of representatives. "For," says he, "though
few can tell the exact degree of men's capacities, yet there
are none but are capable of knowing in general whether
the person they choose is better qualified than most of
his neighbors."* The plainest men have an inbred
shrewdness in judging human nature which makes them
good critics of persons even when impenetrable to ideas.
This shrewdness is fostered by a free society, in which
every one has to make and hold his own place among his
fellows; and it is used with much effect in politics and
elsewhere as a guide to sound ideas.

Some years ago, for instance, occurred a national election in which the main issue was whether silver should or
should not be coined freely at a rate much above its bullion
value. Two facts were impressed upon the observer of
this campaign: first, the inability of most men, even of
education, to reason clearly on a somewhat abstract question lying outside of their daily experience, and, second,
the sound instinct which all sorts of people showed in
choosing sides through leadership. The flow of nonsense

* The Spirit of Laws, book xi, chap. 6.

142

on both parts was remarkable, but personality was the determining influence. It was common to hear men say that they should vote for or against the proposition because they did or did not trust its conspicuous advocates; and it was evident that many were controlled in this way who did not acknowledge it, even to themselves. The general result was that the more conservative men were united on one side, and the more radical and shifting elements on the other.

The real interest of the voter at our elections is usually in personality. One likes or dislikes A, who is running for alderman, and votes accordingly, without knowing or caring what he is likely to do if elected. Or one opposes B, because he is believed to be in league with the obnoxious C, and so on. It is next to impossible to get a large or intelligent vote on an impersonal matter, such as the constitutional amendments which, in most of our states, have to be submitted to the people. The newspapers, reflecting the public taste, say little about them, and the ordinary voter learns of them for the first time when he comes to the polls. Only a measure which directly affects the interests or passions of the people, like prohibition of the liquor traffic, will call out a large vote.

On this shrewd judgment of persons the advocate of democracy chiefly grounds his faith that the people will be right in the long run. The old argument against him runs as follows: democracy is the rule of the many; the many are incompetent to understand public questions; hence democracy is the rule of incompetence. Thus Macaulay held that institutions purely democratic must

143

sooner or later destroy liberty or civilization or both; and expected a day of spoliation in the United States, "for with you the majority is the government and has the rich absolutely at its mercy."* More recent writers of standing have taken the same view, like Lecky, who declares that the rule of the majority is the rule of ignorance, since the poor and the ignorant are the largest proportion of the population.†

To this our democrat will answer, "The many, whether rich or poor, are incompetent to grasp the truth in its abstractness, but they reach it through personal symbols, they feel their way by sympathy, and their conclusions are at least as apt to be right as those of any artificially selected class." And he will perhaps turn to American history, which is, on the whole, a fairly convincing demonstration that the masses are not incapable of temperate and wise decision, even on matters of much difficulty. That our antecedents and training have been peculiarly fortunate must be conceded.

The crudely pessimistic view is superficial not only in underestimating the masses and overestimating wealth—which is, in our times at least, almost the only possible basis of a privileged class—but in failing to understand the organic character of a mature public judgment. Is it not a rather obvious fallacy to say that because the ignorant outnumber the educated, therefore the rule of the majority is the rule of ignorance? If fifty men consult

* From a letter written to an American correspondent in 1857 and printed in the appendix to Trevelyan's Macaulay.

† Democracy and Liberty, vol. i, chap. 1, page 25 and *passim*. Some of Lecky's expressions, however, are more favorable to democracy.

144

together, forty of whom are ignorant regarding the matter in hand and ten informed, will their conclusions necessarily be those of ignorance? Evidently not, unless in some improbable manner the forty separate from the ten and refuse to be guided by them. Savages and gangs of boys on the street choose the most sagacious to lead in counsel, and even pirates will put the best navigators in charge of the ship. The natural thing, as we have seen, is for a group to defer to its most competent members. Lecky would himself have maintained this in the case of Parliament, and why should it not be true of other groups? I see no reason why the rule of the majority should be the rule of ignorance, unless they are not only ignorant but fools; and I do not suppose the common people of any capable race are that.

I was born and have lived nearly all my life in the shadow of an institution of higher learning, a university, supported out of the taxes of a democratic state and governed by a board elected directly by the people. So far back as I can remember there have not been wanting pessimists to say that the institution could not prosper on such a basis. "What," they said, "do the farmers know or care about the university? how can we expect that they should support astronomy and Sanscrit and the higher mathematics?" In fact there have been troublous times, especially in the earlier days, but the higher learning has steadily won its way in open discussion, and the university is now far larger, higher in its standards, better supported and apparently more firmly established in popular approval than ever before. What more exacting test of the power of democracy to pursue and effectuate high and rather abstract ideals could there well be than this? One who lives in the midst of such facts cannot but discover something rather doctrinaire in the views of Macaulay and Lecky.

If it be true that most people judge men rather than ideas, we may say that democratic society is representative not only in politics but in all its thought. Everywhere a few are allowed to think and act for the rest, and the essence of democratic method is not in the direct choice of the people in many matters, but in their retaining a conscious power to change their representatives, or to exercise direct choice, when they wish to do so. All tolerable government is representative, but democracy is voluntarily so, and differs from oligarchy in preserving the definite responsibility of the few to the many. It may even happen, as in England, that a hereditary ruling class retains much of its power by the consent of a democratized electorate, or, as in France, that a conception of the state, generated under absolute monarchy, is cherished under the rule of the people.

As for popular suffrage, it is a crude but practical device for ascertaining the preponderant bent of opinion on a definite issue. It is in a sense superficial, mechanical, almost absurd, when we consider the difference in real significance among the units; but it is simple, educative, and has that palpable sort of justice that allays contention. No doubt spiritual weight is the great thing, but as there is no accepted way to measure this, we count one man one vote, and trust that spiritual differences will be expressed through persuasion.

There is, then, no essential conflict between democracy and specialization in any sphere. It is true that as the vital unity of a group becomes more conscious each member tends to feel a claim on everything the group does. Thus the citizen not only wishes the government—of the village, the state or the nation—to be an expression of himself; but he wishes the same regarding the schools, manufactures, trade, religion and the advance of knowledge. He desires all these things to go on in the best way possible, so as to express to the fullest that human nature that is in himself. And as a guaranty of this he demands that they shall be conducted on an open principle, which shall give control of them to the fittest individuals. Hating all privilege not based on function, he desires power to suppress such privilege when it becomes flagrant. And to make everything amenable, directly or indirectly, to popular suffrage, seems to him a practical step in this direction.

Something like this is in the mind of the plain man of our time; but he is quite aware of his incompetence to carry on these varied activities directly, either in government or elsewhere, and common-sense teaches him to seek his end by a shrewd choice of representatives, and by developing a system of open and just competition for all functions. The picture of the democratic citizen as one who thinks he can do anything as well as anybody is, of course, a caricature, and in the United States, at least, there is a great and increasing respect for special capacity, and a tendency to trust it as far as it deserves. If people are sometimes sceptical of the specialist—in political economy let us say—and inclined to prefer their own common-sense, it is perhaps because they have had unfortunate experience with the former. On the whole, our time is one of the "rise of the expert," when, on account of the rapid elaboration of nearly all activities, there is an ever greater demand for trained capacity. Far from being undemocratic, this is a phase of that effective organization of the public intelligence which real democracy calls for. In short, as already suggested, to be democratic, or even to be ignorant, is not necessarily to be a fool.

So in answer to the question, Just what do the undistinguished masses of the people contribute to the general thought? we may say, They contribute sentiment and common-sense, which gives momentum and general direction to progress, and, as regards particulars, finds its way by a shrewd choice of leaders. It is into the obscure and inarticulate sense of the multitude that the man of genius looks in order to find those vital tendencies whose utterance is his originality. As men in business get rich by divining and supplying a potential want, so it is a great part of all leadership to perceive and express what the people have already felt.

CHAPTER XIV

DEMOCRACY AND CROWD EXCITEMENT

THE CROWD-THEORY OF MODERN LIFE—THE PSYCHOLOGY OF
CROWDS—MODERN CONDITIONS FAVOR PSYCHOLOGICAL CON-
TAGION—DEMOCRACY A TRAINING IN SELF-CONTROL—THE
CROWD NOT ALWAYS IN THE WRONG—CONCLUSION; THE CASE
OF FRANCE.

CERTAIN writers, impressed with the rise of vast democracies within which space is almost eliminated by
ease of communication, hold that we are falling under the
rule of Crowds, that is to say, of bodies of men subject
by their proximity to waves of impulsive sentiment and
action, quite like multitudes in physical contiguity. A
crowd is well known to be emotional, irrational and sup-
pressive of individuality: democracy, being the rule of
the crowd, will show the same traits.

The psychology of crowds has been treated at length
by Sighele,* Le Bon† and other authors who, having
made a specialty of the man in the throng, are perhaps

* Scipio Sighele, La folla delinquente. French translation La
foule criminelle.

† Gustave Le Bon, Psychologie des foules. English translation
The Crowd.

The whole subject, including the question of "prophylactics"
against the mob-mind, is well discussed in Professor E. A. Ross's
Social Psychology

somewhat inclined to exaggerate the degree in which he departs from ordinary personality. The crowd mind is not, as is sometimes said, a quite different thing from that of the individual (unless by individual is meant the higher self), but is merely a collective mind of a low order which stimulates and unifies the cruder impulses of its members. The men are there but they "descend to meet." The loss of rational control and liability to be stampeded which are its main traits are no greater than attend almost any state of excitement—the anger, fear, love and the like, of the man not in the crowd.

And the intimidating effect of a throng on the individual —the stage-fright, let us say, of an inexperienced speaker —is nothing unique, but closely resembles that which we have all felt on first approaching an imposing person; seeming to spring from that vague dread of unknown power which pervades all conscious life. And like the latter, it readily wears off, so that the practised orator is never more self-possessed than with the crowd before him.

The peculiarity of the crowd-mind is mainly in the readiness with which any communicable feeling is spread and augmented. Just as a heap of firebrands will blaze when one or two alone will chill and go out, so the units of a crowd "inflame each other by mutual sympathy and mutual consciousness of it."* This is much facilitated by the circumstance that habitual activities are usually in abeyance, the man in a throng being like one fallen overboard in that he is removed from his ordinary surroundings and plunged into a strange and alarming element. At once excited and intimidated, he readily takes on a sug-

* Whately in his note to Bacon's essay on Discourse.

gested emotion—as of panic, anger or self-devotion—and proceeds to reckless action.

It must be admitted that modern conditions enable such contagion to work upon a larger scale than ever before, so that a wave of feeling now passes through the people, by the aid of the newspaper, very much as if they were physically a crowd—like the wave of resentment, for instance, that swept over America when the battle-ship Maine was destroyed in Havana harbor. The popular excitement over athletic contests is a familiar example. During the foot-ball season the emotion of the crowd actually present at a famous game is diffused throughout the country by prompt and ingenious devices that depict the progress of the play; and, indeed, it is just to get into this excitement, and out of themselves and the humdrum of routine, that thousands of people, most of whom know next to nothing of the game, read the newspapers and stand about the bulletin boards. And when a war breaks out, the people read the papers in quite the same spirit that the Roman populace went to the arena, not so much from any depraved taste for blood, as to be in the thrill. Even the so-called "individualism" of our time, and the unresting pursuit of "business," are in great part due to a contagion of the crowd. People become excited by the game and want to be in it, whether they have any definite object or not; and once in they think they must keep up the pace or go under.

Is democracy, then, the rule of the crowd, and is there a tendency in modern times toward the subjection of society to an irrational and degenerate phase of the mind?

151

This question, like others relating to the trend of modern life, looks differently according to the points of view from which it is approached. In general we may say that the very changes which are drawing modern populations together into denser wholes bring also a discipline in organization and self-control which should remove them further and further from the mob state.

It is agreed by writers on the crowd that men are little likely to be stampeded in matters regarding which they have a trained habit of thought—as a fireman, for instance, will be apt to keep his head when the fire-alarm sounds. And it is just the absence of this that is the mark of a crowd, which is not made by mere numbers and contiguity, but by group excitability arising from lack of stable organization. A veteran army is not a crowd, however numerous and concentrated; and no more perhaps is a veteran democracy, though it number twenty million voters.

A healthy democracy is indeed a training in judgment and self-control as applied to political action; and just as a fireman is at home on trembling ladders and amidst choking fumes, so the free citizen learns to keep his head amid the contending passions and opinions of a "fierce democratie." Having passed safely through many disturbances, he has acquired a confidence in cool judgment and in the underlying stability of things impossible to men who, living under a stricter control, have had no such education. He knows well how to discount superficial sentiment and "the spawn of the press on the gossip of the hour." It is, then, the nature of ordered freedom to train veterans of politics, secure against the wild impulses of a rabble—such as made havoc in Paris at the close of the Franco-Prussian war—and in modern times, when power cannot be kept away from the people, such a training is the main guaranty of social stability. Is it not apparent to judicious observers that our tough-fibred, loose-jointed society takes agitation more safely than the more rigid structures of Europe?

Nor is it merely in politics that this is true, for it is the whole tendency of a free system to train men to stand on their own feet and resist the rush. In a fixed order, with little opening for initiative or differentiated development, they scarcely realize themselves as distinct and self-directing individuals, and from them one may expect the traits of Le Bon's *foules;* hardly from the shrewd farmers and mechanics of American democracy.

It looks at first sight as if, because of their dense humanity, the great cities in which the majority of the population are apparently to live must tend to a mob like state of mind; but except in so far as cities attract the worse elements of the people this is probably not the case. Mob phenomena generally come from crowd excitement ensuing upon a sluggish habit of life and serving as an outlet to the passions which such a life stores up. We find the mob and the mob-like religious revival in the back counties rather than among the cheerful and animated people that throng the open places of New York or Chicago.

Moreover, it is hardly true that "the multitude is always in the wrong";* and conclusions may be no less

* Attributed to the Earl of Roscommon. See Bartlett's Familiar Quotations.

Sir Thomas Browne characteristically describes the multitude as "that numerous piece of monstrosity, which, taken asunder, sound and vital for being reached under a certain exaltation of popular enthusiasm. The individual engaged in private affairs and without the thrill of the common life is not more apt to be at the height of his mental being than the man in the crowd. A mingling of these influences seems to produce the best results, and the highest rationality, while it involves much plodding thought in its preparation, is likely to come to definite consciousness and expression in moments of some excitement. As it is the common experience of artists, poets and saints that their best achievements are the outcome of long brooding culminating in a kind of ecstasy, so the clearest notes of democracy may be struck in times of exaltation like that which, in the Northern United States, followed the attack on Fort Sumter. The impulsiveness which marks popular feeling may express some brutal or trivial phase of human nature, or some profound moral intuition, the only definite test being the persistence of the sentiment which thus comes to light; and if it proves to have the lasting warrant of the general conscience it may be one of those voices of the people in which posterity will discover the voice of God.

The view that the crowd is irrational and degenerate is characteristic of an intricate society where reading has largely taken the place of assembly as a stimulus to thought. In primitive times the social excitement of religious and other festivals represented the higher life; as it still does

seem men, and the reasonable creatures of God, but confused together, make but one great beast, and a monstrosity more prodigious than Hydra." Religio Medici, part ii, sec. 1. This is the very man that urged the burning of witches after the multitude was ready to give it up.

in backwoods communities, and to sluggish temperaments everywhere. Even in the towns our higher sentiments are largely formed in social meetings of one sort or another, accompanied by music, acting, dancing or speech-making, which draw one out of the more solitary currents of his thought and bring him into livelier unity with his fellows.

There is really no solid basis in fact or theory for the view that established democracy is the rule of an irresponsible crowd. If not true of America, it fails as a general principle; and no authoritative observer has found it to be the case here. Those who hold the crowd-theory seem to be chiefly writers, whether French or not, who generalize from the history of France. Without attempting any discussion of this, I may suggest one or two points that we are perhaps apt to overlook. It is, for one thing, by no means clear that French democracy has shown itself to lack the power of self-control and deliberate progress. Its difficulties—the presence of ancient class divisions, of inevitable militarism, and the like—have been immeasurably greater than ours, and its spirit one with which we do not readily sympathize. France, I suppose, is little understood in England or the United States, and we probably get our views too much from a school of French writers whose zeal to correct her faults may tend to exaggerate them. The more notorious excesses of the French or Parisian populace—such as are real and not a fiction of hostile critics—seem to have sprung from that exercise of power without training inevitable in a country where democracy had to come by revolution. And, again, a certain

155

tendency to act in masses, and lack of vigorous local and private initiative, which appears to characterize France, is much older than the Revolution, and seems due partly to race traits and partly to such historical conditions as the centralized structure inherited from absolute monarchy.

CHAPTER XV

DEMOCRACY AND DISTINCTION

THE PROBLEM—DEMOCRACY SHOULD BE DISTINGUISHED FROM
TRANSITION—THE DEAD-LEVEL THEORY OF DEMOCRACY—
CONFUSION AND ITS EFFECTS—"INDIVIDUALISM" MAY NOT
BE FAVORABLE TO DISTINGUISHED INDIVIDUALITY—CON-
TEMPORARY UNIFORMITY—RELATIVE ADVANTAGES OF AMERICA
AND EUROPE—HASTE, SUPERFICIALITY, STRAIN—SPIRITUAL
ECONOMY OF A SETTLED ORDER—COMMERCIALISM—ZEAL FOR
DIFFUSION—CONCLUSION.

WHAT shall we say of the democratic trend of the modern world as it affects the finer sort of intellectual achievement? While the conscious sway of the masses seems
not uncongenial to the more popular and obvious kinds
of eminence, as of statesmen, inventors, soldiers, financiers and the like, there are many who believe it to be
hostile to distinction in literature, art or science. Is
there hope for this also, or must we be content to offset
the dearth of greatness by the abundance of mediocrity?

This, I take it, is a matter for *a priori* psychological
reasoning rather than for close induction from fact. The
present democratic movement is so different from anything in the past that historical comparison of any large
sort is nearly or quite worthless. And, moreover, it is
so bound up with other conditions which are not essential
to it and may well prove transient, that even contemporary fact gives us very little secure guidance. All that is
really practicable is a survey of the broad principles at
work and a rough attempt to forecast how they may

157

work out. An inquiry of this sort seems to me to lead to conclusions somewhat as follows.

First, there is, I believe, no sound reason for thinking that the democratic spirit or organization is in its essential nature hostile to distinguished production. Indeed, one who holds that the opposite is the case, while he will not be able to silence the pessimist, will find little in fact or theory to shake his own faith.

Second, although democracy itself is not hostile, so far as we can make out its nature by general reasoning, there is much that is so in the present state of thought, both in the world at large and, more particularly, in the United States.

In this, as in all discussions regarding contemporary tendency, we need to discriminate between democracy and transition. At present the two go together because democracy is new; but there is no reason in the nature of things why they should remain together. As popular rule becomes established it proves capable of developing a stability, even a rigidity, of its own; and it is already apparent that the United States, for instance, just because democracy has had its way there, is less liable to sudden transitions than perhaps any other of the great nations.

It is true that democracy involves some elements of permanent unrest. Thus, by demanding open opportunity and resisting hereditary stratification, it will probably maintain a competition of persons more general, and as regards personal status more unsettling, than anything the world has been used to in the past. But personal competition alone is the cause of only a small part of the

158

stress and disorder of our time; much more being due to general changes in the social system, particularly in industry, which we may describe as transition. And moreover, competition itself is in a specially disordered or transitional state at present, and will be less disquieting when a more settled state of society permits it to be carried on under established rules of justice, and when a discriminating education shall do a large part of its work. In short, democracy is not necessarily confusion, and we shall find reason to think that it is the latter, chiefly, that is opposed to distinction.

The view that popular rule is in its nature unsuited to foster genius rests chiefly on the dead-level theory. Equality not distinction is said to be the passion of the masses, diffusion not concentration. Everything moves on a vast and vaster scale: the facility of intercourse is melting the world into one fluid whole in which the single individual is more and more submerged. The era of salient personalities is passing away, and the principle of equality, which ensures the elevation of men in general, is fatal to particular greatness. "In modern society," said De Tocqueville, the chief begetter of this doctrine, "everything threatens to become so much alike that the peculiar characteristics of each individual will soon be entirely lost in the general aspect of the world." * Shall we agree with this or maintain with Plato that a democracy will have the greatest variety of human nature? †

* Democracy in America, vol. ii, book iv, chap. 7. But elsewhere he expresses the opinion that this levelling and confusion is only temporary. See, for example, book iii, chap. 21.
† Republic, book viii.

Perhaps the most plausible basis for this theory is the levelling effect ascribed by many to the facilities for communication that have grown up so surprisingly within the past century. In a former chapter I have said much upon this matter, holding that we must distinguish between the individuality of choice and that of isolation, and giving reasons why the modern facility of intercourse should be favorable to the former.

To this we may add that the mere fact of popular rule has no inevitable connection, either friendly or hostile, with variety and vigor of individuality. If France is somewhat lacking in these, it is not because she is democratic, but because of the race traits of her people and her peculiar antecedents; if America abounds in a certain kind of individuality, it is chiefly because she inherited it from England and developed it in a frontier life. In either case democracy, in the sense of popular government, is a secondary matter.

Certainly, America is a rather convincing proof that democracy does not necessarily suppress salient personality. So far as individuality of spirit is concerned, our life leaves little to be desired, and no trait impresses itself more than this upon observers from the continent of Europe. "All things grow clear in the United States," says Paul Bourget, "when one understands them as an immense act of faith in the social beneficence of individual energy left to itself." * The "individualism" of our social system is a commonplace of contemporary writers. Nowhere else, not even in England, I suppose, is there more respect for non-conformity or more disposition to

* Outre-Mer. English Translation, 306.

160

assert it. In our intensely competitive life men learn to value character above similarity, and one who has character may hold what opinions he pleases. Personality, as Mr. Brownell points out in contrasting the Americans with the French, is the one thing of universal interest here: our conversation, our newspapers, our elections are dominated by it, and our great commercial transactions are largely a struggle for supremacy among rival leaders.* The augmenting numbers of the people, far from obscuring the salient individual, only make for him a larger theatre of success; and personal reputation—whether for wealth, statesmanship, literary achievement, or for mere singularity—is organized on a greater scale than ever before. One who is familiar with any province of American life, as for example, that of charitable and penal reform, is aware that almost every advance is made through the embodiment of timely ideas in one or a few energetic individuals who set an example for the country to follow. Experience with numbers, instead of showing the insignificance of the individual, proves that if he has faith and a worthy aim there is no limit to what he may do; and we find, accordingly, plenty of courage in starting new projects. The country is full of men who find the joys of self-assertion, if not always of outward success, in the bold pursuit of hazardous enterprises.

If there is a deficiency of literary and artistic achievement in a democracy of this kind, it is due to some other cause than a general submergence of the individual in the mass.

The dead-level theory, then, is sufficiently discredited

* See the final chapter of his French Traits.

as a general law by the undiminished ascendency of salient individualities in every province of activity. The enlargement of social consciousness does not alter the essential relation of individuality to life, but simply gives it a greater field of success or failure. The man of genius may meet with more competition, but if he is truly great a larger world is his. To imagine that the mass will submerge the individual is to suppose that one aspect of society will stand still while the other grows. It rests upon a superficial, numerical way of thinking, which regards individuals as fixed units each of which must become less conspicuous the more they are multiplied. But if the man of genius represents a spiritual principle his influence is not fixed but grows with the growth of life itself, and is limited only by the vitality of what he stands for. Surely the great men of the past—Plato, Dante, Shakespeare and the rest—are not submerged, nor in danger of being; nor is it apparent why their successors should be.

The real cause of literary and artistic weakness (in so far as it exists) I take to be chiefly the spiritual disorganization incident to a time of rather sudden transition. How this condition, and others closely associated with it, are unfavorable to great æsthetic production, I shall try to point out under the four heads, confusion, commercialism, haste and zeal for diffusion.

With reference to the higher products of culture, not only the United States, but in some degree contemporary civilization in general, is a confused, a raw, society, not as being democratic but as being new. It is our whole newspaper and factory epoch that is crude, and scarcely more so in America than in England or Germany; the main difference in favor of European countries being that the present cannot so easily be separated from the conditions of an earlier culture. It is a general trait of the time that social types are disintegrated, old ones going to pieces and new ones not perfected, leaving the individual without adequate discipline either in the old or in the new.

Now works of enduring greatness seem to depend, among other things, on a certain ripeness of historical conditions. No matter how gifted an individual may be, he is in no way apart from his time, but has to take that and make the best of it he can; the man of genius is in one point of view only a twig upon which a mature tendency bears its perfect fruit. In the new epoch the vast things in process are as yet so unfinished that individual gifts are scarce sufficient to bring anything to a classical completeness; so that our life remains somewhat inarticulate, our literature, and still more our plastic art, being inadequate exponents of what is most vital in the modern spirit.

The psychological effect of confusion is a lack of mature culture groups, and of what they only can do for intellectual or æsthetic production. What this means may, perhaps, be made clearer by a comparison drawn from athletic sports. We find in our colleges that to produce a winning foot-ball team, or distinguished performance in running or jumping, it is essential first of all to have a spirit of intense interest in these things, which shall arouse the ambition of those having natural gifts, support them in their training and reward their success. Without this group spirit no efficient organization, no high standard of achievement, can exist, and a small institution that has this will easily surpass a large one that lacks it. And experience shows that it takes much time to perfect such a spirit and the organizations through which it is expressed.

In quite the same way any ripe development of productive power in literary or other art implies not merely capable individuals but the perfection of a social group, whose traditions and spirit the individual absorbs, and which floats him up to a point whence he can reach unique achievement. The unity of this group or type is spiritual, not necessarily local or temporal, and so may be difficult to trace, but its reality is as sure as the principle that man is a social being and cannot think sanely and steadfastly except in some sort of sympathy with his fellows. There must be others whom we can conceive as sharing, corroborating and enhancing our ideals, and to no one is such association more necessary than the man of genius.

The group is likely to be more apparent or tangible in some arts than in others: it is generally quite evident in painting, sculpture, architecture and music, where a regular development by the passage of inspiration from one artist to another can almost always be traced. In literature the connections are less obvious, chiefly because this art is in its methods more disengaged from time and place, so that it is easier to draw inspiration from distant sources. It is also partly a matter of temperament, men of somewhat solitary imagination being able to form their group out of remote personalities, and so to be almost independent of time and place. Thus Thoreau

164

lived with the Greek and Hindoo classics, with the old English poets, and with the suggestions of nature; but even he owed much to contemporary influences, and the more he is studied the less solitary he appears. Is not this the case also with Wordsworth, with Dante, with all men who are supposed to have stood alone?

The most competent of all authorities on this question —Goethe—was a full believer in the dependence of genius on influences. "People are always talking about originality," he says, "but what do they mean? As soon as we are born the world begins to work upon us, and this goes on to the end. And after all what can we call our own except energy, strength and will? If I could give an account of all that I owe to great predecessors and contemporaries, there would be but a small balance in my favor."* He even held that men of genius are more dependent upon their environment than others; for, being thinner-skinned, they are more suggestible, more perturbable, and peculiarly in need of the right sort of surroundings to keep their delicate machinery in fruitful action.

No doubt such questions afford ground for infinite debate, but the underlying principle that the thought of every man is one with that of a group, visible or invisible, is sure, I think, to prove sound; and if so it is indispensable that a great capacity should find access to a group whose ideals and standards are of a sort to make the most of it.

Another reason why the rawness of the modern world is unfavorable to great production is that the ideals themselves which a great art should express share in the gen-

* Conversation with Eckermann, May 12, 1825.

eral incompleteness of things and do not present themselves to the mind clearly defined and incarnate in vivid symbols. Perhaps a certain fragmentariness and pettiness in contemporary art and literature is due more to this cause than to any other—to the fact that the aspirations of the time, large enough, certainly, are too much obscured in smoke to be clearly and steadily regarded. We may believe, for example, in democracy, but it can hardly be said that we *see* democracy, as the middle ages, in their art, saw the Christian religion.

From this point of view of groups and organization it is easy to understand why the "individualism" of our epoch does not necessarily produce great individuals. Individuality may easily be aggressive and yet futile, because not based on the training afforded by well-organized types—like the fruitless valor of an isolated soldier. Mr. Brownell points out that the prevalence of this sort of individuality in our art and life is a point of contrast between us and the French. Paris, compared with New York, has the "organic quality which results from variety of types," as distinguished from variety of individuals. "We do far better in the production of striking artistic personalities than we do in the general medium of taste and culture. We figure well, invariably, at the Salon. . . . Comparatively speaking, of course, we have no *milieu*."*

The same conditions underlie that comparative uniformity of American life which wearies the visitor and implants in the native such a passion for Europe. When

* French Traits, 385, 387, 393.

166

a populous society springs up rapidly from a few transplanted seeds, its structure, however vast, is necessarily somewhat simple and monotonous. A thousand towns, ten thousand churches, a million houses, are built on the same models, and the people and the social institutions do not altogether escape a similar poverty of types. No doubt this is sometimes exaggerated, and America does present many picturesque variations, but only a reckless enthusiasm will equal them with those of Europe. How unspeakably inferior in exterior aspect and in many inner conditions of culture must any recent civilization be to that, let us say, of Italy, whose accumulated riches represent the deposit of several thousand years.

Such deposits, however, belong to the past; and as regards contemporary accretions the sameness of London or Rome is hardly less than that of Chicago. It is a matter of the epoch, more conspicuous here chiefly because it has had fuller sweep. A heavy fall of crude commercialism is rapidly obscuring the contours of history.

In comparison with Europe America has the advantages that come from being more completely in the newer current of things. It is nearer, perhaps, to the spirit of the coming order, and so perhaps more likely, in due time, to give it adequate utterance in art. Another benefit of being new is the attitude of confidence that it fosters. If America could hardly have sustained the assured mastery of Tennyson, neither, perhaps, could England an optimism like that of Emerson. In contrast to the latter, Carlyle, Ruskin and Tolstoi—prophets of an older world—are shadowed by a feeling of the ascendency and inertia of ancient and somewhat decadent institutions. They are afraid of them, and so are apt to be rather shrill in protest. An American, accustomed to see human nature have pretty much its own way, has seldom any serious mistrust of the outcome. Nearly all of our writers—as Emerson, Longfellow, Lowell, Whittier, Holmes, Thoreau, Whitman, even Hawthorne—have been of a cheerful and wholesome personality.*

On the other hand, an old civilization has from its mere antiquity a richness and complexity of spiritual life that cannot be transplanted to a new world. The immigrants bring with them the traditions of which they feel in immediate need, such as those necessary to found the state, the church and the family; but even these lose something of their original flavor, while much of what is subtler and less evidently useful is left behind. We must remember, too, that the culture of the Old World is chiefly a class culture, and that the immigrants have mostly come from a class that had no great part in it.

With this goes loss of the visible monuments of culture inherited from the past—architecture, painting, sculpture, ancient universities and the like. Burne-Jones, the English painter, speaking of the commercial city in which he spent his youth, says: . . . "if there had been one cast from ancient Greek sculpture, or one faithful copy of a great Italian picture, to be seen in Birmingham when I was a boy, I should have begun to paint ten years before I did . . . even the silent presence of great works in your town will produce an impression on those who see them, and the next generation will, without knowing

* Poe is the only notable exception that occurs to me.

168

how or why, find it easier to learn than this one does whose surroundings are so unlovely."*

Nor is American life favorable to the rapid crystallization of a new artistic culture; it is too transient and restless; transatlantic migration is followed by internal movements from east to west and from city to country; while on top of these we have a continuous subversion of industrial relations.†

Another element of special confusion in our life is the headlong mixture of races, temperaments and traditions that comes from the new immigration, from the irruption by millions of peoples from the south and east of the Old World. If they were wholly inferior, as we sometimes imagine, it would perhaps not matter so much; but the truth is that they contest every intellectual function with the older stock, and, in the universities for instance, are shortly found teaching our children their own history and literature. They assimilate, but always with a difference, and in the northern United States, formerly dominated by New England influences, a revolution from this cause is well under way. It is as if a kettle of broth were cooking quietly on the fire, when some one should come in and add suddenly a great pailful of raw meats, vegetables and spices—a rich combination, possibly, but likely to require much boiling. That fine English sentiment that came down to us through the colonists more purely, perhaps, than to the English in the old country, is passing

---

*Memorials of Edward Burne-Jones, ii, 100, 101.

† Our most notable group of writers—flourishing at Concord and Boston about 1850—is, of course, connected with the maturing, in partial isolation, of a local type of culture, now disintegrated and dispersed on the wider currents of the time.

away—as a distinct current, that is—lost in a flood of cosmopolitan life. Before us, no doubt, is a larger humanity, but behind is a cherished spirit that can hardly live again; and, like the boy who leaves home, we must turn our thoughts from an irrevocable past and go hopefully on to we know not what.

In short, our world lacks maturity of culture organization. What we sometimes call—truly enough as regards its economic life—our complex civilization, is simple to the point of poverty in spiritual structure. We have cast off much rubbish and decay and are preparing, we may reasonably hope, to produce an art and literature worthy of our vigor and aspiration, but in the past, certainly, we have hardly done so.

Haste and the superficiality and strain which attend upon it are widely and insidiously destructive of good work in our day. No other condition of mind or of society— not ignorance, poverty, oppression or hate—kills art as haste does. Almost any phase of life may be ennobled if there is only calm enough in which the brooding mind may do its perfect work upon it; but out of hurry nothing noble ever did or can emerge. In art human nature should come to a total, adequate expression; a spiritual tendency should be perfected and recorded in calmness and joy. But ours is, on the whole, a time of stress, of the habit of incomplete work; its products are unlovely and unrestful and such as the future will have no joy in. The pace is suited only to turn out mediocre goods on a vast scale.

It is, to put the matter otherwise, a *loud* time. The

newspapers, the advertising, the general insistence of suggestion, have an effect of din, so that one feels that he must raise his voice to be heard, and the whispers of the gods are hard to catch. Men whose voices are naturally low and fine easily lose this trait in the world and begin to shout like the rest. That is to say, they exaggerate and repeat and advertise and caricature, saying too much in the hope that a little may be heard. Of course, in the long run this is a fatal delusion; nothing will really be listened to except that whose quiet truth makes it worth hearing; but it is one so rooted in the general state of things that few escape it. Even those who preserve the lower tone do so with an effort which is in itself disquieting.

A strenuous state of mind is always partial and special, sacrificing scope to intensity and more fitted for execution than insight. It is useful at times, but if habitual cuts us off from that sea of subconscious spirit from which all original power flows. "The world of art," says Paul Bourget, speaking of America, "requires less self-consciousness—an impulse of life which forgets itself, the alternations of dreamy idleness with fervid execution."* So Henry James† remarks that we have practically lost the faculty of attention, meaning, I suppose, that unstrenuous, brooding sort of attention required to produce or appreciate works of art—and as regards the prevalent type of business or professional mind this seems quite true.

It comes mainly from having too many things to think of, from the urgency and distraction of an epoch and a

* Outre-Mer, 25.
† In his essay on Balzac.

171

country in which the traditional structures that support the mind and save its energy have largely gone to pieces. The endeavor to supply by will functions that in other conditions would be automatic creates a rush which imitation renders epidemic, and from which it is not easy to escape in order to mature one's powers in fruitful quiet.

There is an immense spiritual economy in any settled state of society, sufficient, so far as production is concerned, to offset much that is stagnant or oppressive; the will is saved and concentrated; while freedom, as De Tocqueville noted, sometimes produces "a small, distressing motion, a sort of incessant jostling of men, which annoys and disturbs the mind without exciting or elevating it."* The modern artist has too much choice. If he attempts to deal largely with life, his will is overworked at the expense of æsthetic synthesis. Freedom and opportunity are without limit, all cultures within his reach and splendid service awaiting performance. But the task of creating a glad whole seems beyond any ordinary measure of talent. The result in most cases—as has been said of architecture —is "confusion of types, illiterate combinations, an evident breathlessness of effort and striving for effect, with the inevitable loss of repose, dignity and style."† A mediæval cathedral or a Greek temple was the culmination of a long social growth, a gradual, deliberate, corporate achievement, to which the individual talent added only the finishing touch. The modern architect has, no

* Democracy in America, vol. ii, book i, chap. 10.
† Henry Van Brunt, Greek Lines, 225. Some of these phrases, such as "illiterate combinations," could never apply to the work of good architects.

doubt, as much personal ability, but the demands upon it are excessive; it would seem that only a transcendent synthetic genius of the calibre of Dante could deal adequately with our scattered conditions.

The cause of strain is radical and somewhat feverish change, not democracy as such. A large part of the people, particularly the farming class, are little affected by it, and there are indications that in America, where it has been greater than elsewhere, the worst is now over.

By commercialism, in this connection, we may understand a preoccupation of the ability of the people with material production and with the trade and finance based upon it. This again is in part a trait of the period, in part a peculiarity of America, in its character as a new country with stumps to get out and material civilization to erect from the ground up.

The result of it is that ability finds constant opportunity and incitement to take a commercial direction, and little to follow pure art or letters. A man likes to succeed in something, and if he is conscious of the capacity to make his way in business or professional life, he is indisposed to endure the poverty, uncertainty and indifference which attend the pursuit of an artistic calling. Less prosperous societies owe something to that very lack of opportunity which makes it less easy for artistic ability to take another direction.

An even greater peril is the debasing of art by an uncultured market. There seem to be plenty of artists of every kind, but their standard of success is mostly low. The beginner too early gets commercial employment in

173

which he is not held up to any high ideal. This brings us back to the lack of a well-knit artistic tradition to educate both the artist and the public, the lack of a type, "the non-existence," as Mr. Russell Sturgis says, "of an artistic community with a mind of its own and a certain general agreement as to what a work of art ought to be." This lack involves the weakness of the criticism which is required to make the artist see himself as he ought to be. "That criticism is nowhere in proportion to the need of it," says Henry James, "is the visiting observer's first and last impression—an impression so constant that it at times swallows up or elbows out every other."

The antipathy between art and the commercial spirit, however, is often much overstated. As a matter of history art and literature have flourished most conspicuously in prosperous commercial societies, such as Athens, Florence, Venice, the communes of the thirteenth and fourteenth centuries, the trading cities of Germany, the Dutch Republic and the England of Elizabeth. Nothing does more than commerce to awaken intelligence, enterprise and a free spirit, and these are favorable to ideal production. It is only the extreme one-sidedness of our civilization in this regard that is prejudicial.

It is also true—and here we touch upon something pertaining more to the very nature of democracy than the matters so far mentioned—that the zeal for diffusion which springs from communication and sympathy has in it much that is not directly favorable to the finer sorts of production.

Which is the better, fellowship or distinction? There

is much to be said on both sides, but the finer spirits of our day lean toward the former, and find it more human and exhilarating to spread abroad the good things the world already has than to prosecute a lonesome search for new ones. I notice among the choicest people I know—those who seem to me most representative of the inner trend of democracy—a certain generous contempt for distinction and a passion to cast their lives heartily on the general current. But the highest things are largely those which do not immediately yield fellowship or diffuse joy. Though making in the end for a general good, they are as private in their direct action as selfishness itself, from which they are not always easily distinguished. They involve intense self-consciousness. Probably men who follow the whispers of genius will always be more or less at odds with their fellows.

Ours, then, is an Age of Diffusion. The best minds and hearts seek joy and self-forgetfulness in active service, as in another time they might seek it in solitary worship; God, as we often hear, being sought more through human fellowship and less by way of isolate self-consciousness than was the case a short time since.

I need hardly particularize the educational and philanthropic zeal that, in one form or another, incites the better minds among our contemporaries and makes them feel guilty when they are not in some way exerting themselves to spread abroad material or spiritual goods. No one would wish to see this zeal diminished; and perhaps it makes in the long run for every kind of worthy achievement; but its immediate effect is often to multiply the commonplace, giving point to De Tocqueville's reflection

175

that "in aristocracies a few great pictures are produced, in democratic countries a vast number of insignificant ones."* In a spiritual as well as a material sense there is a tendency to fabricate cheap goods for an uncritical market.

"Men and gods are too extense." †

Finally, all theories that aim to deduce from social conditions the limits of personal achievement must be received with much caution. It is the very nature of a virile sense of self to revolt from the usual and the expected and pursue a lonesome road. Of course it must have support, but it may find this in literature and imaginative intercourse. So, in spite of everything, we have had in America men of signal distinction—such, for instance, as Emerson, Thoreau and Whitman—and we shall no doubt have more. We need fear no dearth of inspiring issues; for if old ones disappear energetic minds will always create new ones by making greater demands upon life.

The very fact that our time has so largely cast off all sorts of structure is in one way favorable to enduring production, since it means that we have fallen back upon human nature, upon that which is permanent and essential, the adequate record of which is the chief agent in giving life to any product of the mind.

* Democracy in America, vol. ii, book i, chap. 11.
† Emerson, Alphonso of Castile.

CHAPTER XVI

THE TREND OF SENTIMENT

Meaning and General Trend of Sentiment—Attenuation—
Refinement—Sense of Justice—Truth as Justice—As
Realism—As Expediency—As Economy of Attention—
Hopefulness.

By sentiment I mean socialized feeling, feeling which
has been raised by thought and intercourse out of its
merely instinctive state and become properly human.
It implies imagination, and the medium in which it chiefly
lives is sympathetic contact with the minds of others.
Thus love is a sentiment, while lust is not; resentment is,
but not rage; the fear of disgrace or ridicule, but not
animal terror, and so on. Sentiment is the chief motive-
power of life, and as a rule lies deeper in our minds and
is less subject to essential change than thought, from
which, however, it is not to be too sharply separated.

Two traits in the growth of sentiment are perhaps
characteristic of modern life, both of which, as will appear, are closely bound up with the other psychological
changes that have already been discussed.

First a trend toward diversification: under the impulse of a growing diversity of suggestion and intercourse
many new varieties and shades of sentiment are developed. Like a stream which is distributed for irrigation,

177

the general current of social feeling is drawn off into many small channels.

Second a trend toward humanism, meaning by this a wider reach and application of the sentiments that naturally prevail in the familiar intercourse of primary groups. Following a tendency evident in all phases of the social mind, these expand and organize themselves at the expense of sentiments that go with the more formal or oppressive structures of an earlier epoch.

The diversification of sentiment seems to involve some degree of attenuation, or decline in volume, and also some growth of refinement.

By the former I mean that the constant and varied demands upon feeling which modern life makes—in contrast to the occasional but often severe demands of a more primitive society—give rise, very much as in the case of the irrigating stream, to the need and practice of more economy and regularity in the flow, so that "animated moderation"* in feeling succeeds the alternations of apathy and explosion characteristic of a ruder condition. Thus our emotional experience is made up of diverse but for the most part rather mild excitements, so that the man most at home in our civilization, though more nimble in sentiment than the man of an earlier order, is perhaps somewhat inferior in depth. Something of the same difference can be seen between the city man and the farmer; while the latter is inferior in versatility and readiness of feeling, he has a greater store of it laid up, which is apt to give superior depth and momentum to such

* Bagehot's phrase. See his Physics and Politics.

178

sentiment as he does cherish. Who has not experienced the long-minded faithfulness and kindness, or perhaps resentment, of country people, and contrasted them with the less stable feelings of those who live a more urbane life?

In saying that life tends toward refinement it is only a general trend that is asserted. We must admit that many phases of refined sentiment have been more perfectly felt and expressed in the past than they are now; but this is a matter of the maturity of special types of culture, rather than of general progress. Thus the Italian Renaissance produced wonders of refinement in art, as in the painting, let us say, of Botticelli; but it was, on the whole, a bloody, harsh and sensual time compared with ours, a time when assassination, torture and rape were matters of every day. So, also, there is a refinement of the sense of language in Shakespeare and his contemporaries which we can only admire, while their plays depict a rather gross state of feeling. A course of reading in English fiction, beginning with Chaucer and ending with James, Howells and Mrs. Ward, would certainly leave the impression that our sensibilities had, on the whole, grown finer.

And this is even more true of the common people than of the well-to-do class with which literature is chiefly occupied: the tendency to the diffusion of refinement being more marked than its increase in a favored order. The sharp contrast in manners and feelings between the "gentleman," as formerly understood, and the peasant, artisan and trading classes has partly disappeared.

179

Differences in wealth and occupation no longer necessitate differences in real culture, the opportunities for which are coming to be open to all classes, and in America, at least, the native-bred farmer or handworker is not uncommonly, in essential qualities, a gentleman.

The general fact is that the activities of life, to which feeling responds, have become more various and subtle and less crudely determined by animal conditions. Material variety and comfort is one phase of this: we become habituated to a comparatively delicate existence and so are trained to shun coarseness. Communication, by giving abundance and choice of social contacts, also acts to diversify and refine sentiment; the growth of order disaccustoms us to violence, and democracy tends to remove the degrading spectacle of personal or class oppression.

This modern refinement has the advantage that, being a general rise in level rather than the achievement of a class or a nation, it is probably secure. It is not, like the refinement of Greece, the somewhat precarious fruit of transient conditions, but a possession of the race, in no more danger of dying out than the steam-engine.

To the trend toward humanism and the sentiments—such as justice, truth, kindness and service—that go with it, I shall devote the rest of this chapter and the one that follows:

The basis of all sentiment of this kind is the sense of community, or of sharing in a common social or spiritual whole, membership in which gives to all a kind of inner equality, no matter what their special parts may be. It is felt, however, that the differences among men should be

180

functional and intrinsic, not arbitrary or accidental. The sense of justice is usually strong among the members of a sympathetic group, the basis for determining what is just being the perception of some purpose which every one is to serve, each in his own way, so that he who rightly holds a higher place is the one who can function best for the common good. It does not hurt my self-respect or my allegiance to remain a common seaman while another becomes captain of the ship, provided I recognize that he is the fitter man for the place; and if the distribution of stations in society were evidently of this sort there would be no serious protest against it. What makes trouble is the growth of an ideal of fair play which the actual system of things does not satisfy.

The widening of sympathy and the consciousness of larger unity have brought the hope and demand for a corresponding extension of justice; and all sorts of humanity—not to speak of the lower animals—profit by this wider sentiment. Classes seek to understand each other; the personality of women and children is recognized and fostered; there is some attempt to sympathize with alien nations and races, civilized or savage, and to help them to their just place in the common life of mankind.

Our conception of international rights reflects the same view, and the American, at least, desires that his country should treat other countries as one just man treats another, and is proud when he can believe that she has done so. It is surely of scme significance that in the most powerful of democracies national selfishness, in the judgment of a competent European observer, is less cynical and obtrusive than in any of the great states of Europe.*

Truth is a kind of justice, and wherever there is identification of oneself with the life of the group it is fostered, and lying tends to be felt as mean and impolitic. Serious falsehood among friends is, I believe, universally abhorred —by savages and children as well as by civilized adults. To lie to a friend is to hit him from behind, to trip him up in the dark, and so the moral sentiment of every group attempts to suppress falsehood among its members, however it may be encouraged as against outsiders. "Wherefore," says St. Paul, "putting away lying, speak every man truth with his neighbor, for we are members one of another."†

Our democratic system aims to be a larger organization of moral unity, and so far as it is so, in the feeling of the individual, it fosters this open and downright attitude toward his fellows. In idea, and largely in fact, we are a commonwealth, of which each one is a member by his will and intelligence, as well as by necessity, and with which, accordingly, the human sentiment of loyalty among those who are members one of another is naturally in force. The very disgust with which, in a matter like assessment for taxation, men contemplate the incompatibility that sometimes exists between truth and fairness, is a tribute to the prevailing sentiment of sincerity.

An artificial system, that is one which, however solid

* See James Bryce, The American Commonwealth, chap. 87.
† Ephesians, iv, 25.

its hidden foundations—and of course all systems rest on fact of some sort—does not visibly flow from principles of truth and fairness, fails to arouse this loyalty of partnership. One may be devoted to it, but his devotion will be based rather on reverence for something above him than on a sense of participation, and will call for submission rather than for straightforward dealing. It would seem that lying and servility are natural in the attitude of a subject toward a master, that is toward a superior but uncomprehending power; while truth is generated in sympathy. Tyranny may be said to make falsehood a virtue, and in contemporary Russia, for instance, stealth and evasion are the necessary and justifiable means of pursuing the aims of human nature.

Another reason for the association of freedom with truth is that the former is a training in the sense of social cause and effect; the free play of human forces being a constant demonstration of the power of reality as against sham. The more men experiment intelligently with life, the more they come to believe in definite causation and the less in trickery. Freedom means continuous experiment, a constant testing of the individual and of all kinds of social ideas and arrangements. It tends, then, to a social realism; "Her open eyes desire the truth." The best people I know are pervaded by the feeling that life is so real that it is not worth while to make believe. "Knights of the unshielded heart," they desire nothing so much as to escape from all pretense and prudery and confront things as they really are—confident that they are not irremediably bad. I read in a current newspaper that

183

"brutal, unvarnished, careless frankness is the pose of
the new type of girl. She has not been developed in a
school of evasion. To pretend you gave a hundred dollars for a gown when you really gave fifty for it, is a sorry
jest for her and a waste of time. . . . If she owns to the
new gown she tells you its cost, the name of the inexpen-
sive dressmaker who made it, and just where she econo-
mized in its price."

There is a tribute to truth in the very cynicism and
shamelessness with which flagitious politicians and financiers declare and defend their practices. Like Napoleon
or Macchiavelli they have at least cast off superstition and
are dealing with reality, though they apprehend it only in a
low and partial aspect. If they lie, they do so deliberately,
scientifically, with a view to producing a certain effect upon
people whom they regard as fools. It only needs that this
rational spirit should ally itself with higher sentiment and
deeper insight in order that it should become a source of
virtue.

I will not here inquire minutely how far or in what
sense honesty is the best policy, but it is safe to say that
the more life is organized upon a basis of freedom and
justice the more truth there is in the proverb. When
the general state of things is anarchical, as in the time of
Macchiavelli, rationalism may lead to the cynical use
of falsehood as the tool suited to the material; nor is it
deniable that this is often the case at the present day.
But modern democracy aims to organize justice, and in
so far as it succeeds it creates a medium in which truth
tends to survive and falsehood to perish. We all wish to

live in such a medium: there is nothing more grateful than the conviction that the order of things is sincere, is founded on reality of some sort; and in a good measure the American, for instance, does have this conviction. It makes democracy a soft couch for the soul: one can let himself go and does not have to make believe; pretence is no part of the system; be your real self and you will find your right place.

> "I know how the great basement of all power
> Is frankness, and a true tongue to the world;
> And how intriguing secrecy is proof
> Of fear and weakness, and a hollow state."

An artificial system must maintain itself by suppressing the free play of social forces and inculcating its own artificial ideas in place of those derived from experience. Free association, free speech, free thinking, in so far as they touch upon matters vital to authority, are and always have been put down under such systems, and this means that the whole mind of the people is emasculated, as the mind of Italy was by Spanish rule and religious reaction in the seventeenth and eighteenth centuries. "Oriental mendacity" is ascribed to the insecurity of life and property under arbitrary rule; but it is not merely life and property that are affected. The very idea of truth and reason in human affairs can hardly prevail under a system which affords no observation to corroborate it. The fact that in diplomacy, for instance, there is a growing belief that it pays to be simple and honest, I take to be a reflection of the fact that the international system, based more and more on intelligent public opinion, is

185

gradually coming to be a medium in which truth is fit to live.

Perhaps something of this hostility to truth will linger in all establishments, however they may be humanized: they all involve a kind of vested interest in certain ideas which is not favorable to entire frankness. It sometimes appears that one who would be quite honest and stand for human nature should avoid not only religious, political and educational allegiance, but law, journalism, and all positions where one has to speak as part of an institution. As a rule the great seers and thinkers have stood as much aside from institutions as the nature of the human mind permits.

Still another reason for the keener sense of truth in our day is the need to economize attention. In societies where life is dull, fiction, circumlocution and elaborate forms of intercourse serve as a sort of pastime; and the first arouses no resentment unless some definite injury is attempted by it. Although the Chinese are upright in keeping their pecuniary engagements, we are told that mere truth is not valued by them, and is not inculcated by their classic moralists. So in Italy the people seem to think that a courteous and encouraging lie is kinder than the bare truth, as when a man will pretend to give you information when he knows nothing about the matter. A strenuous civilization like ours makes one intolerant of all this. It is not that we are always hurried; but we are so often made to feel the limitations of our attention that we dislike to waste it. Thought is life, and we wish to get the most reality for a given outlay of it that is to be had. We wish to come at once to the Real Thing, whether it be a business proposition or the most subtle theory.

Another sentiment favored by the times is social courage and hopefulness, a disposition to push forward with confidence regarding the future both of the individual and of society at large. That this attitude is the prevalent one, in American democracy at least, nearly all observers are agreed. "Let any one," says Dr. Lyman Abbott, "stand on one of our great highways and watch the countenances of the passers-by; the language written on most of them is that of eagerness, ambition, expectation, hope."* There is something ruthless about this headlong optimism, which is apt to deny and neglect failure and despair, as certain religious sects of the day deny and neglect physical injury; but it answers its purpose of sustaining the combatants. It springs from a condition in which the individual, not supported in any one place by a rigid system, is impelled from childhood to trust himself to the common current of life, to make experiments, to acquire a habit of venture and a working knowledge of social forces. The state of things instigates endeavor, and, as a rule, rewards it sufficiently to keep up one's courage, while occasional failure at least takes away that vague dread of the unknown which is often worse than the reality. Life is natural and vivid, not the wax-works of an artificial order, and has that enlivening effect that comes from being thrown back upon human nature. A real pessimism—one which despairs of the general trend

* In Shaler's United States, ii, 594.

of things—is rare and without much influence, even the revolutionary sects maintaining that the changes they desire are in the line of a natural evolution. Discontent is affirmative and constructive rather than stagnant: it works out programmes and hopefully agitates for their realization. There is a kind of piety and trust in God to be seen in the confidence with which small bodies of men anticipate the success of principles they believe to be right.

CHAPTER XVII

THE TREND OF SENTIMENT; Continued

Nature of the Sentiment of Brotherhood—Favored by Communication and Settled Principles—How Far Contemporary Life Fosters It—How Far Uncongenial To It—General Outcome in this Regard—The Spirit of Service—The Trend of Manners—Brotherhood in Relation to Conflict—Blame—Democracy and Christianity.

THE sentiment of mutual kindness or brotherhood is a simple and widespread thing, belonging not only to man in every stage of his development, but extending, in a crude form, over a great part of animal life. Prince Kropotkin, in his Mutual Aid a Factor in Evolution, has collected illustrations of its universality and significance. ". . . the necessity of communicating impressions," he says, "of playing, of chattering, or of simply feeling the proximity of other kindred living beings pervades nature, and is, as much as any other physiological function, a distinctive feature of life and impressionability."* Darwin perceived, what Kropotkin and others have illustrated with convincing fulness, that this fusing kindliness underlies all higher phases of evolution, and is essential to the coöperative life in which thought and power are developed. The popular notion that kindly sentiment can only be a hindrance to the survival of the fittest is a somewhat pernicious misapprehension.

This sentiment flourishes most in primary groups, where, as we have seen, it contributes to an ideal of moral unity of which kindness is a main part. Under its in-

* Page 55.

189

fluence the I-feeling becomes a we-feeling, which seeks no good that is not also the good of the group. And the humanism of our time strives with renewed energy to make the we-feeling prevail also in the larger phases of life. "We must demand," says a writer who lives very close to the heart of the people,* "that the individual shall be willing to lose the sense of personal achievement, and shall be content to realize his activity only in connection with the activity of the many." Huxley at one time felt this so strongly as to say, "If I had 400 pounds a year I would never let my name appear to anything I did or shall do."†

Such utterances, though significant, are one-sided, and it is perhaps more in the way of real progress to demand, not that the sense of personal achievement shall be given up, but that it shall be more allied with fellow-feeling. The sort of ambition congenial to the we-feeling is one directed toward those common aims in which the success of one is the success of all, not toward admiration or riches. Material goods, one feels, should not be appropriated for pride or luxury, but, being limited in amount, should be used in a consciousness of the general need, and apportioned by rules of justice framed to promote a higher life in the whole.

Much might be said of the we-feeling as joy:

> Perchè quanto si dice piu li nostro,
> Tanto possiede piu di ben ciascuno,
> E piu di caritate arde in quel chiostro.‡

* Jane Addams, Democracy and Social Ethics, 275.
† Quoted in The Commons, October, 1903.
‡ Dante, Purgatorio, 15, 55–57. He is speaking of Paradise.

For there, as much the more as one says *Our*,
So much the more of good each one possesseth,
And more of charity in that cloister burns.*

There is nothing more wholesome or less pursued by compunction. To mingle our emotions with fellowship enlarges and soothes them; even resentment on behalf of *us* is less rankling than on behalf of only *me*, and there is something cheerful in suffering wrong in friendly company. One of the most obvious things about selfishness is the unhappiness of it, the lack of imaginative expatiation, of the inspiration of working consciously with a vast whole, of "the exhilaration and uplift which come when the individual sympathy and intelligence is caught into the forward intuitive movement of the mass."†
Fellowship is thus a good kind of joy in that it is indefinitely diffusible; though by no means incapable of abuse, since it may be cultivated at the expense of truth, sanity and individuality.

Everything that tends to bring mankind together in larger wholes of sympathy and understanding tends to enlarge the reach of kindly feeling. Among the conditions that most evidently have this effect are facility of communication and the acceptance of common principles. These permit the contact and fusion of minds and tend to mould the group into a moral whole.

In times of settled principles and of progress in the arts of communication the idea of the brotherhood of man has a natural growth; as it had under the Roman Empire. On the other hand, it is dissipated by whatever breaks up

* Longfellow's Translation.
† Jane Addams, Democracy and Social Ethics, 272.

the moral unity and makes human interests seem inconsistent. Not only war, but all kinds of destructive or unregulated competition, in which the good of one party appears to be a private good gained by the harm of another, are reflected in the mind by unkindly feeling. What human nature needs is—not the disappearance of opposition, which would be death—but the suppression of destructive forms, and the control of all forms by principles of justice and kindness, so that men may feel that the good survives.

As regards the bearing of contemporary conditions upon the spirit of brotherhood, we find forces at work so conflicting that it is easy to reach opposite conclusions, according to the bias of the observer.

The enlargement of consciousness has brought a broadening of sentiment in all directions. As a rule kindly feeling follows understanding, and there was never such opportunity and encouragement to understand as there is now. Distant peoples—Russians, Chinese and South Sea Islanders; alienated classes—criminals, vagrants, idiots and the insane, are brought close to us, and the natural curiosity of man about his fellows is exploited and stimulated by the press. Indeed, the decried habit of reading the newspapers contributes much to a general we-feeling, since the newspaper is a reservoir of commonplace thought of which every one partakes—and which he knows he may impute to every one else—pervading the world with a conscious community of sentiment which tends toward kindliness.

Even more potent, perhaps, is the indirect action of

communication in making it possible to organize all phases of life on a larger scale and on a more human basis; in promoting democracy and breaking down caste. Under a democratic system the masses have means of self-expression; they vote, strike, and print their views. They have power, and this, at bottom, is the source of all respect and consideration. People of other classes have to think of them, feel with them and recognize them as of a common humanity. Moreover, in tending to wipe out conventional distinctions and leave only those that are functional, democracy fosters the notion of an organic whole, from which all derive and in which they find their value. A sense of common nature and purpose is thus nourished, a conscious unity of action which gives the sense of fellowship. It comes to be assumed that men are of the same stuff, and a kind of universal sympathy—not incompatible with opposition—is spread abroad. It is realized that "there are diversities of gifts but the same spirit."

On the other hand, our life is full of a confusion which often leaves the individual conscious only of his separateness, engaged in a struggle which, so far as he sees, has no more relation to justice and the common good than a dog-fight. Whether he win or lose makes, in this case, little difference as to the effect upon his general view of life: he infers that the world is a place where one must either eat or be eaten; the idea of the brotherhood of man appears to be an enervating sentimentalism, and the true philosophy that of the struggle for existence, which he understands in a brutal sense opposite to the real teaching of science. Nothing could be more uncongenial to the we-feeling than this view, which unfortunate experience has prepared many to embrace, taking from life, as it does, its breadth and hopefulness, the joy and inspiration of working in a vast and friendly whole.

Probably most of us are under the sway of both of these tendencies. We feel the new idealism, the sweep and exhilaration of democracy, but we practise, nevertheless, a thrifty exploitation of all the private advantages we can decently lay our hands on; nor have we the moral vigor to work out any reconciliation of these principles. Experience shows, I think, that until a higher sentiment, like brotherly kindness, attains some definite organization and programme, so that men are held up to it, it is remarkably ineffective in checking selfish activities. People drift on and on in lower courses, which at bottom they despise and dislike, simply because they lack energy and initiative to get out of them. How true it is that many of us would like to be *made* to be better than we are. I have seen promising idealists grow narrow, greedy and sensual—and of course unhappy—as they prospered in the world; for no reason, apparently, but lack of definite stimulation to a higher life. There is firm ground for the opinion that human nature is prepared for a higher organization than we have worked out.

Certainly there is, on the whole, a more lively and hopeful pursuit of the brotherhood of man in modern democracy than there ever was, on a large scale, before. One who is not deaf to the voices of literature, of social agitation, of ordinary intercourse, can hardly doubt this. The social settlement and similar movements express it, and so, more and more, does the whole feeling of our society regarding richer and poorer. Philanthropy is not only extending, but undergoing a revolution of principle from alms to justice and from condescension to fellowship. The wealthy and the educated classes feel, however vaguely, that they must justify their advantages to their fellow men and their own consciences by making some public use of them. Gifts—well meant if not always wise—to education, science and philanthropy are increasing, and there was never, perhaps, a more prevalent disposition to make unusual mental acquirements available toward general culture.

Even the love of publicity and display, said to mark our rich people, has its amiable side as indicating a desire to impress general opinion, rather than that of an exclusive class. Indeed, if there is anywhere in American society an exclusive and self-sufficient kind of people, they are not a kind who have much influence upon the general spirit.

The same sentiment incites us, in our better moments, to shun habits, modes of dress and the like that are not good in themselves and merely accentuate class lines; to save on private and material objects so as to have the more energy to be humanly, spiritually, alive. This, for example, is the teaching of Thoreau, whose works, especially his Walden, have latterly a wide circulation. If Thoreau seems a little too aloof and fastidious to represent democracy, this is not the case with Whitman, who had joy in the press of cities, and whose passion was to "utter the word Democratic, the word En Masse."* His chants express a great gusto in common life: "All this I

* Leaves of Grass (1884), page 9.

195

swallow, it tastes good, I like it well, it becomes mine; I am the man, I suffered, I was there."* "Whoever degrades another degrades me."† "By God! I will accept nothing which all cannot have their counterpart of on the same terms." ‡ "I believe the main purport of these states is to found a superb friendship, exalté, previously unknown." §

On the whole, Americans may surely claim that there was never before a great nation in which the people felt so much like a family, had so kindly and cheerful a sense of a common life. It is not only that the sentiment has a wider range; there is also more faith in its future, more belief that government and other institutions can be made to express it. And the popular agitation of all countries manifests the same belief—socialism, and even anarchism, as well as the labor movement and the struggle against monopoly and corruption.

A larger spirit of service is the active side of democratic feeling. A life of service of some sort—in behalf of the clan or tribe, of the chief, of the sovereign, of the mistress, of the Church, of God—has always been the ideal life, since no imaginative and truly human mind contents itself with a separate good: what is new is that the object of this service tends to become wider, with the modern expansion of the imagination, and to include all classes, all nations and races, in its ideal scope. The narrower boundaries do not disappear, but as they become less distinct the greater whole becomes more so. As the child grows until he can see over the hedges bounding his early

* *Idem,* 59.   † *Idem,* 48.   ‡ *Idem,* 48.   § *Idem,* 110.

playground, so the democratized individual has outgrown the limits of the clan or the caste.

In the United States, at least, the feeling that everybody ought to be doing something useful is so established that there is no influential class within which idleness is respectable. Whatever narrowness there may be in this spirit, in the way of undervaluing activities whose usefulness is of an inobvious sort, it is sound on the whole and does incalculable service in redeeming riches from vulgarity and corruption. If it be true, as is asserted, that the children of the wealthy, with us, are on the whole less given to sloth and vice than the same class in older countries, the reason is to be found in a healthier, more organic state of public opinion which penetrates all classes with the perception that the significance of the individual lies in his service to the whole. That this sentiment is gaining in our colleges is evident to those who know anything of these institutions. Studies that throw light on the nature and working of society, past or present, and upon the opportunities of service or distinction which it offers to the individual, are rapidly taking the place, for purposes of culture, of studies whose human value is less, or not so apparent. Classes in history—political, industrial and social—in economics, in government and administration, in sociology and ethics, in charities and penology, are larger year by year. And the young people, chiefly from the well-to-do classes, who seek these studies, are one and all adherents of the democratic idea that privilege must be earned by function.

The tendency of manners well expresses that of sentiment, and seems to be toward a spontaneous courtesy,

197

expressing truth and equality as against the concealment and, sometimes, the arrogance, of mere polish. The best practice appears to be to put yourself, on approaching another, into as open and kindly a frame of mind toward him as you can, but not to try to express more than you feel, preferring coldness to affected warmth. Democracy is too busy and too fond of truth and human nature to like formality, except as an occasional amusement. A merely formal politeness goes with a crystallized society, indicating a certain distrust of human nature and desire to cloak or supplant it by propriety. Thus a Chinese teacher, having a rare opportunity to send a message to his old mother, called one of his pupils saying, "Here, take this paper and write me a letter to my mother." This proceeding struck the observer as singular, and he enquired if the lad was acquainted with the teacher's mother, learning that the boy did not even know there was such a person. "How, then, was he to know what to say, not having been told?" To this the schoolmaster made reply: "Doesn't he know quite well what to say? For more than a year he has been studying literary composition, and he is acquainted with a number of elegant formulas. Do you think he does not know perfectly well how a son ought to write to a mother?" The letter would have answered equally well for any other mother in the Empire.* Here is one extreme, and the kindly frontiersman with "no manners at all" is at the other.

No doubt form, in manners as well as elsewhere, is capable of a beauty and refinement of its own, and probably raw democracy goes to an anarchic excess in depreci-

* Arthur H. Smith, Chinese Characteristics, 181.

198

ating it; but the sentiment of reality which demands that form and content should agree, is perhaps a permanent factor in the best manners.

Conflict, of some sort, is the life of society, and progress emerges from a struggle in which each individual, class or institution seeks to realize its own idea of good. The intensity of this struggle varies directly as the vigor of the people, and its cessation, if conceivable, would be death. There is, then, no prospect of an amiable unanimity, and the question arises, What change, if any, in the nature of opposition and of hostility, accompanies the alleged growth of the sense of brotherhood?

The answer to this is probably best sought by asking ourselves what is the difference between the opposition of friends and that of enemies. Evidently the former may be as energetic as the latter, but it is less personal: that is, it is not directed against the opponent as a whole, but against certain views or purposes which the opponent— toward whom a kindly feeling is still cherished—for the time being represents. The opposition of enemies, on the other hand, involves a personal antagonism and is gratified by a personal injury.

Well-conducted sports are a lesson to every one that fair and orderly opposition may even promote good fellowship; and familiarity with them, in primary groups, is an excellent preparation for the friendly competition that ought to prevail in society at large. Indeed it is only through opposition that we learn to understand one another. In the moment of struggle the opposing agent may arouse anger, but afterward the mind, more at ease,

199

views with respect and interest that which has exhibited
so much force. It seems evident, for instance, that the
self-assertion of the wage-earning class, so far as it is
orderly and pursuant of ideals which all classes share,
has commanded not only the respect but the good will of
the people at large. Weakness—intrinsic weakness, the
failure of the member to assert its function—is instinctively
despised. I am so far in sympathy with the struggle for
existence as to think that passive kindliness alone, apart
from self-assertion, is a demoralizing ideal, or would be
if it were likely to become ascendant. But the self which
is asserted, the ideal fought for, must be a generous one—
involving perhaps self-sacrifice as that is ordinarily understood—or the struggle is degrading.

The wider contact which marks modern life, the sup-
pling of the imagination which enables it to appreciate
diverse phases of human nature, the more instructed sense
of justice, brings in a larger good will which economizes
personal hostility without necessarily diminishing opposition. In primitive life the reaction of man against man
is crude, impulsive, wasteful. Violent anger is felt against
the opponent as a whole and expressed by a general as-
sault. Civilized man, trained to be more discriminating,
strikes at tendencies rather than persons, and avoids
so far as possible hostile emotion, which he finds painful
and exhausting. As an opponent he is at once kinder
and more formidable than the savage.

Perhaps the most urgent need of the present time, so
far as regards the assuaging of antipathy, is some clearer
consciousness of what may be called, in the widest sense,
the rules of the game; that is, for accepted ideals of justice

which conscience and public opinion may impose upon reasonable men, and law upon the unreasonable. In the lack of clear notions of right and duty the orderly test of strength degenerates into a scuffle, in which the worst passions are released and low forms of power tend to prevail—just as brutal and tricky methods prevail in ill-regulated sports. We need a popular ethics which is at once Christian and evolutionary, recognizing unity of spirit alongside of diversity of standpoint; a coöperative competition, giving each individual, group or race a fair chance for higher self-assertion under conditions so just as to give the least possible occasion for ill-feeling. Something of this sort is in fact the ideal in accordance with which modern democracy hopes to reconstruct a somewhat disordered world.

There is a French maxim, much quoted of late, to the effect that to understand all is to pardon all: all animosity, as some interpret this, is a mistake; when we fully understand we cease to blame. This, however, is only a half-truth, and becomes a harmful fallacy when it is made to stand for the whole. It is true that if we wholly lose ourselves in another's state of mind blame must disappear: perhaps nothing is felt as wrong by him who does it at the very instant it is done. But this is more than we have a right to do: it involves that we renounce our moral individuality, the highest part of our being, and become a mere intelligence. The fact that every choice is natural to the mind that chooses does not make it right.

The truth is that we must distinguish, in such questions as this, two attitudes of mind, the active and the con-

201

templative, both natural and having important functions, but neither by itself sufficient. Pure contemplation sees things and their relations as a picture and with no sense of better or worse; it does not care; it is the ideal of science and speculative philosophy. If one could be completely in this state of mind he would cease to be a self altogether. All active personality, and especially all sense of right and wrong, of duty, responsibility, blame, praise and the like, depend upon the mind taking sides and having particular desires and purposes.

The unhappiness of bad men, maintained by Socrates, depends upon their badness being brought home to them in conscience. If, because of their insensibility or lack of proper reproof, the error of their way is not impressed upon them, they have no motive to reform. The fact that the evil-doer has become such gradually, and does not realize the evil in him, is no reason why we should not blame him; it is the function of blame to make him and others realize it, to define evil and declare it in the sight of men. We may pardon the evil-doer when he is dead, or has sincerely and openly repented, not while he remains a force for wrong.

It seems that the right way lies between the old vindictiveness and the view now somewhat prevalent that crime should be regarded without resentment, quite like a disease of the flesh. The resentment of society, if just and moderate, is a moral force, and definite forms of punishment are required to impress it upon the general mind. If crime is a disease it is a moral disease and calls for moral remedies, among which is effective resentment. It is right that one who harms the state should go to prison

202

in the sight of all; but it is right also that all should understand that this is done for the defence of society, and not because the offender is imagined to be another kind of man from the rest of us.

The democratic movement, insomuch as it feels a common spirit in all men, is of the same nature as Christianity; and it is said with truth that while the world was never so careless as now of the mechanism of religion, it was never so Christian in feeling. A deeper sense of a common life, both as incarnated in the men about us and as inferred in some larger whole behind and above them—in God—belongs to the higher spirit of democracy as it does to the teaching of Jesus.

He calls the mind out of the narrow and transient self of sensual appetites and visible appurtenances, which all of us in our awakened moments feel to be inferior, and fills it with the incorrupt good of higher sentiment. We are to love men as brothers, to fix our attention upon the best that is in them, and to make their good our own ambition.

Such ideals are perennial in the human heart and as sound in psychology as in religion. The mind, in its best moments, is naturally Christian; because when we are most fully alive to the life about us the sympathetic becomes the rational; what is good for you is good for me because I share your life; and I need no urging to do by you as I would have you do by me. Justice and kindness are matters of course, and also humility, which comes from being aware of something superior to your ordinary self. To one in whom human nature is fully awake "Love your enemies and do good to them that despitefully use you" is natural and easy, because despiteful people are seen to be in a state of unhappy aberration from the higher life of kindness, and there is an impulse to help them to get back. The awakened mind identifies itself with other persons, living the sympathetic life and following the golden rule by impulse.

To put it otherwise, Christ and modern democracy alike represent a protest against whatever is dead in institutions, and an attempt to bring life closer to the higher impulses of human nature. There is a common aspiration to effectuate homely ideals of justice and kindness. The modern democrat is a plain man and Jesus was another. It is no wonder, then, that the characteristic thought of the day is preponderantly Christian, in the sense of sharing the ideals of Christ, and that in so far as it distrusts the Church it is on the ground that the Church is not Christian enough.

But how far, after all, is this brotherly and peaceful sentiment, ancient or modern, applicable to life as we know it? Is it feasible, is it really right, is it not a sentiment of submission in a world that grows by strife? After what has already been said on this, it is perhaps enough to add here that neither in the life of Christ nor in modern democracy do we find sanction for submission to essential, moral wrong. Christ brought a sword which the good man of our day can by no means sheathe: his counsels of submission seem to refer to merely personal injuries, which it may be better to overlook in order to keep the conflict on a higher plane. If we mean by Christianity an understanding and brotherly spirit toward all men

204

and a reverence for the higher Life behind them, expressed in an infinite variety of conduct according to conditions, it would seem to be always right, and always feasible, so far as we have strength to rise to it.

The most notable reaction of democracy upon religious sentiment is no doubt a tendency to secularize it, to fix it upon human life rather than upon a vague other world. So soon as men come to feel that society is not a machine, controlled chiefly by the powers of darkness, but an expression of human nature, capable of reflecting whatever good human nature can rise to; so soon, that is, as there comes to be a public will, the religious spirit is drawn into social idealism. Why dream of a world to come when there is hopeful activity in this? God, it seems, is to be found in human life as well as beyond it, and social service is a method of his worship. "If ye love not your brother whom ye have seen, how can ye love God whom ye have not seen?"

An ideal democracy is in its nature religious, and its true sovereign may be said to be the higher nature, or God, which it aspires to incarnate in human institutions.

PART IV

SOCIAL CLASSES

CHAPTER XVIII

THE HEREDITARY OR CASTE PRINCIPLE

NATURE AND USE OF CLASSES—INHERITANCE AND COMPETITION THE TWO PRINCIPLES UPON WHICH CLASSES ARE BASED—CONDITIONS IN HUMAN NATURE MAKING FOR HEREDITARY CLASSES —CASTE SPIRIT.

SPEAKING roughly, we may call any persistent social group, other than the family, existing within a larger group, a class. And every society, except possibly the most primitive, is more or less distinctly composed of classes. Even in savage tribes there are, besides families and clans, almost always other associations: of warriors, of magicians and so on; and these continue throughout all phases of development until we reach the intricate group structure of our own time. Individuals never achieve their life in separation, but always in coöperation with a group of other minds, and in proportion as these coöperating groups stand out from one another with some distinctness they constitute social classes.

We may say of this differentiation, speaking generally, that it is useful. The various functions of life require special influences and organization, and without some class spirit, some speciality in traditions and standards, nothing is well performed. Thus, if our physicians were not, as regards their professional activities, something of a psychological unit, building up knowledge and sentiment by communication, desiring the approval and dreading the censure of their colleagues, it would be worse not only for them but for the rest of us. There are no doubt class divisions that are useless or harmful, but something of this nature there should be, and I have already tried to show that our own society suffers considerably from a lack of adequate group differentiation in its higher mental activities.

Fundamental to all study of classes are the two principles, of inheritance and of competition, according to which their membership is determined. The rule of descent, as in the hereditary nobility of England or Germany, gives a fixed system, the alternative to which is some kind of selection—by election or appointment as in our politics; by purchase, as formerly in the British army and navy; or by the informal action of preference, opportunity and endeavor, as in the case of most trades and professions at the present day.

Evidently these two principles are very much intermingled in their working. The hereditary distinctions must have a beginning in some sort of selective struggle, such as the military and commercial competition from which privileged families have emerged in the past, and never become so rigid as not to be modified by similar processes. On the other hand, inherited advantages, even in the freest society, enter powerfully into every kind of competition.

Another consideration of much interest is that the strict rule of descent is a biological principle, making the social organization subordinate to physical continuity of life,

210

while selection or competition brings in psychical elements, of the most various qualities to be sure, but capable at the best of forming society on a truly rational method.

Finally it is well to recognize that there is a vast sum of influences governed by no ascertainable principle at all, which go to assign the individual his place in the class system. After allowing for inheritance and for everything which can fairly be called selection (that is, for all definite and orderly interaction between the man and the system), there remains a large part which can be assigned only to chance. This is particularly true in the somewhat tumultuous changes of modern life.

When a class is somewhat strictly hereditary, we may call it a caste—a name originally applied to the hereditary classes of India, but to which it is common, and certainly convenient, to give a wider meaning.

Perhaps the best way to understand caste is to open our eyes and note those forces at work among ourselves which might conceivably give rise to it.

On every side we may see that differences arise, and that these tend to be perpetuated through inherited associations, opportunities and culture. The endeavor to secure for one's children whatever desirable thing one has gained for oneself is a perennial source of caste, and this endeavor flows from human nature and the moral unity of the family. If a man has been able to save money, he anxiously invests it to yield an income after his death; if he has built up a business, it is his hope that his children may succeed him in it; if he has a good handicraft, he wishes his boys to learn it. And so with less tangible

211

goods—education, culture, religious and moral ideas—
there is no good parent but desires his children to have
more than the common inheritance of what is best in these
things. It is, perhaps, safe to say that if the good of his
children could be set on one side and the good of all the rest
of the world over against it on the other, the average parent
would desire that evil might befall the latter rather than
the former. And much of the wider social spirit of recent
times comes from the belief that we cannot make this separation, and that to secure the real good of our children we
must work for the common advancement.

That this endeavor to secure a succession in desirable
function is not confined to the rich we may see, for instance,
in the fact that labor unions often have regulations tending to secure to the children of members a complete or partial monopoly of the opportunities of apprenticeship. In
Chicago, not long since, only the son of a plumber could
learn the plumber's trade.

As being the actual possessor of the advantages in question, the parent is usually in a position either to hand
them over directly to his children, or to make their acqui-
sition comparatively easy. Wealth, the most obvious
and tangible source of caste, is transmissible, even in the
freest societies, under the sanction and protection of law.
And wealth is convertible not only into material goods
but, if the holder has a little tact and sense, into other
and finer advantages—educational opportunities, business
and professional openings, travel and intercourse with
people of refinement and culture. Against this we must,
of course, offset the diminished motive to exertion, the
lack of rough-and-tumble experience, and other disad-

212

vantages which inherited wealth, especially if large, is apt to bring with it; but that it does, as a rule, perpetuate the more conventional sorts of superiority is undeniable.

And such intangible advantages as culture, manners, good associations and the like, whether associated with wealth or not, are practically heritable, since they are chiefly derived by children from a social environment determined by the personality and standing of their parents.

Indeed, irrespective of any intention toward or from inheritance, there is a strong drift toward it due to mere familiarity. It is commonly the line of least resistance. The father knows much about his own trade and those closely related to it, little about others; and the son shares his point of view. So when the latter comes to fix upon a career he is likely, in the absence of any decided individuality of preference, to take the way that lies most open to him. Of course he may lack the ability to carry the paternal function; but this, though common enough, does not affect the majority of cases. The functions that require a peculiar type of natural ability, while of the first importance, since they include all marked originality, are not very numerous, sound character and training, with fair intelligence, being ordinarily sufficient. Even in the learned professions, such as law, medicine, teaching and the ministry, the great majority of practitioners hold their own by common sense and assiduity rather than by special aptitude. To the best of my observation, there are many men serving as foremen in various sorts of handicraft, or as farmers, who have natural capacity adequate for success in law, commerce or politics. A man of good, all-round ability will succeed in that line of work which

he finds ready to his hand, but only a few will break
away from their antecedents and seek a wholly different
line.   And if their work affords them health, thought and
mastery, why should they wish to change it if they could?

I would not have it supposed, however (because I dwell
thus upon opportunity), that I agree with those whose
zeal for education and training leads them to depreciate
natural differences.   I do not know how to talk with men
who believe in native equality: it seems to me that they
lack common sense and observation.   How can they fail
to see that children in the same family, even twins, as
Mr. Galton has shown,* are often widely divergent in
ability, one destined to leadership and another to obscurity?

The two variables of personality, "nature and nurture,"
are without doubt of equal diversity and importance, and
they must work together to bring about any notable
achievement.   Natural ability is essential; but, no matter
how great, it cannot know or develop its power without
opportunity.   Indeed, great natural faculty is often more
dependent on circumstance than is mediocrity—because
of some trait, like extreme sensitiveness, that unfits it for
miscelianeous competition.   Opportunity, moreover, means
different things in different cases, and is not to be identified
with wealth or facile circumstances of any sort.   Some
degrees and kinds of difficulty are helpful, others not.

And yet, leaving out, on the one hand, unusual talent
or energy, and, on the other, decided weakness or dulness,
the mass of men are guided chiefly by early surroundings
and training, which determine for them, in a general way,

* See the memoir on the subject in his Inquiries into Human
Faculty.

214

what sort of life they will take up, and contribute much to their success or failure in it. Society, even in a comparatively free country, is thus vaguely divided into hereditary strata or sections, from which the majority do not depart.

If the transmission of function from father to son has become established, a caste spirit, a sentiment in favor of such transmission and opposed to the passage from one class into another, may arise and be shared even by the unprivileged classes. The individual then thinks of himself and his family as identified with his caste, and sympathizes with others who have the same feeling. The caste thus becomes a psychical organism, consolidated by community of sentiment and tradition. In some measure the ruling class in England, for example, has hung together in this way, and the same is partly true of the lower orders. No doubt there is generally some protest against a hereditary system on the part of restless members of the lower castes—certainly this was always the case in Europe —but it may be practically insignificant.

And out of caste sentiment arise institutions, social, political and economic—like the mediæval system in Europe, much of which still survives—whose tendency is to define and perpetuate hereditary distinctions.

I have, perhaps, said enough to make it clear that an impulse toward caste is found in human nature itself. Whether it spreads through and dominates the system of life, as in India, or remains subordinate, as with us, depends upon the strength or weakness of other impulses which limit its operation. As certain types of vegetation,

215

like the ferns, which at one time were dominant in the forests, are now overshadowed by plants of higher organization, so caste, which we must, on the whole, reckon to be an inferior principle, tends to be supplanted by something freer and more rational.

CHAPTER XIX

CONDITIONS FAVORING OR OPPOSING THE GROWTH OF CASTE

Three Conditions Affecting the Increase or Diminution of Caste—Race Caste—Immigration and Conquest—Gradual Differentiation of Functions; Mediæval Caste; India—Influence of Settled Conditions—Influence of the State of Communication and Enlightenment—Conclusion.

There seem to be three conditions which, chiefly, make for the increase or diminution of the caste principle. These are, first, likeness or unlikeness in the constituents of the population; second, the rate of social change (whether we have to do with a settled or a shifting system), and, finally, the state of communication and enlightenment. Unlikeness in the constituents, a settled system and a low state of communication and enlightenment favor the growth of caste, and *vice versa*. The first provides natural lines of cleavage and so makes it easier to split into hereditary groups; the second gives inheritance time to consolidate its power, while the third means the absence of those conscious and rational forces which are its chief rivals.

The most important sorts of unlikeness in the constituents of the population are perhaps three: differences in

217

race; differences, apart from race, due to immigration or conquest, and unlikeness due to the gradual differentiation of social functions within a population originally homogeneous.

Two races of different temperament and capacity, distinct to the eye and living side by side in the same community, tend strongly to become castes, no matter how equal the social system may otherwise be. The difference, as being hereditary, answers in its nature to the idea of caste, and the external sign serves to make it conscious and definite.

The race caste existing in the Southern United States illustrates the impotence of democratic traditions to overcome the caste spirit when fostered by obvious physical and psychical differences. This spirit is immeasurably strong on the part of the whites, and there is no apparent prospect of its diminution.

The specially caste nature of the division—as distinguished from those personal differences which democratic tradition recognizes—is seen in the feeling, universal among the whites, that the Negro must be held apart and subordinate not merely as an individual, or any number of individuals, but as a race, a social whole. That is, the fact that many individuals of this race are equal, and some superior, to the majority of whites does not, in the opinion of the latter, make it just or expedient to treat them apart from the mass of their race. To dine with a Negro, to work or play by his side, or to associate in any relation where superiority cannot be asserted, is held to be degrading and of evil example, no matter what kind of Negro he may be. It is the practice and policy of the dominant race to impress upon the Negro that he belongs by birth to a distinct order out of which he can in no way depart. There or nowhere he must find his destiny. If he wishes to mingle with whites it must be as an acknowledged inferior. As a servant he may ride in the same railway car, but as a citizen he may not do so.

Thoughtful whites justify this attitude on the ground, substantially, that a race *is* an organic whole—bound together by heredity and social connection—and that it is practically necessary to recognize this in dealing with race questions. The integrity of the white race and of white civilization, they say, requires Negro subordination (separation being impracticable), and the only available line of distinction is the definite one of color. A division on this line is even held to be less invidious—as involving no judgment of individuals—as well as more feasible, than one based on personal traits. Particular persons cannot, in practice, be separated from their families and other antecedents, and if they could be the example of mixture on an equal footing would be demoralizing.

This argument is probably sound in so far as it requires the recognition of the two races as being, for some purposes, distinct organisms. In this regard it is perhaps better sociology than the view that every one should be considered solely on his merits as an individual.

At the same time it is only too apparent that our application of this doctrine is deeply colored with that caste arrogance which does not recognize in the Negro a spiritual brotherhood underlying all race difference and possible "inferiority." The matter of unequal ability, in races as in individuals, is quite distinct from that sharing in a

219

common spirit and service from which no human being can rightly or Christianly be excluded. The idea that he is fundamentally a man like the rest of us cannot and should not be kept from the Negro any more than from other lowly orders of people. Science, religion and the democratic spirit all give him a right to it; and the white man cannot deny it to him without being false to his own best self. Anything in our present attitude which does deny it we must hope to be transitory, since it is calculated, in a modern atmosphere, to generate continuing disquiet and hatred. It belonged with slavery and is incongruous with the newer world.

These may be subtleties, but subtlety is the very substance of the race question, the most vital matter being not so much what is done as the spirit in which it is done.

The practical question here is not that of abolishing castes but of securing just and kindly relations between them, of reconciling the fact of caste with ideals of freedom and right. This is difficult but not evidently impossible, and a right spirit, together with a government firmly repressive of the lower passions of both races, should go far to achieve it. There seems to be no reason in the nature of things why divergent races, like divergent individuals, should not unite in a common service of the ideals to which all human nature bears allegiance—I mean ideals of kindness, fair play and so on. And the white man, in claiming superiority, assumes the chief responsibility for bringing this state of things to pass.

When peoples of the same race mingle by migration, the effect, as regards classes, depends chiefly on their states of civilization and the character of the migration, as hostile or friendly. The peaceful advent of kindred settlers, like the English immigrants to the United States, creates no class divisions. If they differ in language and customs, like the Germans, or are extremely poor and ignorant, like many of the Irish, they are held apart for a time and looked down upon, but as they establish themselves and gradually prove their substantial equality with the natives, they may become indistinguishable from the latter. Of recent years, however, the arrival by millions of peoples somewhat more divergent—especially Italians, Slavs and Jews—has introduced distinctions in which race as well as culture plays an appreciable part.

Much depends, of course, upon the special character of the institutions and traditions that thus come into contact. Some societies are rigid and repellent in their structure, while others, like the United States, are almost ideally constituted to invite and hasten assimilation.

Conquest has been one of the main sources of caste the world over. The hostile tradition it leaves may continue indefinitely; servile functions are commonly forced upon the conquered, and the consciousness of superiority leads the conquerors to regard intermarriage as shameful. A servile caste, strictly hereditary, existed even among the primitive German tribes from which most of us are descended, and intermarriage with freemen was severely punished. "The Lombard," says Mr. Gummere, "killed a serf who ventured to marry a free woman, . . . West Goths and Burgundians scourged and burnt them both, while the Saxons punished an unequal marriage of any sort with death of man and wife."*

The unlikeness out of which caste grows may not be original, as in the case of race difference or conquest, but may arise gradually by the differentiation of a homogeneous people. Any distinct social group, having its special group sympathies and traditions, has some tendency to pass on its functions and ideas to the children of its members, promoting association and intermarriage among them, and thus taking on a caste character.

Accordingly, any increase in the complexity of social functions—political, religious, military or industrial—such as necessarily accompanies the enlargement of a social system, may have a caste tendency, because it separates the population into groups corresponding to the several functions; and this alone may without doubt produce caste if the conditions are otherwise favorable.

Something of this sort seems to have followed upon the conquest by the Germanic tribes of Roman territory, and the consequent necessity of administering a more complex system than their own. As the new order took shape it showed a tendency toward more definite inheritance of rank and function than existed in the tribal society. This was due partly, no doubt, to the influence of Roman traditions, but the very nature of the civilization required it. That is, functions became more diverse and of such a character as to separate the citizens into distinct classes, the principal ones being warriors of various degrees (combining military functions with the control of land), clergy,

* Germanic Origins, 154

222

artisans and peasants. The military and landholding class, uniting the force of arms with that of wealth, naturally dominated the others; the artisans, especially in the towns, maintained a free status which served later as the nucleus of a democratic tendency; the peasants became serfs. As the conditions did not permit organization on any free or open principle—there being little facility of travel, diffusion of knowledge or unfixed wealth—the hereditary principle naturally prevailed. Only the clergy, monopolizing most of the knowledge and communication of the time and fortified by celibacy against inheritance, maintained a comparatively open organization. It is well known that lands, and the local rule that went with them, held at first as a personal trust, gradually became a family property, and we are told that when the Emperor Conrad, in 1037, issued his edict making chiefs hereditary in Italy, he only did for the south "by a single stroke what gradual custom and policy had slowly procured for the north."* Offices, armorial devices and other privileges generally followed the same course, and the servile status of serfs was also transmitted to children.

The feudal system was based on inheritance of function, and had two well-defined castes, the knightly, consisting originally of those whose ability to maintain a horse and equipment placed them in the rank of effective warriors, and the servile. Between these marriage was impossible. Intercourse of any kind was scanty and, on the part of the superior order, contemptuous. "A boy of knightly birth was reared in ceremony. From his earliest childhood he learnt to look upon himself and his equals as of a differ-

* Tout, The Empire and The Papacy, 59.

ent degree and almost of a different nature from his fellow creatures who were not of gentle condition. Heraldic pride and the distinction of degree were among his first impressions."* Socially and psychologically the mediæval nobility lived in their caste, not in the world at large. It was the sphere of the social self; the knight looked to it and not to a general public for sympathy and recognition: he was far closer in spirit to the chivalry of hostile nations than to the commons of his own. But the plain people were out of all this, and were regarded with a contempt at least as great as that felt in our day for the Negro at the South. The whole institution of chivalry, with its attendant ideas, ideals and literature, was a thing of caste which recognized no common humanity in the lower orders of society, and whatever it did for the world in the way of developing the knightly ideal of valor, devotion and courtesy—an ideal later transformed into that of the gentleman and now coming to pervade all classes—was a product of caste spirit.

The feudal courts, large and small, the tournaments, festivals and military expeditions, including the crusades, were facilities of communication through which this caste, not only in single countries but throughout Europe, was enabled to have a common thought and sentiment.

Without doubt, however, the lower caste had also its unity and organization, its group traditions, customs and standards; mostly lost to us because they never achieved a literary record. This was an inarticulate caste; but it is probable that village communities were the spheres of a

* Cornish, Chivalry, 183.

vigorous coöperative life in which the best traits of human nature were fostered.

In India also the elaborate caste systems, although due in part to conquest, seem also to have come about by the hardening of occupation-classes. The priests, powerful because of their supposed intercourse with superhuman powers, taught their mystic traditions to their children and so built up a hereditary corporation, known, finally, as the Brahman caste. The military caste was apparently formed in a similar manner, while in industry "veneration for parental example and the need of an exact transmission of methods"* rendered all employments hereditary. In fact, says one writer, the caste system was in its origin "simply an instinctive effort for the organization of labor."† In the case of so intricate a caste society as that of India much may also be ascribed to the reaction of the theory upon the system. When the idea that caste is natural had become prevalent and sanctified, it tended to create caste where it would not otherwise have existed.

A settled state of society is favorable, and change hostile, to the growth of caste, because it is necessary that functions should be continuous through several generations before the principle of inheritance can become fixed. Whatever breaks up existing customs and traditions tends to abolish hereditary privilege and throw men into a rough struggle, out of which strong, coarse natures emerge as victors, to found, perhaps, a new aristocracy. Thus the conquest of southern Europe by northern

* Samuel Johnson, Oriental Religions, India, 241.   † *Ibid.*

tribes led to a period of somewhat confused readjustment, in which men of natural power bettered their status. The classes which emerged were as much the result of competition as derived by inheritance from those of tribal society. And so the openness of classes in our own day *may* be due as much to confusion as to a permanent decline in the caste principle.

That a low state of communication and of enlightenment are favorable to caste, while intelligence—especially political intelligence—and facility of intercourse antagonize it, becomes evident when we consider what, psychologically speaking, caste is. It is an organization of the social mind on a biological principle. That functions should follow the line of descent instead of adjusting themselves to individual capacity and preference, evidently means the subordination of reason to convenience, of freedom to order. The ideal principle is not biological but moral, based, that is, on the spiritual gifts of individuals without regard to descent. Caste, then, is something which, we may assume, will give way to this higher principle whenever the conditions are such as to permit the latter to work successfully; and this will be the case when the population is so mobilized by free training and institutions that just and orderly selection is practicable.

The diffusion of intelligence, rapid communication, the mobilization of wealth by means of money, and the like, mark the ascendency of the human mind over material and biological conditions. Popular government becomes possible, commercial and industrial functions—other things equal—come under more open competition, and

226

free personal development of all sorts is fostered. The general sentiment also, perceiving the superiority of free organization to caste, becomes definitely hostile to the latter and antagonizes it by public educational and other opportunities. The most effective agent in keeping classes comparatively open is an adequate system of free training for the young, tending to make all careers accessible to those who are naturally fit for them. In so far as there is such a system early education becomes a process of selection and discipline which permits ability to serve its possessor and the world in its proper place. In our own society—we may note in passing—this calls for a great development of public education, especially in the way of trade schools and the like, and also for an effective campaign against child-labor, bad housing and whatever else shuts off opportunity.

But before this mobility is achieved, caste is perhaps the only possible basis for an elaborate social structure; the main flow of thought is then necessarily in local channels. The people cannot grasp the life of which they are a part in any large way, or have a free and responsible share in it, but are somewhat mechanically held in place by habit and tradition. Those special relations to the system of government, religion or industry which are implied in classes, since they cannot be determined by rational selection, must be fixed in some traditional way, and the most available is the inheritance of functions.

We may expect, then, that complex, stationary societies of low mental organization will tend toward caste. That this is true, in a general way, is shown by the prevalence of caste in Oriental nations to-day, and in the later history of the great empires of antiquity. It goes without saying that each society has its peculiarities which only special study could elucidate.

CHAPTER XX

THE OUTLOOK REGARDING CASTE

THE QUESTION—HOW FAR THE INHERITANCE PRINCIPLE ACTUALLY
PREVAILS—INFLUENCES FAVORING ITS GROWTH—THOSE AN-
TAGONIZING IT—THE PRINCIPLES OF INHERITANCE AND EQUAL
OPPORTUNITY AS AFFECTING SOCIAL EFFICIENCY—CONCLUSION.

A VERY pertinent question is that of the part which the
hereditary or caste principle is likely to play in the coming
life; whether it is probable that caste, other than that due
to race, will arise in modern society; or that the hereditary
principle will, to any degree, have increased ascendency.

The answer should probably be that the principle is always powerful, and may gain somewhat as conditions become more settled, but certainly can never produce true
caste in the modern world.

As regards the power, in general, of the inheritance
tendency, I have perhaps said enough already. The inheritance of property, notwithstanding the perennial
agitation of communism, is probably as secure as any
institution can be—because there is apparently nothing
practicable to take its place as a means to economic stability. And with inheritance of property goes, in all
prosperous countries, a class of people who come without
effort into wealth and all its advantages: their number
and riches are certainly on the rapid increase. The less
formal inheritance of culture, opportunity and position is
equally real.

229

As to occupation, even now a census would perhaps show that the majority of young men follow that of their father, or one cognate to it. Most farmers' sons probably remain farmers (in spite of the well-known drift to the towns), most mechanics' sons become mechanics, and a large proportion of the children of professional men enter the professions. The child of a well-to-do parent is given, as a matter of course, the education, often long and expensive, which is required for entrance upon a profession, and is coming to be necessary also for commerce. Not only this, but he is made to feel from childhood that success in achieving a professional or business position is expected of him; he *must* get it or lose the respect of his family and friends. In the majority of cases—though the minority on the other side is no small one—these opportunities and incitements, together with the power to wait and choose which judicious paternal support gives him, are effective in drawing out his energies and directing them continuously upon the desired point. Certainly they will not make a good lawyer or a captain of industry out of a fool, nor will the lack of them keep decisive natural ability from exercising these functions; but with the common run of men, having fair capacity not very definitely inclined in a special direction, they are potent. Paternal suggestion and backing must be used with great discretion and often fail entirely, but no man of the world, so far as I know, regards them as unimportant.

If we ask whether the influence of inheritance is likely to increase or diminish, we find, on studying the situation

230

as a whole, a conflict of tendencies the precise outcome of which can only be guessed at.

As favoring the growth of the principle and the crystallization of classes, we have chiefly two considerations: the probability of more settled conditions, and the influence of that sharper differentiation of functions which modern life involves.

Social change, as already pointed out, is a main force in breaking up the inheritance of function, and to this must largely be attributed the comparative weakness of the principle in the United States. The changes incident to the settlement of a new country, coinciding with those incident to an economic revolution, have set everything afloat and brought in a somewhat confused and disorderly sort of competition. Our cities, especially, are aggregates of immigrants, most of whom have broken away from early associations, and a large part of whom are performing functions unheard of by their fathers. It is hardly possible that trades should become hereditary when most of them endure less than one man's lifetime. And something of the same uncertainty runs through commerce and the professions.

Without predicting any great decline in the pace of invention, we may yet expect that the next fifty years will see a great deal of the consolidation that comes with maturity. The population will be comparatively established, in place at least, and the forces making for inheritance will have a chance to work. An immense body of transmitted wealth will exist, and democratic influences will have all they can do to keep it from generating an aristocratic spirit. Industries, professions and trades can hardly

231

fail to be more stable than they have been, and the rural population, as always, will be a stronghold of the forces that favor inheritance.

The sentiment of regard for ancestry, of which caste is the extreme expression, is likely to increase in this and in all new countries. As communities grow older the family line comes more and more under public observation. It is *seen*, and displayed in memory, wherever any sort of continuity is preserved, and, being seen, it is judged, and the individual shares the credit or discredit of his kin. While this influence is now weak in the United States, on the whole, and is almost absent in the recent and confused life of our cities, it is gaining rapidly wherever—as is generally the case in the East and Southeast outside of large towns—the conditions are settled enough to make the family as a whole a matter of observation. And there can be little doubt that it is increasing in the West wherever it has a similar chance.

In some ways this greater recognition of descent is wholesome. A sense of being part of a kindred, of bearing the honor of a continuing group as well as of a perishing individual, tends to make one a better man; and from this point of view our somewhat disintegrated society might well have more of it.

As to the sharper differentiation that goes with modern life, we see it on all hands. The city is more clearly marked off from the country, in its functions, and is itself broken up into quarters the inhabitants of which have often little or no intercourse with those of other quarters. Trades and professions subdivide into specialties, and, a more elaborate training being demanded, it is more necessary

232

than formerly that a man should know from the start what he wants to do and assiduously prepare himself to do it. Not forgetting that there is another side to this, a side of unification implied in these differences, one may yet say that in themselves they tend to separate people more sharply into social groups which might conceivably become hereditary.

The forces antagonizing inheritance of function come chiefly under two heads, the opposition of ambitious young men and the general current of democratic sentiment.

Caste means restriction of opportunity, and consequently lies across the path of the most energetic part of the people. Its rule can prevail only where individual self-assertion is restrained by ignorance and formal institutions. Under our flexible modern conditions, it is safe to say, no system can endure that does not make a point of propitiating the formidable ambition of youth by at least an apparent freedom of opportunity. Even the inheritance of property is constantly questioned in the minds of the young, and nothing but the lack of a plausible alternative prevents its being more seriously assailed. And since this stronghold of inequality can hardly be shaken, there is all the more demand that it be offset by opening every other kind of advantage, especially in the way of education and training, to whomsoever may be fit to profit by it.

Somewhat vaguer but perhaps even more effective than the resistance of young men is the opposition of the general current of sentiment to any growth of inheritance at

233

the expense of opportunity. To abolish extrinsic inequalities and give each a chance to serve all in his own fit way, is undoubtedly the democratic ideal. In politics this is expressed by doing away with hereditary privilege and basing everything on popular suffrage; in education it is seeking an expression quite as vital by striving to open to every one the training to any function for which he may show fitness. But the spirit of unity and brotherhood is far from satisfied with what has been achieved in these directions, and aspires to bring home to every child that fair access to the fruits of progress which, in spite of theoretical liberty, is now widely lacking. It calls for *social* democracy, the real presence of freedom and justice in every fibre of the social fabric. To this spirit any increase of the privileges, already unavoidably great, which come by inheritance, is evidently hateful.

In America at least this sentiment is not that of a struggling lower class but of, practically, the whole community. With reference to so vital a part of our traditional ideal there are no classes; all the people feel substantially alike; and there is no public purpose for which wealth is so freely spent as in the support of institutions whose purpose is to keep open the path of opportunity from any condition of life to any other.

There is also, back of this sentiment, a belief that equal opportunity makes for the general good, since that system of society will be most efficient, other things equal, in which each individual is required to prove that he has more fitness than others for his special function. Every one can see, at times, the deteriorating effect of family influence—as upon business establishments when a less competent son succeeds his father, or upon military service, as in the British army at the outbreak of the Boer war.

On the other hand, the results of a confused competition may be worse than those of order, even if the latter rests upon an artificial principle.

Thus it is said with some truth—and this is perhaps the most considerable argument for caste in modern life— that a class having hereditary wealth and position, like the English aristocracy, makes a permanent channel for high traditions of culture and public service, and that it is well to preserve such traditions even at the cost of a somewhat exclusive order to contain and cherish them. De Tocqueville, himself imbued with the best traditions of the old French aristocracy, held this view, and ascribed the lack of intellectual distinction in the America of his day largely to the fact that there was no class "in which the taste for intellectual pleasures is transmitted with hereditary fortune and leisure, and by which the labors of the intellect are held in honor."*

The answer, of course, is that there are other means than caste for securing the continuity of special traditions, and, more particularly, that voluntary associations are capable of supplanting inherited wealth as channels of culture. In the various branches of science, for example, we have vigorous and continuing groups, with plenty of *esprit de corps*, by which the labors of the intellect are held in honor. If libraries, associations and educational institutions can do this for one phase of culture, why not for others?

* Democracy in America, vol. i, chap. 3.

It would be unfair, however, not to acknowledge that great services are constantly rendered to society by persons whom inherited wealth enables to devote themselves earlier and more independently to high aims than would otherwise be possible. There is certainly something favorable to originality in an inherited competence, without which one is more apt to be coerced into seeking a kind of success already in vogue, and so having a market value. And the movement to foster originality by endowments depending upon merit rather than birth will be most difficult to make effectual, since such endowments almost inevitably fall into the control of an institutional sort of men who cannot be expected to subsidize heresy. Funds for this purpose will probably aid only those sorts of originality already recognized, and in a manner established; not the radical innovations from which important movements usually start. It is hard to see how they can do much outside of experimental science, in which there is a sort of conventional test of originality.

On the whole, whatever is good in the principle of descent may be appropriated by a democratic society without going back to formal rank or exclusive opportunity. Freedom offers no bar to continuity of function in the family, so long as efficiency is maintained, but merely requires this, like everything else, to meet the test of service. There is no adequate reason why a hereditary group, transmitting special culture and fitness, should not continue their functions under a democratic system—as is actually the case to a certain extent with the political families of England. They will do their work all the better for not being too sure of their position. I see nothing but good in the fact that a military career has become traditional in a number of American families who have rendered distinguished service of this sort. The more special family ambitions we have, of a noble kind, the better for the country.

No sober observer will imagine that the opposing forces are to abolish the power of inheritance; they merely set reasonable limits to its scope. When the way of ambition is opened to the most energetic individuals, the sharpest teeth of discontent are drawn, and the mass of men very willingly avoid trouble to themselves and to society by keeping on in the paternal road. The family is after all too natural and too convenient a channel of social continuity not to play a great part in every phase of organization, and there seems little reason to depart from the opinion of Comte that it must ordinarily be the main influence in determining occupation.

I am inclined to expect that, owing to somewhat more settled conditions of life, inheritance of function will be rather more common, and the tendency to see the individual as one of a stock rather greater, in the future than in the immediate past. On the other hand it is nearly certain that educational opportunities will become more open and varied, making it easier than now for special aptitude to find its place. These things are not inconsistent, and both will make for order and contentment.

Also much more endeavor will be directed to the welfare of the less privileged classes as classes—that is, of those who are content to remain in the ancestral status instead of trying to get into one more favored. Heretofore we have given too much thought, relatively, to the one man who aims at distinction, and too little to the ninety and nine who do not.

CHAPTER XXI

OPEN CLASSES

THE NATURE OF OPEN CLASSES—WHETHER CLASS-CONSCIOUSNESS IS DESIRABLE—FELLOWSHIP AND COÖPERATION DEFICIENT IN OUR SOCIETY—CLASS ORGANIZATION IN RELATION TO FREEDOM.

WITH the growth of freedom classes come to be more open, that is, more based on individual traits and less upon descent. Competition comes actively into play and more or less efficiently fulfils its function* of assigning to each one an appropriate place in the whole. The theory of a free order is that every one is born to serve mankind in a certain way, that he finds out through a wise system of education and experiment what that way is, and is trained to enter upon it. In following it he does the best possible both for the service of society and his own happiness. So far as classes exist they are merely groups for the furtherance of efficiency through coöperation, and their membership is determined entirely by natural fitness.

This ideal condition is never attained on a large scale. In practice the men who find work exactly suited to them and at the same time acceptable to society are at the best somewhat exceptional—though habit reconciles most of us—and classes are never wholly open or wholly devoted to the general good.

The problem of finding where men belong, of adapting personal gifts to a complex system, is indeed one of ex-

* I make frequent use of this word to mean an activity which furthers some general interest of the social group. It differs from "purpose" in not necessarily implying intention.

239

treme difficulty, and is in no way solved by facile schemes
of any sort. There are, fundamentally, only two principles
available to meet it, that of inheritance or caste and that of
competition. While the former is a low principle, the
latter is also, in many of its phases, objectionable, involving waste of energy and apt to degenerate into anarchy.
There are always difficulties on either hand, and the actual
organization of life is ever a compromise between the aspiration toward freedom and the convenience of status.

We may assume, then, that in contemporary life we have
to do with a society in which the constitution of classes,
so far as we have them, is partly determined by inheritance
and partly by a more or less open competition, which is,
again, more or less effective in placing men where they
rightly belong.

If classes are open and men make their way from one
into another, it is plain that they cannot be separate mental wholes as may be the case with castes. The general
state of things becomes one of facile intercourse, and those
who change class will not forget the ideas and associations
of youth. Non-hereditary classes may have plenty of
solidarity and class spirit—consider, for instance, the
mediæval clergy—and their activity may also be of a
special and remote sort, like that of an astronomical
society, but after all there will be something democratic
about them; they will share the general spirit of the whole
in which they are rooted. They mean only specialization
in consciousness, where caste means separation.

The question whether there is or ought to be "class-
consciousness" in a democratic society is a matter of defi-

nitions. If we mean a division of feeling that goes deeper than the sense of national unity and separates the people into alien sections, then there is no such thing in the United States on any important scale (leaving aside the race question), and we may hope there never will be. But if we mean that along with an underlying unity of sentiment and ideals there are currents of thought and feeling somewhat distinct and often antagonistic, the answer is that class-consciousness in this sense exists and is more likely to increase than to diminish. A country of newspapers, popular education and manhood suffrage has passed the stage in which sentiments or interests can flow in separate channels; but there is nothing to prevent the people forming self-assertive groups in reference to economic and social questions, as they do in politics.

Class-consciousness along these lines will probably increase with growing interest in the underlying controversies, but I do not anticipate that this increase will prove the dreadful thing which some imagine. A "class-war" would indeed be a calamity, but why expect it? I see no reason unless it be a guilty conscience or an unbelief in moral forces. A certain sort of agitators expect and desire a violent struggle, because they see privilege defiant and violence seems to them the shortest way to get at it; and on the other hand, there are many in the enjoyment of privilege who feel in their hearts that they deserve nothing better than to have it taken away from them: but these are naïve views that ignore the solidity of the present order, which ensures that any change must be gradual and make its way by reason. Orderly struggle is the time-honored method of adjusting controversies among a free people,

241

and why should we assume that it will degenerate into anarchy and violence at just this point? Will not feeling be rather better than worse when a vague sense of injustice has had a chance to try itself out in a definite and positive self-assertion?

It is to be remembered, moreover, that in a society where groups interlace as much as they do with us a conflict of class interests is, in great degree, not a conflict of persons but rather one of ideas in a common social medium—since many persons belong to more than one class. Only under conditions of caste would a class war of the sort predicted by some theorists be likely to come to pass. I am not sure that it would be more fantastic to expect a literal war between Democrats and Republicans than between the parties—hardly less united by common social and economic interests—of Labor and Capital.

It seems equally mistaken to say, on the one hand, that all class-consciousness is bad, or, on the other, that we ought above all things to gird ourselves for the class-struggle. The just view apparently is that we should have in this matter, as elsewhere, difference on a basis of unity. Class loyalty in the pursuit of right ends is good; but like all such sentiments it should be subordinate to a broad justice and kindness. If there is no class-consciousness men become isolated, degraded and ineffective; if there is too much, or the wrong kind, the group becomes separate and forgets the whole. Let there be "diversities of gifts but the same spirit."

The present state of things as regards fellowship and coöperation in special groups is, on the whole, one of de-

242

ficiency rather than excess. The confusion or "individualism" that we see in literature, art, religion and industry means a want of the right kind of class unity and spirit. There is a lack of mutual aid and support not only among hand-workers, where it is much needed, but also among scholars, artists, professional men, writers and men of affairs. The ordinary business or professional man hardly feels himself a member of any brotherhood larger than the family; with his wife and children about him he stands in the midst of a somewhat cold and jostling world, keeping his feet as best he can and seeking a mechanical security in bank-account and life insurance—being less fortunate in this regard, perhaps, than the trades-unionist, who has been forced by necessity to stand shoulder-to-shoulder with his fellows and give and take sacrifice for the common good. And much the same is true of scholars and artists: they are likely not to draw close enough together to keep one another warm and foster the class ideals which lead the individual on to a particular kind of efficiency: there is a lack of those snug nests of special tradition and association in which more settled civilizations are rich.

Organization, of certain kinds, is no doubt more extensive and elaborate than ever before, and organization, it may be said, involves the interdependence, the unity, of parts. But will this be a conscious and moral unity? In a high kind of organization it will; but rapid growth may give us a system that is mechanical rather than, in the higher sense, social. When organization quickly extends there is a tendency to lower its type, as a rubber band becomes thinner the more you stretch it; the rela-

243

tions grow less human, and so may degrade instead of elevating the individual's relation to his whole. In a measure this has taken place in our life. The vast structure of industry and commerce remains, for the most part, unhumanized, and whether it proves a real good or not depends upon our success or failure in making it vital, conscious, moral. There is union on a low plane and isolation on a higher. The progress of communication has supplied the mechanical basis for a spiritual organization far beyond anything in the past; but this remains unachieved. On the whole, in the words of Miss Jane Addams, with whom this is a cherished idea, "The situation demands the consciousness of participation and well-being which comes to the individual when he is able to see himself 'in connection and coöperation with the whole'; it needs the solace of collective art inherent in collective labor."*

It is indeed probable that the growth of class fellowship will help to foster that spirit of art in work which we so notably lack, and the repose and content which this brings. There is truth in the view that a confused and standardless competition destroys art, which requires not only a group ideal but a certain deliberation, a chance to brood over things and work perfection into them. When the workman is more sure of his position, when he feels his fellows at his shoulder and knows that the quality of his work will be appreciated, he will have more courage and patience to be an artist. We all draw our impulse toward perfection not from vulgar opinion or from our pay, but from the approval of fellow craftsmen. The truth, little

* Democracy and Social Ethics, 219.

seen in our day, is that all work should be done in the spirit of art, and that no society is humanly organized in which this is not chiefly the case.

It is also true that closer fellowship—dominated by good ideals—should bring the sympathetic and moral motives to diligence and efficiency into more general action, and relegate the 'work or starve' motive more to the background. Some of us love our work and are eager to do it well; others have to be driven. Is this because the former are naturally a superior sort of people, because the work itself is essentially more inviting, or because the social conditions are such that sympathy and fellowship are more enlisted with it? Allowing something for the first two, I suspect the third is the principal reason. What work is there that would not be pleasant in moderate quantities, in good fellowship, and in the feeling of service? No great proportion, I imagine, of our task. Washing dishes is not thought desirable, and yet men do it joyfully when they go camping together.

Class organization is not, as some people assert, necessarily hostile to freedom. All organization is, properly, a means through which freedom is sought. As conditions change, men are compelled to find new forms of union through which to express themselves, and the rise of industrial classes is of this nature.

In fact, the question of freedom, as applied to class conditions, has two somewhat distinct aspects. These are:

1. Freedom to rise from one class into another, freedom of individual opportunity, or *carrière ouverte aux talents*. This is chiefly for the man of exceptional capacity and am-

bition. It is important, but not more so than the other, namely:

2. Freedom of classes, or, what is the same thing, of those individuals who have not the wish or power to depart from the sphere of life in which circumstance has placed them. It means justice, opportunity, humane living, for the less privileged groups as groups; not opportunity to get out of them but to be something in them; a chance for the teamster to have comfort, culture and good surroundings for himself and his family without ceasing to be a teamster.

The first of these has been much better understood in America than the second. That it is wrong to keep a man down who might rise is quite familiar, but that those who cannot rise, or do not care to, have also just claims is almost a novel idea, though they are evidently that majority for whom our institutions are supposed to exist. Owing to a too exclusive preoccupation with ideals of enterprise and ambition, a certain neglect, and even reproach, have rested upon those who do quietly the plain work of life.

Ours, if you think of it, is rather too much success on the tontine plan, where one puts all he has into a pool in the hope of being one of a few survivors to get what the rest lose; it would be better to take to heart that idea of Emerson's that each may succeed in his own way, without putting others down. It is a great thing that every American boy may aspire to be president of the United States, or of the Standard Oil Company, but it is equally important that he should have a chance for full and wholesome life in the more probable condition of clerk or mill hand. While we must admire the heroes of Samuel Smiles, we may remember that they do and should constitute only a small minority of the human race.

And the main guaranty for freedom of this latter sort is some kind of class organization which shall resist the encroachment and neglect of which the weaker parties in society are in constant danger. Those who have wealth, position, knowledge, leisure, may perhaps dispense with formal organization (though in fact it is those who are strong already who most readily extend their strength in this way), but the multitudes who have nothing but their human nature to go upon must evidently stand together or go to the wall.

CHAPTER XXII

HOW FAR WEALTH IS THE BASIS OF OPEN CLASSES

IMPERSONAL CHARACTER OF OPEN CLASSES—VARIOUS CLASSIFI-
CATIONS—CLASSES, AS COMMONLY UNDERSTOOD, BASED ON
OBVIOUS DISTINCTIONS—WEALTH AS GENERALIZED POWER—
ECONOMIC BETTERMENT AS AN IDEAL OF THE ILL-PAID CLASSES
—CONCLUSION.

WHERE classes do not mean separate currents of thought, as in the case of caste, but are merely differentiations in a common mental whole, there are likely to be several kinds of classes overlapping one another, so that men who fall in the same class from one point of view are separated in another. The groups are like circles which, instead of standing apart, interlace with one another so that several of them may pass through the same individual. Classes become numerous and, so to speak, impersonal; that is, each one absorbs only a part of the life of the individual and does not sufficiently dominate him to mould him to a special type. This is one of the things that distinguish our American order from that, say, of Germany, where caste is still so dominant as to carry many other differences with it and create unmistakable types of men. As a newspaper writer puts it, "The one thing we may be sure of every day is that not a man whom we shall meet in it will belong to his type. The purse-proud aristocrat turns out to be a humble-minded young fellow anxiously envious of our knowledge of golf; the comic actor in private life is dull and shy, and reddens to the tips of his

248

ears when he speaks; the murderer taken out of the dock in a quiet hob-and-nob turns out to be a likable young chap who reminds you of your cousin Bob."

And this independence of particular classes should give one the more opportunity to achieve a truly personal individuality by combining a variety of class affiliations, each one suited to a particular phase of his character.

It is, then, easy to see why different classifiers discover different class divisions in our society, according to their points of view; namely, because there are in fact an indefinite number of possible collocations. This would not have been the case anywhere in the Middle Ages, nor is it nearly as much the case in England at the present time as in the United States.

We might, to take three of the most conspicuous lines of division, classify the people about us according to trade or profession, according to income, and according to culture. The first gives us lawyers, grocers, plumbers, bankers and the like, and also, more generally, the hand-laboring class, skilled and unskilled, the mercantile class, the professional class and the farming class. The division by income is, of course, related to this, though by no means identical. We might reckon paupers, the poor, the comfortable, the well-to-do and the rich. Culture and refinement have with us no very close or essential connection with occupation or wealth, and a classification based upon the former would show a very general rearrangement. There are many scholars and philosophers among us who, like Thoreau, follow humble trades and live upon the income of day labor.

249

And virtue, the most important distinction of all, is independent alike of wealth, calling and culture. The real upper class, that which is doing the most for the onward movement of human life, is not to be discerned by any visible sign. The more inward or spiritual a trait is, the less it is dependent upon what are ordinarily understood as class distinctions.

It is, however, upon the grosser and more obvious differences of wealth and rank, and not upon intellectual or moral traits, that classes, in the ordinary meaning of the word, are based. The reasons for this are, first, that something obvious and unquestionable is requisite as a symbol and unfailing mark of class, and, second, that the tangible distinctions alone are usual matters of controversy. Culture and character have more intrinsic importance, but are too uncertain to mark a class, and even if they were stamped upon the forehead they are not matter to quarrel over like wealth or titles; since those who have them not cannot hope to get them by depriving those who have.

Income, for instance, classifies people through creating different standards of living, those who fall into the same class in this respect being likely to adopt about the same external mode of life. It usually decides whether men live in one quarter of the city or another, what sort of houses or apartments they inhabit, how they dress, whether the wife "does all her own work" or employs household help (and, if the latter, how much and of what sort), whether they keep a carriage, whether they go into the country for the summer, whether they travel abroad, whether they send their sons to college, and so on. And such likeness leads to likeness of ideas, especially in that commonplace sort of people—the most numerous of course —who have not sufficient definiteness or energy of character to associate on any other basis. Note how difficult it is for two people, congenial in other respects, to converse freely when one has an income of $5,000, the other of $500. Few topics can be touched upon without accentuating the superficial but troublesome discrepancy. Amusements, household and the like are hardly possible; the weather may supply a remark or two, perhaps also politics, though here the economic point of view is likely to appear. Religion or philosophy, if the parties could soar so high, would be best of all. Of course, serious discussion should be all the more practicable and fruitful because of difference of viewpoint. What I mean, however, is light, offhand, sociable talk that does not stir any depths. As between their wives the situation would be harder still, and only an unusual tact and magnanimity would make it tolerable.

The result is that we ordinarily find it most comfortable to associate on a basis of income, combined with and modified by the influence of occupation, culture and special tastes. And yet to do this is perhaps a confession of failure, a confession that we do not know how to cast off the adventitious and meet as men. The most superficial differences, being the most apparent, impose themselves upon our commonly indolent and sensuous states of mind.

In proportion to their energy men will always seek power. It is, perhaps, the deepest of instincts, resting directly on the primary need for self-expression. But the kind of power sought will take many forms.

251

Wealth stands, in modern society, for nearly all the grosser and more tangible forms; for power over material goods, primarily, and secondarily over the more purchasable kinds of human activity—hand labor, professional services, newspaper commendation, political assiduity and so on. The class that has it is, in all such matters, the strong class, and naturally our coarser thought concludes that this is the kind of power most worth consideration. In all the obvious details of life, in that seeking for petty advantages and immunities in which most of our time is passed, at the store or the railway station, we are measured by money and are apt to measure others so. The ascendency of wealth is too natural to disappear. Children prize possessions before they can talk, and readily learn that money is possession generalized. Indeed, only the taste for finer possessions can or should drive out that for lower.

And yet all clear minds, or rather all minds in their clearer moments, may see that wealth is not the chief good that the commonplace and superficial estimate makes it. It is simply a low form of power, important in measure to the group and to the individual, but easily preoccupying the mind beyond its just claim. If society gets material prosperity too fast, its spiritual life suffers, as is somewhat the case in our day: and the individual is in peril of moral isolation and decay as soon as he seeks to get richer than his fellows.

The finest and, in the long run, the most influential minds, have for the most part not cared for riches, or not cared enough to go out of their way to seek them, preferring to live on bare necessities if they must rather than spend

252

their lives in an uncongenial scramble. And the distinctively spiritual leaders have always regarded them as inconsistent with their aims. "Provide neither gold, nor silver, nor brass in your purses, nor scrip for your journey, neither two coats, neither shoes, nor yet staves." Not that Christianity is opposed to industrial prosperity—the contrary is the case—but that Christian leadership required the explicit renunciation of prosperity's besetting sin. In our day the life of Thoreau, among others, illustrates how a man may have the finer products of wealth —the culture of all times—while preferring to remain individually poor. He held that for an unmarried student, wishing first of all to preserve the independence of his mind, occasional day labor, which one can do and have done with, is the best way of getting a living. "A man is rich in proportion to the number of things which he can afford to let alone." "It makes but little difference whether you are committed to a farm or the county jail."* The thoroughgoing way in which this doctrine is developed in his Walden and other books makes them a *vade mecum* for the impecunious idealist.

Professor William James asserts that the prevalent fear of poverty among the educated classes is the worst moral disease from which civilization suffers, paralyzing their ideal force. "Think of the strength which personal indifference to poverty would give us if we were devoted to unpopular causes. We need no longer hold our tongues or fear to vote the revolutionary or reformatory ticket. Our stocks might fall, our hopes of promotion vanish, our salaries stop, our club doors close in our faces; yet,

*Walden, 89, 91.

while we lived, we would imperturbably bear witness to the spirit, and our example would help to set free our generation."*

If these considerations do not keep us from greed, it is because most of us have only flashes of the higher ambition. We may believe that we could reconcile ourselves to poverty if we had to—even that it might be good for us—but we do our best to avoid it.

For the ill-paid classes, certainly, the desire for money does not mean "materialism" in any reproachful sense, but is chiefly the means by which they hope to realize, first, health and decency, and then a better chance at the higher life—books, leisure, education and refinement. They are necessarily materialized in a certain sense by the fact that their most strenuous thought must be fixed upon work and product in relation to material needs. It is in those who are already well-to-do that the preoccupation with money is most degrading—as not justified by primary wants. "Meat is sweetest when it is nearest the bone," and it is good to long and strive for money when you have an urgent human need for it; but to do this for accumulation, luxury, or a remote security is not wholesome. This cold-blooded storing up in banks and tin boxes is perilous to the soul, often becoming a kind of secret vice, a disease of narrow minds, feeble imaginations and contracted living.†

In modern life, then, and in a country without formal privilege, the question of classes is practically one of wealth, and of occupation considered in relation to wealth;

* The Varieties of Religious Experience, 368.

† I will not here discuss the question just how far it serves a useful purpose in the economic system.

the reason being not that this distinction really dominates life, but that it is the focus of the more definite and urgent class controversies. Other aims are pursued in peace; wealth, because it is material and appropriable, involves conflict. We may then accept the economic standpoint for this purpose without at all agreeing with those who regard it as more fundamental than others.*

* If the reader cares to know my opinion of that doctrine—sometimes called the economic interpretation of history—which teaches that economic conditions are in a peculiar sense the primary and determining factor in society, he will find it in the following passages:

"The organic view of history [which I hold] denies that any factor or factors are more ultimate than others. Indeed it denies that the so-called factors—such as the mind, the various institutions, the physical environment and so on—have any real existence apart from a total life in which all share in the same way that the members of the body share in the life of the animal organism. It looks upon mind and matter, soil, climate, flora, fauna, thought, language and institutions as aspects of a single rounded whole, one total growth. We may concentrate attention upon some one of these things, but this concentration should never go so far as to overlook the subordination of each to the whole, or to conceive one as precedent to others."

"I cannot see that the getting of food, or whatever else the economic activities may be defined to be, is any more the logical basis of existence than the ideal activities. It is true that there could be no ideas and institutions without a food supply; but no more could we get food if we did not have ideas and institutions. All work together, and each of the principal functions is essential to every other."

"History is not like a tangled skein which you may straighten out by getting hold of the right end and following it with sufficient persistence. It has no straightness, no merely lineal continuity, in its nature. It is a living thing, to be known by sharing its life, very much as you know a person. In the organic world—that is to say in real life—each function is a centre from which causes radiate and to which they converge; all is alike cause and effect; there is no logical primacy, no independent variable, no place where the thread begins. As in the fable of the belly and the members, each is dependent upon all the others. You must see the whole or you do not truly see anything." (Publications of the American Economic Association, Third Series, vol. v, 426 ff.)

CHAPTER XXIII

ON THE ASCENDENCY OF A CAPITALIST CLASS

THE CAPITALIST CLASS—ITS LACK OF CASTE SENTIMENT—IN
WHAT SENSE "THE FITTEST"—MORAL TRAITS—HOW FAR
BASED ON SERVICE—AUTOCRATIC AND DEMOCRATIC PRINCI-
PLES IN THE CONTROL OF INDUSTRY—REASONS FOR EXPECT-
ING AN INCREASE OF THE DEMOCRATIC PRINCIPLE—SOCIAL
POWER IN GENERAL—ORGANIZING CAPACITY—NATURE AND
SOURCES OF CAPITALIST POWER—POWER OVER THE PRESS AND
OVER PUBLIC SENTIMENT—UPPER-CLASS ATMOSPHERE.

SINCE in our age commerce and industry absorb most
of the practical energy of the people, the men that are fore-
most in these activities have a certain ascendency, similar
to that of warriors in a military age.

Although this sort of men is not sharply marked off,
it is well enough indicated by the term capitalist or capitalist-manager class; the large owner of capital being
usually more or less of a manager also, while the large
salaries and other gains of successful managers soon make
them capitalists.

It is not quite accurate to speak of the group in question
as the rich, because, at a given time, a large part of its
most vigorous membership is as yet without wealth—
though in a way to get it—and, on the other hand, many
of the actual possessors of wealth are personally idle or
ineffective. The essential thing is a social tendency or
system of ideas generated in the accumulation of wealth
and having for its nucleus the more active and successful
leaders of commerce and industry.

256

That these are a very small class in proportion to their power is apparent, but not, perhaps, in itself, so fatal a defect in the system that permits it as many imagine. In so far as concentration of control means that wealth is in the hands of those who understand how to use it for the common good, and do in fact so use it, much may be said in its favor. We are all eager to entrust our property to those who will make it profitable to us; and society, under any system that could be devised, must probably do the same. But we may well ask whether there is not some more adequate means than we now have of getting this trust faithfully executed.

For better or for worse, concentration is probably inevitable in any society that has a vast, mobile wealth subject to competition; and the actual inequality is perhaps not much greater than that of political power, which is supposed to be equally distributed by general suffrage. The truth is that equality of power or influence, in any sphere of life, is inconsistent with the free working of human forces, which is ever creating differences, some of which are useful to society and some harmful. A true freedom, a reasonable equality, aims to conserve the former and abolish or limit the latter.

The sentiment of the class is not aristocratic in the ordinary sense. Although its members endeavor to secure their possessions to their children, there is little of the spirit of hereditary caste, which, indeed, is uncongenial to commerce. Freedom of opportunity is the ideal in this as in other parts of American society, and educational or other opportunities designed to maintain or increase it are sincerely approved and supported. There is, in fact, an almost inevitable dualism which makes it natural that a man should strive to aggrandize himself, his family and his class even though he truly wishes for greater equality of privilege. He floats on two currents, and as a man and a brother may be glad of restraints upon his own class which are in the interest of justice.

The ideal of freedom prevalent in the managing class is, however, somewhat narrow and hardly hospitable to the group self-assertion of the less privileged classes. The labor movement has made its way by its energy and reasonableness in the face of a rather general mistrust and opposition—sometimes justified by its aberrations—on the part of the masters of industry. Yet even in this regard, as it comes to be seen that organization is an element of fair play, and as experience shows that union may become an instrument of stability, a broader sentiment makes headway.

Like everything else that has power in human life, the money-strong represent, in some sense, the survival of the fittest—not necessarily of the best. That is, their success, certainly no guaranty of righteousness, does prove a certain adaptation to conditions, those who get rich being in general the ablest, for this purpose, of the many who devote their energies to it with about the same opportunities. They are not necessarily the ablest in other regards, since only certain kinds of ability count in making money; other kinds, and those often the highest, such as devotion to intellectual or moral ideals, being even a hindrance. Men of genius will seldom shine in this way, because, as a rule, only a somewhat commonplace mind will give itself whole-heartedly to the commercial ideal.

There is much likeness in the persons and methods by which, in all ages, the cruder sort of power is acquired. When the military system is ascendent over the industrial it is acquired in one way, when property is secure from force in another, but this makes less difference than might be supposed. In either case it is not mere personal prowess, with the sword or with the tool, that gains large success, but power in organization. Aggressiveness, single-minded devotion to the end and, above all, organizing faculty—these were the methods of Clovis and Pepin and William of Normandy, as they are of our rulers of finance. And now, as formerly, much of the power that is alive in such men falls by inheritance into weaker hands.

As to righteousness, in the sense of good intention, they probably do not, on the whole, differ much from the average. Some may be found of the highest character, some of gross unscrupulousness. The majority are doubtless without moral distinction and take the color of their associates. The view sometimes set forth on behalf of men of wealth that riches go with virtue, and the view, more popular among non-possessors, that it comes by wickedness, are equally untrustworthy. The great mass of wealth is accumulated by solid qualities—energy, tenacity, shrewdness and the like—which may coexist with great moral refinement or with the opposite.

As a group, however, they are liable to moral deficiencies analogous to those of the conquerors and organizers of states just referred to. There is, especially, a certain

259

moral irresponsibility which is natural to those who have broken away from customary limitations and restraints and are coursing almost at will over an unfenced territory. I mean that business enterprise, like military enterprise, deals largely with relations as to which there are no settled rules of morality, no constraining law or public opinion. Such conditions breed in the ordinary actor a Macchiavellian opportunism. Since it is hard to say what *is* just and honest in the vast and abstract operations of finance, human nature is apt to cease looking for a standard and to seize booty wherever and however it safely can. Hence the truly piratical character of many of our great transactions. And in smaller matters also, as in escaping taxation, it is often fatally easy for the rich to steal.

It must be allowed that such ascendency as the capitalist class has rests, in part at least, upon service. That is to say, its members have had an important function to perform, and in performing that function have found themselves in a position to grasp wealth. The great work of the time has been, or has seemed to be, the extension and reconstruction of industry. In this work leadership and organization have been needed on a great scale, and our captains of industry have nobly met this demand. That their somewhat autocratic control of production was called for by the situation seems to be shown by the rather general failure of coöperative enterprises intended to dispense with it. Why is it that America abounds in opportunity, and that every sort of industrial capacity is eagerly sought out and rewarded? Of course natural advantages play a great part, but much must also be ascribed to the energy and imaginative daring of our entrepreneurs, many of whom have spent great faculty and tireless zeal upon business, in a spirit of adventure and achievement rather than of gain. Where the general is aggressive the soldier will be kept busy.

I have no sympathy with the general abuse of commercialism, but hold with Montesquieu that "The spirit of commerce is naturally attended with that of frugality, economy, moderation, labor, prudence, tranquillity, order and rule. So long as this spirit subsists the riches it produces have no ill effect. The mischief is when excessive wealth destroys the spirit of commerce; then it is that the inconveniences of inequality begin to be felt."*

The conception of keen adaptation of means to ends, of exact social workmanship, inculcated by "business" is of untold value to our civilization and capable of very general application. It is a very proper demand that government, education and philanthropy should, in this sense, be conducted on business principles.

At the same time it is plain that a large part of the accumulation of wealth—hard unfortunately to distinguish from other parts—is accomplished not by social service but, as just intimated, by something akin to piracy. This is not so much the peculiar wickedness of a predatory class as a tendency in all of us to abuse power when not under definite legal or moral control. The vast transactions associated with modern industry have come very little under such control, and offer a field for freebooting such as the world has never seen.

Nor need we affirm that even the gains of the great

* The Spirit of Laws, book v, chap. 6.

261

organizers are in the highest sense right, only that they are natural and do not necessarily involve conscious wrong-doing.

The question of the rather arbitrary control of industry by the capitalist-manager, which now prevails, and of the possibility of this control being diminished or modified in the future, calls for some analysis of underlying forces. Evidently there is a conflict of principles here—the democratic or popular and the autocratic. The latter, now ascendant, has the advantages of concentration, secrecy and promptness—the same which give it superiority in war. On the other hand, the democratic principle should have the same merit in industry and commerce that it has in politics; namely that of enlisting the pride and ambition of the individual and so getting him to put himself into his work. Other things being equal, a free system is a more vital and energetic organism than one in which the initiative and choice come from a central authority.

And it is apparent that the working of the autocratic system in our economic life shows just the strength and weakness that would naturally be expected. The prompt undertaking and execution of vast schemes at a favorable moment, and the equally prompt recession when conditions alter; the investment of great resources in enterprises which yield no immediate return; the decision and secrecy important in overcoming competitors; the unhesitating sacrifice of workmen and their families when the market calls for a shut-down of production—such traits as these are of the utmost importance to commercial success, and belong to arbitrary control rather than to anything of a more popular sort. On the other hand, it would be easy to show at any length desired that such control is accompanied by a wide-spread disaffection of spirit on the part of the working classes, which, expressed in unwilling labor, strikes and agitation, is a commercial disadvantage, and a social problem so urgent as to unsettle the whole economic system.

The autocratic system has evidently a special advantage in a time of rapid and confused development, when conditions are little understood or regulated, and the state of things is one of somewhat blind and ruthless warfare; but it is quite possible that as the new industries become established and comparatively stable, there will be a commercial as well as a social demand for a system that shall invite and utilize more of the good-will and self-activity of the workman. "The system which comes nearest to calling out all the self-interests and using all the faculties and sharing all the benefits will outcompete any system that strikes a lower level of motive faculty and profit."* And the penetrating thinker who wrote this sentence believed that the function of the autocratic "captain of industry" was essentially that of an explorer and conqueror of new domains destined to come later under the rule of a commonwealth. Indeed the rise, on purely commercial grounds, of a more humane and individualizing tendency, aiming in one way or another to propitiate the self-feeling of the workman and get him to identify himself with his work, is well ascertained. Among the familiar phases of this are the notable growth of coöperative

* Henry D. Lloyd, Man the Social Creator, 255.

263

production and exchange in Belgium, Russia and other European countries, the increasing respect for labor unions and the development by large concerns of devices for insurance, for pensions, for profit-sharing and for the material and social comfort of their employees. "As a better government has come up from the people than came down from the kings, so a better industry appears to be coming up from the people than came down from the capitalists."*

In some form or other the democratic principle is sure to make its way into the economic system. Coöperation, labor unions, public regulation, public ownership and the informal control of opinion will no doubt all have a part; the general outcome being that the citizen becomes a more vital agent in the life of the whole.

Before discussing further the power of the capitalist-manager class, we ought to think out clearly just what we mean by social power, since nowhere are we more likely to go astray than in vagueness regarding such notions.

Evidently the essence of it is control over the human spirit, and the most direct phases of power are immediately spiritual, such as one mind exercises over another by virtue of what it is, without any means but the ordinary symbols of communication. This is live, human power, and those who have it in great degree are the prime movers of society, whether they gain any more formal or conventional sort or not. Such, for instance, are the poets, prophets, philosophers, inventors and men of science of all ages, the great political, military and religious organ-

---

* *Idem*, 246. Lloyd was rather a prophet than a man of science, but there is a shrewd sense of fact back of his visions.

izers, and even the real captains of industry and commerce. All power involves in its origin mental or spiritual force of some sort; and so far as it attaches to passive attributes, like hereditary social position, offices, bank-accounts, and the like, it does so through the aid of conventions and habits which regard these things as repositories of spiritual force and allow them to exercise its function.

In its immediate spiritual phase power is at a maximum of vitality and a minimum of establishment. Only a few can recognize it. Its possessors, then, strive to establish and organize it, to give it social expression and efficacy, to gain position, reputation or wealth. Since power is not apparent to the common mind until it takes on these forms, they are, to superficial observation and in all the conventional business of life, the only valid evidence of it. And yet by the time these symbols appear, the spiritual basis has often passed away. Primary power goes for the most part unseen, much of it taking on no palpable form until late in life, much yielding only posthumous reputation, and much, and that perhaps the finest sort, having never any vulgar recognition whatever.

Regarding money-value we may say, in general, that it is one expression of the conventional or institutional phase of society, and exhibits all that mixture of grandeur and confusion with which nature usually presents herself to our understanding. I mean that its appraisal of men and things is partly expressive of great principles, and partly, so far as we can see, unjust, trivial or accidental. Some gains are vital or organic, springing from the very nature of life and justified as we come to understand that life; some are fanciful, springing from the tastes or whims of the rich, like the value of diamonds or first editions, and some parasitical, like those of the legally-protected swindler. In general the values of the market are those of the habitual world in all its grossness; spiritual values, except those that have become conventional, being little felt in it. These appeal to the future. The detailed working of market value has no ascertainable connection with moral worth, and we must not expect it to have. If a man's work is moral, in the higher sense, it is in its nature an attack upon the habitual world which the latter is more likely to resent than reward. One can only take up that useful work that seems best suited to him, trying to be content if its value is small, and, if large, to feel that the power over money it gives him is rightly his only in so far as he uses it for the general good.

The more tangible kind of social power—so far as it is intrinsic to the man and not adventitious like inherited wealth—depends chiefly upon organizing capacity, which may be described as the ability to build and operate human machinery. It has its roots in tact and skill in dealing with men, in tenacity, and in a certain instinct for construction. One who possesses it sees a new person as social material, and is likely to know what can be made of him better than he knows himself.*

* Such a one
> "Lässt jeden ganz das bleiben was er ist;
> Er wacht nur drüber das er's immer sei
> Am rechten Ort; so weiss er aller Menschen
> Vermögen zu dem seinigen zu machen."

"He lets every one remain just what he is, but takes care that he shall always be it in the right place: thus he knows how to make all men's power his own." Schiller, Wallenstein's Lager, I, 4.

Of all kinds of leadership this has the readiest recognition and the highest market value; and naturally so, since it is essential to every sort of coöperative achievement. Its possessors understand the immediate control of the world, which they will exercise no matter what the apparent forms of organization may be. In all ages they have gained and held the grosser forms of power, whenever these were at all open to competition. Thus, during the early Middle Age, men of energy and management, more or less favored by situation, built up for themselves local authority and estate, or perhaps exploited the opportunities for still wider organization, like the founders of Burgundy and Brittany and the early kings of France; very much in the same manner as men of our own day build up commercial and industrial systems and become senators and railway presidents.

Indeed, this type of ability was never in such demand as it now is, for the conduct of the vast and diverse social structures rising about us—industrial enterprises, political parties, labor unions, newspapers, universities and philanthropies.

It has its high money value partly because of its rarity and partly because there is a regular market for it; the need being so urgent and obvious as to create a steady and intelligent demand. In this latter respect it contrasts with services, like moral leadership, which people need but will seldom pay for. A third reason is that its possessors are almost always clever enough to know their own value and secure its recognition.

In discussing the power of the capitalist class there is no question of the finer and higher forms of power. We shall rarely find among the rich any pregnant spiritual leadership, theirs being a pedestrian kind of authority which has a great deal to do with the every-day comfort of their contemporaries but does not attempt to sway the profounder destinies of the race. Nor does the world often accord them enduring fame: lacking spiritual significance their names are writ in water. Even in industry the creative thought, the inventions which are the germs of a new era, seldom come from money-winners, since they require a different kind of insight.

The capitalist represents power over those social values that are tangible and obvious enough to have a definite standing in the market. His money and prestige will command food, houses, clothes, tools and all conventional and standard sorts of personal service, from lawn-mowing to the administration of a railroad, not genius or love or anything of that nature. That wealth means social power of this coarser sort is apparent in a general way, and yet merits a somewhat closer examination.

We have, first, its immediate power over goods and services: the master of riches goes attended by an invisible army of potential servitors, ready to do for him anything that the law allows, and often more. He is in this way, as in so many others, the successor of the nobleman of mediæval and early modern history, who went about with a band of visible retainers eager to work his will upon all opposers. He is the ruler of a social system wherever he may be.

The political power of wealth is due only in part to direct corruption, vast as that is, but is even more an indirect and perfectly legal pressure in the shape of inducements which its adroit use can always bring to bear—trade to the business man, practice to the lawyer and employment to the handworker: every one when he thinks of his income wishes to conciliate the rich. Influence of this sort makes almost every rich man a political power, even without his especially wishing to be. But when wealth is united to a shrewd and unscrupulous political ambition, when it sets out to control legislation or the administration of the laws, it becomes truly perilous. We cannot fail to see that a large part of our high offices are held by men who have no marked qualification but wealth, and would be insignificant without it; also that our legislation —municipal, state and national—and most of our administrative machinery, feel constantly the grasp of pecuniary power. Probably it is not too much to say that except when public opinion is unusually aroused wealth can generally have its way in our politics if it makes an effort to do so.

As to the influence of the rich over the professional classes—lawyers, doctors, clergymen, teachers, civil and mechanical engineers and the like—we may say in general that it is potent but somewhat indirect, implying not conscious subservience but a moral ascendency through habit and suggestion. The abler men of this sort are generally educated and self-respecting, have a good deal of professional spirit and are not wholly dependent upon any one employer. At the same time, they get their living largely through the rich, from whom the most lucrative employment comes, and who have many indirect ways of making and marring careers. The ablest men in the legal profession are in close relations with the rich and commonly become capitalists themselves; physicians are more independent, because their art is not directly concerned with property, yet look to wealthy patients for their most profitable practice; clergymen are under pressure to satisfy wealthy parishioners, and teachers must win the good will of the opulent citizens who control educational boards.

Now there is nothing in social psychology surer than that if there is a man by whose good will we desire to profit, we are likely to adapt our way of thinking to his. Impelled to imagine frequently his state of mind, and to desire that it should be favorable to our aims, we are unconsciously swayed by his thought, the more so if he treats us with a courtesy which does not alarm our self-respect. It is in this way that wealth imposes upon intellect. Who can deny it?

Newspapers are generally owned by men of wealth, which has no doubt an important influence upon the sentiments expressed in them; but a weightier consideration is the fact that they depend for profit chiefly upon advertisements, the most lucrative of which come from rich merchants who naturally resent doctrines that threaten their interest. Of course the papers must reach the people, in order to have a value for advertising or any other purpose, and this requires adaptation to public opinion; but the public of what are known as the better class of papers are chiefly the comparatively well-to-do. And even that portion of the press which aims to please the hand-working class is usually more willing to carry on a loud but vague agitation, not intended to accomplish anything but increase circulation, than to push real and definite reform.

All phases of opinion, including the most earnest and honest inquiry into social questions, finds some voice in print, but—leaving aside times when public opinion is greatly aroused—those phases that are backed by wealthy interests have a great advantage in the urgency, persistence and cleverness with which they are presented. At least, this has been the case in the past. It is a general feeling of thoughtful men among the hand-working class that it is hard to get a really fair statement of their view of industrial questions from that portion of the newspaper and magazine press that is read by well-to-do people. The reason seems to be mainly that the writers live unconsciously in an atmosphere of upper-class ideas from which they do not free themselves by thorough inquiry. Besides this, there is a sense of what their readers expect, and also, perhaps, a vague feeling that the sentiments of the hand-working class may threaten public order.

Since the public has supplanted the patron, a man of letters has least of all to hope or fear from the rich—if he accepts the opinion of Mr. Howells that the latter can do nothing toward making or marring a new book.

The power of wealth over public sentiment is exercised partly through sway over the educated classes and the press, but also by the more direct channel of prestige. Minds of no great insight, that is to say the majority, mould their ideals from the spectacle of visible and tangible success. In a commercial epoch this pertains to the rich; who consequently add to the other sources of their influence power over the imagination. Millions accept the money-making ideal who are unsuited to attain it, and run themselves out of breath and courage in a race they should never have entered; it is as if the thin-legged and flat-chested people of the land should seek glory in football. The money-game is mere foolishness and mortification for most of us, and there is a madness of the crowd in the way we enter into it. Even those who most abuse the rich commonly show mental subservience in that they assume that the rich have, in fact, gotten what is best worth having.

As hinted above, there is such a thing as an upper-class atmosphere, in the sense of a state of mind regarding social questions, initiated by the more successful money-winners and consciously or unconsciously imposed upon business and professional people at large. Most of us exist in this atmosphere and are so pervaded by it that it is not easy for us to understand or fairly judge the sentiment of the hand-working classes. The spokesmen of radical doctrines are, in this regard, doing good service to the public mind by setting in motion counterbalancing, if not more trustworthy, currents of opinion.

If any one of business or professional antecedents doubts that he breathes a class atmosphere, let him live for a time at a social settlement in the industrial part of one of our cities—not a real escape but as near it as most of us have the resolution to achieve—reading working-class literature (he will be surprised to find how well worth reading it is), talking with hand-working people, attending meetings, and in general opening his mind as wide as possible to the influences about him. He will presently become aware of being in a new medium of thought and feeling; which may or may not be congenial but cannot fail to be instructive.

272

CHAPTER XXIV

ON THE ASCENDENCY OF A CAPITALIST CLASS— ### Continued

The Influence of Ambitious Young Men—Security of the Dominant Class in an Open System—Is there Danger of Anarchy and Spoliation?—Whether the Sway of Riches is Greater now than Formerly—Whether Greater in America than in England.

In any society where there is some freedom of opportunity ambitious young men are an element of extreme importance. Their numbers are formidable and their intelligence and aggressiveness much more so: in short, they want an opening and are bound to get it.

As the members of this class are mainly impecunious, it might be supposed that they would be a notable offset to the power of wealth; and in a sense they are. It is their interest to keep open the opportunity to rise, and they are accordingly inimical to caste and everything which tends toward it. But it by no means follows that they are opposed to the ascendency of an upper class based on wealth and position. This becomes evident when one remembers that their aim is *not to raise the lower class, but to get out of it.* The rising young man does not identify himself with the lowly stratum of society in which he is born, but, dissatisfied with his antecedents, he strikes out for wealth, power or fame. In doing so he fixes his eyes on those who have these things, and from whose example

273

he may learn how to gain them; thus tending to accept the ideals and standards of the actual upper class. He gives a great deal of attention to the points of view of A, a railroad president, B, a senator, and even of C, head of a labor organization, but to a mere farmer or laborer, whose hand is on no levers, he is indifferent.

The students of our universities are subject to a conflict between the healthy idealism of youth, which prevails with the more generous, and the influences just indicated, which become stronger as education draws closer to practical affairs. On the whole, possessed of one great privilege and eager to gain others, they are not so close in spirit to the unprivileged classes as might be imagined.

Thus the force of ambitious youth goes largely to support the ascendency of the money-getting class; directly, in that it accepts the ideals of this class and looks forward to sharing its power; indirectly, in that it is withdrawn from the resources of the humbler class. How long will the rising lawyer retain his college enthusiasm for social reform if the powers that be welcome him and pay him salaries?

We have then the fact, rather paradoxical at first sight, that the dominant class in a competitive society, although unstable as to its individual membership, may well be more secure as a whole than the corresponding class under any other system—precisely because it continually draws into itself most of the natural ability from the other classes. Throughout English history, we are told, the salvation of the aristocracy has been its comparative openness, the fact that ability could percolate into it, instead of rising up behind it like water behind a dam, as was the case in pre-revolutionary France. And the same principle is working even more effectually in our own economic order. A great weakness of the trades-union movement, as of all attempts at self-assertion on the part of the less privileged classes, is that it is constantly losing able leaders. As soon as a man shows that marked capacity which would fit him to do something for his fellows, it is ten to one that he accepts a remunerative position, and so passes into the upper class. It is increasingly the practice —perhaps in some degree the deliberate policy—of organized wealth to win over in this way the more promising leaders from the side of labor; and this is one respect in which a greater class-consciousness and loyalty on the part of the latter would add to its strength.

Thus it is possible to have freedom to rise and yet have at the same time a miserable and perhaps degraded lower class—degraded because the social system is administered with little regard to its just needs. This is more the case with our own industrial system, and with modern society in general, than our self-satisfaction commonly perceives. Our one-sided ideal of freedom, excellent so far as it goes, has somewhat blinded us to the encroachments of slavery on an unguarded flank. I mean such things as bad housing, insecurity, excessive and deadening work, child labor and the lack of any education suited to the industrial masses—the last likely to be remedied now that it is seen to threaten industrial prosperity.

It is hard to say how much of the timidity noticeable in the discussion of questions of this sort by the comfortable classes is due to a vague dread of anarchy and spoliation by an organized and self-conscious lower class; but probably a good deal. If power, under democracy, goes with numbers, and the many are poor, it would seem at first glance that they would despoil the few.

To conservative thinkers a hundred, or even fifty, years ago this seemed almost an axiom, but a less superficial philosophy has combined with experience to show that anarchy, in Mr. Bryce's words, "is of all dangers or bugbears the one which the modern world has least cause to fear."*

The most apparent reason for this is the one already discussed, namely, that power does not go with mere numbers, under a democracy more than under any other form of government; a democratic aristocracy, that is, one whose members maintain their position in an open struggle, being without doubt the strongest that can exist. We shall never have a revolution until we have caste; which, as I have tried to show, is but a remote possibility. And as an ally of established power we have to reckon with the inertia of social structure, something so massive and profound that the loudest agitation is no more than a breeze ruffling the surface of deep waters. Dominated by the habits which it has generated, we all of us, even the agitators, uphold the existing order without knowing it. There may, of course, be sudden changes due to the fall of what has long been rotten, but I see little cause to suppose that the timbers of our system are in this condition: they are rough and unlovely, but far from weak.

Another conservative condition is that economic solid-

* The American Commonwealth, Chapter 94.

276

arity which makes the welfare of all classes hang together, so that any general disturbance causes suffering to all, and more to the weak than to the strong. A sudden change, however reasonable its direction, must in this way discredit its authors and bring about reaction. The hand-working classes may get much less of the economic product than they ought to; but they are not so badly off that they cannot be worse, and, unless they lose their heads, will always unite with other classes to preserve that state of order which is the guaranty of what they have. Anarchy would benefit no one, unless criminals, and anything re-sembling a general strike I take to be a childish expedient not likely to be countenanced by the more sober and hard-headed leaders of the labor movement. All solid better-ment of the workers must be based on and get its nourish-ment from the existing system of production, which must only gradually be changed, however defective it may be. The success of strikes, and of all similar tactics, depends, in the nature of things, on their being partial, and drawing support from the undisturbed remainder of the process. It is the same principle of mingling stability with improvement which governs progress everywhere.

And, finally, effective organization on the part of the less privileged classes goes along with intelligence, with training in orderly methods of self-assertion, and with edu-cation in the necessity of patience and compromise. The more real power they get, the more conservatively, as a rule, they use it. Where free speech exists there will al-ways be a noisy party advocating precipitate change (and a timid party who are afraid of them), but the more the

277

people are trained in real democracy the less will be the influence of this element.

Whatever divisions there may be in our society, it is quite enough an organic whole to unite in casting out tendencies that are clearly anarchic. And it is also evident that such tendencies are to be looked for at least as much among the rich as among the poor. If we have at one extreme anarchists who would like to despoil other people, we have, at the other, monopolists and financiers who actually do so.

It is a common opinion that the sway of riches over the human mind is greater in our time than previously, and greater in America than elsewhere. How far is this really the case?

To understand this matter we must not forget that the ardor of the chase—as in a fox hunt—may have little to do with the value of the quarry. The former, certainly, was never so great in the pursuit of wealth as here and now; chiefly because the commercial trend of the times, due to a variety of causes, supplies unequalled opportunities and incitements to engage in the money-game. In this, therefore, the competitive zeal of an energetic people finds its main expression. But to say that wealth stands for more in the inner thought of men, that to have or not to have it makes a greater intrinsic difference, is another and a questionable proposition, which I am inclined to think opposite to the truth. Such spiritual value as personal wealth has comes from its power over the means of spiritual development. It is, therefore, diminished by everything which tends to make those means common

278

property: and the new order has this tendency. When money was the only way to education, to choice of occupation, to books, leisure and variety of intercourse, it was essential to the intellectual life; there was no belonging to the cultured class without it. But with free schools and libraries, the diffusion of magazines and newspapers, cheap travel, less stupefying labor and shorter hours, culture opportunity is more and more extended, and the best goods of life are opened, if not to all, yet to an ever-growing proportion. Men of the humblest occupations can and do become gentlemen and scholars. Indeed, people are coming more and more to think that exclusive advantages are uncongenial to real culture, since the deepest insight into humanity can belong only to those who share and reflect upon the common life.

The effect is that wealth is shorn of much of that prestige of knowledge, breeding and opportunity which always meant more than its material power. The intellectual and spiritual centre of gravity, like the political, sinks down into the masses of the people. Though our rich are rich beyond the dreams of avarice, they mean less to the inner life of the time, exercise less spiritual authority, perhaps, than the corresponding class in any older society. They are the objects of popular curiosity, resentment, admiration or envy, rather than the moral deference given to a real aristocracy. They are not taken too seriously. Indeed, there could be no better proof that the rich are no overwhelming power with us than the amount of good-natured ridicule expended upon them. Were they really a dominant order, the ridicule, if ventured at all, would not be good-natured. Their ascendency is great

when compared with a theory of equality—and in this
sense the remarks in the last chapter should be understood
—but small compared with that of the ruling classes of
the Old World.

Over a class of frenzied gold-seekers, rich or poor,
chiefly in the towns, the money-idea is no doubt ascendant;
but if you approach the ordinary farmer, mechanic or
sober tradesman you are likely to find that he sets no high
rate on wealth beyond what is necessary for the frugal
support of a family, and that he neither admires nor
envies the rich, but looks at the millionaire and thinks:
"After all, it isn't life. What does he get out of it more
than the rest of us?" The typical American is an idealist, and the people he looks up to are those who stand in
some way for the ideal life—or whom he supposes to do
so—most commonly statesmen, but often writers, scientists
or teachers. Education and culture, as Mr. Bryce and
others have noticed, is cherished by plain people all over
the land, often to a degree that puts to shame its professed
representatives.

We find, then, that agitators who strive to incite the
people against the rich encounter with disgust an idealism which refuses to believe that their advantages are ex-
travagantly great; and one of the main grievances of such
men is what they look upon as the folly or lack of spirit of
the poor in this regard.

Never before, probably, was there so large a class of
people who, having riches, feel that they are a doubtful blessing, especially in relation to the nurture of children. Many
a successful man is at his wits' end to give his children those
advantages of enforced industry, frugality and self-con-

trol which he himself enjoyed. One of the richest men of the day holds that accumulations are generally bad for the children, as well as for society, and favors almost unlimited graduated taxation of inheritances.* According to the philosophy which he supports by practice as well as theory, the man who finds himself rich is to live modestly and use his surplus as a trust fund for the benefit of the public.

What would a man wish for his own son, if he could choose? First, no doubt, some high and engrossing purpose, which should fill his life with the sense of worthy striving and aspiration. After this he would wish for health, friends, peace of mind, the enjoyment of books, a happy family life and material comfort. But the last, beyond that degree which even unskilled labor should bring, he would regard as of secondary importance. Not a straitened house and table but a straitened soul is the real evil, and the two are more separable now than formerly. The more a real democracy prevails, the less is the spiritual ascendency of riches.

There is, for instance, no such settled and institutional deference to wealth in the United States as there seems to be in England; the reason being, in part, that where there are inherited classes there are also class standards of living, costly in the upper class, to which those who would live in good company are under pressure to conform. In England there is actually a ruling order, however ill defined, which is generally looked up to and membership in which is apparently the ambition of a large majority

* Andrew Carnegie.

of all aspiring men who do not belong to it by birth. Its habits and standards are such that only the comparatively rich can be at home in it. There is nothing corresponding to this with us. We have richer men and the pursuit of riches is an even livelier game, but there is no such ascendency in wealth, no such feeling that one must be rich to be respectable. With us, if people have money they enjoy it; if not, they manage with what they have, neither regarding themselves nor regarded by others as essentially inferior.

It is also a general feeling here that wealth should not be a controlling factor in marriage, and it is not common for American parents to object seriously to a proposed son-in-law (much less a daughter-in-law) on the mere ground of lack of means, apart from his capacity to earn a living. The matter-of-fact mercenariness in this regard which, as we are led to believe by the novelists, prevails in the upper circles of England, is as yet somewhat shocking to the American mind.

Hereditary titles, sometimes imagined to be a counterpoise to the ascendency of wealth, are really, in our time at least, a support and sanction to it, giving it an official standing and permanence it cannot have in democracy. We understand that in England wealth—with tact, patience and maybe political services—will procure a title, which, unlike anything one can get for money in America, is indestructible by vice and folly, and can be used over and over to buy wealth in marriage. "Nothing works better in America than the promptness with which the degenerate scions of honored parents drop out of sight."* Rank is not an offset but a reward and bribe to

* T. W. Higginson, Book and Heart, 145.

wealth; perhaps the only merit that can be claimed for it in this connection being that the desire and deference for it imposes a certain discipline on the arrogance of newly acquired riches.

The English idea that those in high offices should have a magnificent style of living, "becoming to their station," is also one that goes with caste feeling. It makes it hardly decent for the poor to hold such offices, and is almost absent here, where, if riches are important to political success, the condition is one of which the people do not approve and would gladly dispense with.

I doubt whether the whole conception which imputes merit to wealth and seeks at least the appearance of the latter in modes of dress, attendance and the like, is not stronger everywhere in Europe than in the United States.

CHAPTER XXV

THE ORGANIZATION OF THE ILL-PAID CLASSES

THE NEED OF CLASS ORGANIZATION—USES AND DANGERS OF UNIONS
—GENERAL DISPOSITION OF THE HAND-WORKING CLASSES.

IT is not the purpose of this book to add anything to
the merely controversial literature of the time; and in
treating the present topic I intend no more than to state
a few simple and perhaps obvious principles designed to
connect it with our general line of thought.

It is quite apparent that an organized and intelligent
class-consciousness in the hand-working people is one of
the primary needs of a democratic society. In so far as
this part of the people is lacking in a knowledge of its
situation and in the practice of orderly self-assertion, a real
freedom will also be lacking, and we shall have some kind
of subjection in its place; freedom being impossible without group organization. That industrial classes exist—in
the sense already explained*—cannot well be denied, and
existing they ought to be conscious and self-directing.

The most obvious need of class-consciousness is for
self-assertion against the pressure of other classes, and
this is both most necessary and most difficult with those
who lack wealth and the command over organized forces
which it implies. In a free society, especially, the Lord
helps those who help themselves; and those who are weak

* See chapter 21.

284

in money must be strong in union, and must also exert themselves to make good any deficiency in leadership that comes from ability deserting to more favored classes.

That the dominant power of wealth has an oppressive action, for the most part involuntary, upon the people below, will hardly be denied by any competent student. The industrial progress of our time is accompanied by sufferings that are involved with the progress. These sufferings—at least in their more tangible forms—fall almost wholly upon the poorer classes, while the richer get a larger share of the increased product which the progress brings. By sufferings I mean not only the physical hardship and liability to disease, early decay, and mutilation or death by accident, which fall to the hand-worker; but also the debasement of children by premature and stunting labor, the comparative lack of intellectual and social opportunities, the ugly and discouraging surroundings, and the insecurity of employment, to which he and his are subject. There is no purpose to inflict these things; but they are inflicted, and the only remedy is a public consciousness, especially in the classes who suffer from them, of their causes and the means by which they can be done away with.

The principal expressions of class-consciousness in the hand-working classes in our day are labor unions and that wider, vaguer, more philosophical or religious movement, too various for definition, which is known as socialism. Regarding the latter I will only say at present that it includes much of what is most vital in the contemporary working of the democratic spirit; the large problems with which its doctrines deal I prefer to discuss in my own way.

Labor unions are a simpler matter. They have arisen out of the urgent need of self-defence, not so much against deliberate aggression as against brutal confusion and neglect. The industrial population has been tossed about on the swirl of economic change like so much sawdust on a river, sometimes prosperous, sometimes miserable, never secure, and living largely under degrading, inhuman conditions. Against this state of things the higher class of artisans—as measured by skill, wages and general intelligence—have made a partly successful struggle through coöperation in associations, which, however, include much less than half of those who might be expected to take advantage of them.* That they are an effective means of class self-assertion is evident from the antagonism they have aroused.

Besides their primary function of group-bargaining, which has come to be generally recognized as essential, unions are performing a variety of services hardly less important to their members, and serviceable to society at large. In the way of influencing legislation they have probably done more than all other agencies together to combat child-labor, excessive hours, and other inhuman and degrading kinds of work; also to provide for safeguards against accident, for proper sanitation of factories, and the like. In this field their work is as much defensive as aggressive, since employing interests, on the other side,

* Professor John R. Commons (Publications of the American Sociological Society, vol. ii, p. 141) estimates 2,000,000 members of unions out of 6,000,000 wage-earners "available for class conflict."

are constantly influencing legislation and administration to their own advantage.

Their function as spheres of fellowship and self-development is equally vital and less understood. To have a we-feeling, to live shoulder to shoulder with one's fellows, is the only human life; we all need it to keep us from selfishness, sensuality and despair, and the hand-worker needs it even more than the rest of us. Usually without pecuniary resource and insecure of his job and his home, he is, in isolation, miserably weak and in a way to be cowed and unmanned by misfortune or mere apprehension. Drifting about in a confused society, unimportant, apparently, to the rest of the world, it is no wonder if he feels

> "I am no link of Thy great chain," *

and loses faith in himself, in life and in God. The union makes him feel that he is part of a whole, one of a fellowship, that there are those who will stand by him in trouble, that he counts for something in the great life. He gets from it that thrill of broader sentiment, the same in kind that men get in fighting for their country; his self is enlarged and enriched and his imagination fed with objects, comparatively, "immense and eternal."

Moreover, the life of labor unions and other class associations, through the training which it gives in democratic organization and discipline, is perhaps the chief guaranty of the healthy political development of the hand-working class — especially those imported from non-democratic civilizations—and the surest barrier against recklessness and disorder. That their members get this training will

* George Herbert.

be evident to anyone who studies their working, and it is not apparent that they would get it in any other way. Men learn most in acting for purposes which they understand and are interested in, and this is more certain to be the case with economic aims than with any other.

Thus, if unions should never raise wages or shorten hours, they would yet be invaluable to the manhood of their members. At worst, they ensure the joy of an open fight and of companionship in defeat. Self-assertion through voluntary organization is of the essence of democracy, and if any part of the people proves incapable of it it is a bad sign for the country. On this ground alone it would seem that patriots should desire to see organization of this sort extend throughout the industrial population.

The danger of these associations is that which besets human nature everywhere—the selfish use of power. It is feared with reason that if they have too much their own way they will monopolize opportunity by restricting apprenticeship and limiting the number of their members; that they will seek their ends through intimidation and violence; that they will be made the instruments of corrupt leaders. These and similar wrongs have from time to time been brought home to them, and, unless their members are superior to the common run of men, they are such as must be expected. But it would be a mistake to regard these or any other kinds of injustice as a part of the essential policy of unions. They are feeling their way in a human, fallible manner, and their eventual policy will be determined by what, in the way of class advancement, they find by experience to be practicable. In so

288

far as they attempt things that are unjust we may expect them, in the long run, to fail, through the resistance of others and through the awakening of their own consciences. It is the part of other people to check their excesses and cherish their benefits.

In general no sort of persons mean better than hand-laboring men. They are simple, honest people, as a rule, with that bent toward integrity which is fostered by working in wood and iron and often lost in the subtleties of business. Moreover, their experience is such as to develop a sense of the brotherhood of man and a desire to realize it in institutions. Not having enjoyed the artificial support of accumulated property, they have the more reason to know the dependence of each on his fellows. Nor have they any great hopes of personal aggrandizement to isolate them and pamper their self-consciousness.

To these we may add that offences from this quarter are likely to be more shocking and less dangerous than those of a more sophisticated sort of people. Occasional outbreaks of violence alarm us and call for prompt enforcement of law, but are not a serious menace to society, because general sentiment and all established interests are against them; while the subtle, respectable, systematic corruption by the rich and powerful threatens the very being of democracy.

The most deplorable fact about labor unions is that they embrace so small a proportion of those that need their benefits. How far into the shifting masses of unskilled labor effective organization can extend only time will show.

CHAPTER XXVI

POVERTY

The Meaning of Poverty—Personal and General Causes—
Poverty in a Prosperous Society Due Chiefly to Mal-
adjustment—Are the Poor the "Unfit"?—Who is to
Blame for Poverty?—Attitude of Society Toward the
Poor—Fundamental Remedies.

THE most practical definition of poverty is that now widely adopted which relates it to function, and calls those the poor whose income is not sufficient to keep up their health and working efficiency. This may be vague but is not too much so to be useful, and is capable of becoming quite definite through exact inquiry. At least it indicates roughly a considerable portion of the people who are poor in an obvious and momentous sense of the word.

Being undernourished, the poor lack energy, physical, intellectual and moral. Whatever the original cause of their poverty, they cannot, being poor, work so hard, think so clearly, plan so hopefully, or resist temptation with so much steadfastness as those who have the primary means of keeping themselves in sound condition.

Moreover, the lack of adequate food, clothing and housing commonly implies other lacks, among which are poor early training and education, the absence of contact with elevating and inspiring personalities, a narrow outlook upon the world, and, in short, a general lack of social opportunity.

POVERTY

The poor are not a class in the sense of having a distinct psychical organization. Absorbed in a discouraging material struggle, or perhaps in the sensuality and apathy to which a discouraging outlook is apt to lead, they have no spirit or surplus energy adequate to effectual coöperative endeavor on their own initiative, or even to grasping the benefits of existing organization. As a rule they get far less from the law and its administration, from the church, the schools, the public libraries and the like, than the classes more capable of self-assertion, and this is particularly true in a *laissez-faire* democracy, such as ours, which gives rights pretty much in proportion to the vigor with which they are demanded. It is this lack of common consciousness and purpose that explains the ease with which, in all ages, the poor have been governed, not to say exploited, from above. And if they are getting some consciousness and purpose at the present time, it is largely for the very reason that they are less inveterately and hopelessly poor now than in the past.

The familiar question whether poverty is due to personal or social causes is in itself somewhat fallacious, as smacking of a philosophy that does not see that the personal and social are inseparable. Everything in personality has roots in social conditions, past or present. So personal poverty is part of an organic whole, the effect in one way or another, by heredity or influence, of the general life. The question has significance, however, when we understand it as asking whether or not the cause is so fixed in personality that it cannot be counteracted by social influences. We find that in a community generally prosper-

291

ous a part of the people—say ten per cent.—are poor in the urgent sense indicated above. The practical question is, Are these people poor from causes so established in their characters (however originating) that the rest of the community can do nothing effectual for them, or are they plastic to forces which might raise them to a normal standard of living?

As to this—leaving out the various extreme opinions which attend all such questions—there is a fair measure of agreement among competent observers somewhat to the following effect: There is a considerable number of individuals and families having intrinsic defects of character which must always keep them poor so long as they are left in the ordinary degree of self-dependence. The great majority of the poor, however, have no ineradicable personal weakness but are capable of responding to influences which might raise them to a normal standard of living. In other words, the nine-tenths of the community which is not poor might conceivably bring influences to bear which would—in a healthy manner and without demoralizing alms-giving—remove all but a small part of the poverty of the other tenth. It is only a question of putting into the matter sufficient knowledge and good will. As to the view, still not uncommon, that the laziness, shiftlessness and vice of the poor are the source of their difficulties, it may be said that these traits, so far as they exist, are now generally regarded by competent students as quite as much the effect as the cause of poverty. If a man is undervitalized he will either appear lazy or will exhaust himself in efforts which are beyond his strength—the latter being common with those of a nervous temperament.

Shiftlessness, also, is the natural outcome of a confused and discouraging experience, especially if added to poor nutrition. And as to drink and other sensual vices, it is well understood that they are the logical resource of those whose life does not meet the needs of human nature in the way of variety, pleasantness and hope. There are other causes of vice besides poverty, as appears from its prevalence among the unresourceful rich, but there can be no doubt that good nurture, moderate work, wholesome amusement and a hopeful outlook would do away with a great, probably the greater, part of it. There are, no doubt, among the poor, as among the well-to-do, many cases of incurable viciousness and incompetence, but it would be no less unjust and foolish to assume that any individual is of this sort than to give up a scarlet fever patient because some will die of that disease in spite of the best treatment.

I find that the ablest and most experienced workers have generally the most confidence as to what may be done even with the apparently lazy, shiftless or vicious by bringing fresh suggestions, encouragements and opportunities to bear upon them. And it is only a small portion of the poor that are even apparently lazy, shiftless or vicious; the majority comparing not unfavorably with the well-to-do classes in these respects.

Leaving aside general conditions which may depress whole nations or races, the main cause of poverty in a prosperous country like the United States is without doubt some sort of maladjustment between the individual, or the family or neighborhood group, and the wider community, by reason of which potential capacity does not yield its proper fruit in efficiency and comfort. This is evidently the case, for example, with the sort of poverty most familiar in our American cities; that due to the transplanting of vast numbers of Europeans to a society, not too good for them as we carelessly assume, but out of connection with their habits and traditions. The Italians, Slavs and Russian Jews who just now throng our cities are by no means deficient, on the whole, either in intelligence, industry or thrift; and those who know them best find them prolific in some qualities, such as artistic sensibility of various kinds, in which America is otherwise rather deficient. But the process of adaptation to our industrial conditions is trying and leaves many in poverty and demoralization.

Among the native population also, poverty and the moral degradation which is often found with it is due largely, perhaps chiefly, to various kinds of maladjustment between the working classes and the industrial system—to loss of employment from periodical depressions or from the introduction of new methods, to the lack of provision for industrial education, to the perils attending migration from country to city, and so on.

What shall we say of the doctrine very widely, though perhaps not very clearly, held that the poor are the "unfit" in course of elimination, and are suffering the painful but necessary consequences of an inferiority that society must get rid of at any cost? A notion of this kind may be discovered in the minds of many men of fair intelligence, and is due to remote, obscure and for the most part mistaken impressions of the teaching of Malthus and Darwin.

The unfit, in the sense of Darwin and of biology in general, are those whose hereditary type is so unsuited to the conditions of life that it tends to die out, or at least suffer relative diminution in numbers, under the action of these conditions—as white families tend to die out in the tropics. In other words, they have an inferiority due to heredity, and this inferiority is of such a character that they do not leave as many children to continue their race as do those of a superior or fitter type.

It is very questionable whether any great part of the poor answer the description in either of these respects. As to the first, it is the prevailing opinion with those most familiar with the matter that their inferiority, except possibly where a distinct race is in question, as with the Negroes, is due chiefly to deficient nurture, training and opportunity, and not to heredity. This view is supported by the fact that under the conditions which a country of opportunity, like the United States, affords, great masses of people rise from poverty to comfort, and many of them to opulence, showing that the stock was as capable as any. Something of this sort has taken place with German and Irish immigrants, and is likely to take place with Jews, Slavs and Italians.

As to elimination, it is well known that only poverty of the most extreme and destructive kinds avails to restrict propagation, and that the moderately poor have a higher rate of increase than the educated and well-to-do classes. It is, in fact, far more the latter that are the "unfit" in a biological sense than the former.

295

The truth is that poverty is unfitness, but in a social and not a biological sense. That is to say, it means that feeding, housing, family life, education and opportunity are below the standards that the social type calls for, and that their existence endangers the latter in a manner analogous to that in which the presence of inferior cattle in a herd endangers the biological type. They threaten, and to a greater or less degree actually bring about, a general degradation of the community, through ignorance, inefficiency, disease, vice, bad government, class hatred (or, still worse, class servility and arrogance) and so on.

But since the unfitness is social rather than biological, the method of elimination must also be social, namely, the reform of housing and neighborhood conditions, improvement of the schools, public teaching of trades, abolition of child-labor and the humanizing of industry.

That there are strains of biological unfitness among the poor—hereditary idiocy, or nervous instability tending toward vice and crime, for example—is not to be denied, and certainly these should be eliminated, but poverty, far from effecting elimination, is perhaps their main cause. This will, no doubt, be duly considered by students of the new science of eugenics, for which those of us who approach social problems from another point of view may yet have the highest regard and expectation. Only a shallow sort of mind will suppose there is any necessary conflict between biological and psychological sociology.

As to the question, who is to blame for poverty, let us remember that the whole question of praise or blame is one of point of view and expediency. Blame the poor if it will do them any good, and sometimes, perhaps, it will, but not so often probably as the well-to-do are apt to imagine. It used to be thought that people must always be held responsible for their condition, and that the main if not the only source of improvement was to prod their sense of this responsibility; but more thoughtful observation shows that it is not always a good thing to urge the will. "Worry," says an experienced worker,* "is one of the direct and all-pervading causes of economic dependence," and he asserts that "Take no thought for the morrow" is often the most practical advice. Many indications, among them the spread of "mind-cure" doctrines and practices, point to a widely felt need to escape from the waste and unrest of an over-stimulated sense of responsibility.

The main blame for poverty must rest upon the prosperous, because they have, on the whole, far more power in the premises. However, poverty being due chiefly to conditions of which society is only just beginning to become conscious, we may say that in the past nobody has been to blame. It is an unintended result of the economic struggle, and is "done with the elbows rather than the fists." But consciousness is arising, and with it comes responsibility. We are becoming aware of what makes poverty and how it can in great part be done away with, and if accomplishment does not keep pace with knowledge we shall be to blame indeed.

All parts of society being interdependent, the evils of

* An editorial writer in Charities and the Commons, presumably Professor Devine, the author of Principles of Relief, and other works on rational charity.

poverty are not confined to one class, but spread throughout the whole; and the influence of a low standard of living is felt in the corruption of politics, the prevalence of vice and the inefficiency of labor. The cause of the poor is therefore the cause of all, and from this point of view those of them who in spite of weakness, discouragement and neglect keep up the fight for a decent life and shun dependence and degradation, should be regarded as heroic defenders of the general welfare, deserving praise as much as the soldier at the front. If we do not so regard them, it is because of our lack of intelligence and social consciousness.

In a truly organic society the struggles and suffering of a poor class would arouse the same affectionate and helping solicitude as is felt when one member of a family falls ill. In contrast to this, the indifference or somewhat contemptuous pity usually felt toward poverty indicates a low state of community sentiment, a deficient we-feeling. Respect and appreciation would seem to be due to those who sustain the struggle successfully, and sympathetic help to those who are broken down by it. Especially brutal, stupid and inexpedient—when we think of it— is the old way of lumping the poor with the degenerate as "the lower class," and either leaving them to bear their discredited existence as best they may, or dealing out to them a contemptuous and unbrotherly alms. The confusion with the degraded of those who are keeping up the social standard in the face of exceptional difficulties is as mean and deadly a wrong as could well be.

In so far as there is an effective, self-conscious Christian

298

spirit in the world, thought, feeling and effort must concentrate wherever there is injustice or avoidable suffering. That this takes place so slowly and imperfectly in the matter of poverty is largely owing to a lack of clear perception of what ought to be done. I suppose there is no doubt that if mere gifts could wipe out poverty it would be wiped out at once. But people are now, for the most part, just sufficiently informed to see the futility of ordinary alms, without being instructed in the possibilities of rational philanthropy. Rational philanthropy is coming, however, along with an excellent literature and a body of expert persons who unite humane enthusiasm with a scientific spirit.*

The fundamental remedy for poverty is, of course, rational organization having for its aim the control of those conditions, near and remote, which lead people into it and prevent their getting out. The most radical measures are those which are educational and protective in a very broad and searching sense of the words—the humanization of the primary school system, industrial education, facilities for play, physical training and healthy amusement, good housing, the restriction by law of child labor and of all vicious and unwholesome conditions, and, finally, the biological precaution of stopping the propagation of really degenerate types of men.

* "Our children's children may learn with amazement how we thought it a natural social phenomenon that men should die in their prime, leaving wives and children in terror of want; that accidents should make an army of maimed dependents; that there should not be enough houses for workers; and that epidemics should sweep away multitudes as autumn frost sweeps away summer insects." Simon N. Patten, The New Basis of Civilization, 197.

If we can give the children of the poor the right start in life, they will themselves, in most cases, develop the intelligence, initiative, self-control and power of organization which will enable them to look out for their own interests when they are mature. The more one thinks of these questions the more he will feel that they can only be solved by helping the weaker classes to a position where they can help themselves.

CHAPTER XXVII

HOSTILE FEELING BETWEEN CLASSES

Conditions Producing Class Animosity—The Spirit of Service Allays Bitterness—Possible Decrease of the Prestige of Wealth—Probability of a More Communal Spirit in the Use of Wealth—Influence of Settled Rules for Social Opposition—Importance of Face-to-Face Discussion.

Class animosity by no means increases in proportion to the separation of classes. On the contrary, where there is a definite and recognized class system which no one thinks of breaking down, a main cause of arrogance and jealousy is absent. Every one takes his position for granted and is not concerned to assert or improve it. In Spain, it is said, "you may give the inch to any peasant; he is sure to be a gentleman, and he never thinks of taking the ell." So in an English tale, written about 1875, I find the following: "The peasantry and little people in country places like to feel the gentry far above them. They do not care to be caught up into the empyrean of an equal humanity, but enjoy the poetry of their self-abasement in the belief that their superiors are indeed their betters." So at the South there was a kind of fellowship between the races under slavery which present conditions make more difficult. A settled inequality is the next best thing, for intercourse, to equality.

But where the ideal of equality has entered, even slight differences may be resented, and class feeling is most bitter, probably, where this ideal is strong but has no regu-

301

lar and hopeful methods of asserting itself. In that case aspiration turns sour and generates hateful passions. Caste countries are safe from this by lacking the ideal of equality, democracies by partly realizing it. But in Germany, for instance, where there is a fierce democratic propaganda on the one hand, and a stone wall of military and aristocratic institutions on the other, one may feel a class bitterness that we hardly know in America. And in England also, at the present time, when classes are still recognized but very ill-defined, there seems to be much of an uneasy preoccupation about rank, and of the elbowing, snubbing and suspicion that go with it. People appear to be more concerned with trying to get into a set above them, or repressing others who are pushing up from below, than with us. In America social position exists, but, having no such definite symbols as in England, is for the most part too intangible to give rise to snobbery, which is based on titles and other externalities which men may covet or gloat over in a way hardly possible when the line is merely one of opinion, congeniality and character.

The feeling between classes will not be very bitter so long as the ideal of service is present in all and mutually recognized. And it is the tendency of the democratic spirit—very imperfectly worked out as yet—to raise this ideal above all others and make it a common standard of conduct. Thus Montesquieu, describing an ideal democracy, says that ambition is limited " to the sole desire, to the sole happiness, of doing greater services to our country than the rest of our fellow citizens. They cannot all render her equal services, but they all ought to serve her

302

with equal alacrity." He thinks also that the love of frugality, by which he means compunction in material self-indulgence, "limits the desire of having to the study of procuring necessities to our family and superfluities to our country."* If it were indeed so in our own world, there would be no danger of a class conflict.

Possibly all states of opinion by which any service is despised are survivals from a caste society, and reminiscent of the domination of one order over another—just as slavery has left a feeling in the South that hand labor is degrading. So soon as all kinds of workers share freely in the social and political order, all work must be respected. The social prestige of idleness, of "conspicuous leisure," that still exists in the Old World, is evidently a survival of this sort, and it can hardly happen in the democratic future that "people will let their nails grow that all may see they do not work." "I do not call one greater and one smaller," says Whitman, "that which fills its period and place is equal to any."† I think, however, that there will always be especial esteem for some sorts of achievement, but the grounds for this will, more and more, be distinction in the common service.

The excessive prestige of wealth, along with much of the ill feeling which it involves, is also, in my opinion, rather a legacy from caste society than a trait congenial to democracy. I have tried to show that the ascendency of riches is really greater in the older and less democratic societies; and it survives in democracy as much as it

* The Spirit of Laws, book v, chap. 3.
† Leaves of Grass, 71.

does partly because of the tradition that associates wealth with an upper caste, and partly because other ideals are as yet crude and unorganized. A real democracy of sentiment and action, a renewed Christianity and a renewed art might make life beautiful and hopeful for those who have little money without diminishing the wholesome operation of the desire for gain. At present the common man is impoverished not merely by an absolute want of money but by a current way of thinking which makes pecuniary success the standard of merit, and so makes him feel that failure to get money is failure of life. As we no longer feel much admiration for mere physical prowess, apart from the use that is made of it, so it seems natural that the same should come true of mere pecuniary strength. The mind of a child, or of any naïve person, bases consideration chiefly on function, on what a man can do in the common life, and it is in the line of democratic development that we should return toward this simple and human view.

It is in accord with this movement that children of all classes are more and more taught the use of tools, cooking and other primary arts of life. This not only makes for economy and independence, but educates the "instinct of workmanship," leading us to feel an interest in all good work and a respect for those who do it.

The main need of men is life, self-expression, not luxury, and if self-expression can be made general material inequalities alone will excite but little resentment.

As to the use of wealth we may expect a growing sense of social responsibility, of which there are already cheerful indications. Since it is no longer respectable to be idle, why may we not hope that it will presently cease to be respectable to indulge one's lower self in other ways—in pecuniary greed, in luxurious eating, in display, rich clothes and other costly and exclusive pleasures?

We must not, however, be so optimistic as to overlook the ease with which narrow or selfish interests may form special groups of their own, encouraging one another in greed or luxury to the neglect of the common life. Such associations cannot altogether shut out general sentiment, but they can and do so far deaden its influence that the more hardened or frivolous are practically unconscious of it. While there are some cheerful givers on a large scale among us, and many on a small one, I am not sure that there was ever, on the whole, a commercial society that contributed a smaller part of its gains to general causes. We have done much in this way; but then we are enormously rich; and the most that has been done has been by taxation, which falls most heavily upon small property-owners. The more communal use of wealth is rather a matter of general probability, and of faith in democratic sentiment, than of demonstrable fact.

Much might be said of the various ways in which more community sentiment might be shown and class resentment alleviated. In the matter of dress, for example; shall one express his community consciousness in it or his class consciousness, assuming that each is natural and creditable? It would seem that when he goes abroad among men the good democrat should prefer to appear a plain citizen, with nothing about him to interrupt intercourse with any class. And in fact, it is a wholesome feature of American life, in notable contrast with, say, Germany, that high as well as low are averse to wearing military or other distinctive costume in public—except at times of festival or display, when class consciousness is in special function. We feel that if a man wants to distinguish himself in general intercourse he should do so in courtesy or wisdom, not in medals or clothes.

And why should not the same principle, of deference to the community in non-essentials, apply to one's house and to one's way of living in general? If he has anything worthy to express in these things, let him express it, but not pride or luxury.

Let us not, however, formulize upon the question what one may rightly spend money for, or imagine that formulism is practicable. The principle that wealth is a trust held for the general good is not to be disputed; but latitude must be left to individual conceptions of what the general good is. These are matters not for formulas or sumptuary laws, but for conscience. To set up any other standard would be to suppress individuality and do more harm than good.

Some of us would be glad to see almost any amount of wealth spent upon beautiful architecture, though we might prefer that the buildings be devoted to some public use. Let us have beauty, even luxury, but let it be public and communicable. It certainly seems at first sight that vast expenditure upon private yachts, private cars, costly balls, display of jewelry, sumptuous eating and the like, indicates a low state of culture; but perhaps this is a mistake; no doubt there is some beneficence in these things not generally understood.

We do not want uniformity in earning and spending, more than elsewhere, only unity of spirit. Some writers praise the emulation that is determined to have as fine things as others have, but while this has its uses it is a social impulse of no high kind and keeps the mass of men feeling poor and inferior. Our dignity and happiness would profit more if each of us were to work out life in a way of his own without invidious comparisons. We shall never be content except as we develop and enjoy our individuality and are willing to forego what does not belong to it. I know that I was not born to get or to use riches, but I am willing to believe that others are.

An essential condition of better feeling in the inevitable struggles of life is that there should be just and accepted "rules of the game" to give moral unity to the whole. Much must be suffered, but men will suffer without bitterness if they believe that they do so under just and necessary principles.

A solid foundation has been laid for this, in free countries, by the establishment of institutions under which all class conflicts are referred, in the last resort, to human nature itself. Through free speech a general will may be organized on any matter urgent enough to attract general attention, and through democratic government this may be tested, recorded and carried out. Thus is provided a tribunal free from class bias before which controversies may be tried and settled in an orderly manner.

It would be hard to exaggerate the importance to social peace of this recognition of the ultimate authority of public opinion, acting slowly but surely through constitutional methods. It means a moral whole which prescribes rules, directs sane agitation into healthy and moderate channels, and takes away all rational ground for violence or revolution. If men, for instance, believe that a particular kind of socialistic state is the cure for the evils of society, let them speak, print and form their party. Perhaps they are right; at least, they get much wholesome self-expression and a kind of happiness out of their aspiration and labors. And if they are partly wrong, yet they may both learn and impart much to the general advantage.

But we have made only a beginning in this. Our ethics is only a vague outline, not a matured system, and in the details of social contact—as between employer and workman, rich and poor, Negro and white, and so on—there is such a lack of accepted standards that men have little to go by but their crude impulses. All this must be worked out, in as much patience and good will as possible, before we can expect to have peace.

Where there is no very radical conflict of essential principles, ill feeling may commonly be alleviated by face-to-face discussion, since the more we come to understand one another the more we get below superficial unlikeness and find essential community. Between fairly reasonable and honest men it is always wholesome to "have it out," and many careful studies of labor troubles agree regarding the large part played by misunderstandings and suspicion that have no cause except lack of opportunity for explanation. "The rioting would not have taken place," says a student of certain mining disorders, "had not the ignorance and suspicion of the Hungarians been supplemented by the ignorance and suspicion of the employers; and the perseverance of this mutual attitude may yet create another riot."* There is a strong temptation for those in authority, especially if they are overworked, or conscious of being a little weak or unready in conference, to fence themselves with formality and the type-written letter. But a man of real fitness in any administrative capacity must have stomach for open and face-to-face dealing with men.

And a democratic system sooner or later brings to pass face-to-face discussion of all vital questions, because the people will be satisfied with no other. An appearance of shirking it will arouse even more distrust and hostility than the open avowal of selfish motives; and accordingly it is more and more the practice of aggressive interests to seek to justify themselves by at least the appearance of frank appeal to popular judgment.

* Spahr, America's Working People, 128.

PART V

INSTITUTIONS

CHAPTER XXVIII

INSTITUTIONS AND THE INDIVIDUAL

THE NATURE OF INSTITUTIONS—HEREDITARY AND SOCIAL FACTORS
—THE CHILD AND THE WORLD—SOCIETY AND PERSONALITY
—PERSONALITY VERSUS THE INSTITUTION—THE INSTITUTION
AS A BASIS OF PERSONALITY—THE MORAL ASPECT—CHOICE
VERSUS MECHANISM—PERSONALITY THE LIFE OF INSTITUTIONS
—INSTITUTIONS BECOMING FREER IN STRUCTURE.

AN institution is simply a definite and established phase
of the public mind, not different in its ultimate nature from
public opinion, though often seeming, on account of its
permanence and the visible customs and symbols in which
it is clothed, to have a somewhat distinct and independent
existence. Thus the political state and the church, with
their venerable associations, their vast and ancient power,
their literature, buildings and offices, hardly appear even
to a democratic people as the mere products of human invention which, of course, they are.

The great institutions are the outcome of that organization which human thought naturally takes on when it is
directed for age after age upon a particular subject, and
so gradually crystallizes in definite forms—enduring sentiments, beliefs, customs and symbols. And this is the
case when there is some deep and abiding interest to hold
the attention of men. Language, government, the church,
laws and customs of property and of the family, systems

of industry and education, are institutions because they are the working out of permanent needs of human nature.

These various institutions are not separable entities, but rather phases of a common and at least partly homogeneous body of thought, just as are the various tendencies and convictions of an individual: they are the "apperceptive systems" or organized attitudes of the public mind, and it is only by abstraction that we can regard them as things by themselves. We are to remember that the social system is above all a whole, no matter how the convenience of study may lead us to divide it.

In the individual the institution exists as a habit of mind and of action, largely unconscious because largely common to all the group: it is only the differential aspect of ourselves of which we are commonly aware. But it is in men and nowhere else that the institution is to be found. The real existence of the Constitution of the United States, for example, is in the traditional ideas of the people and the activities of judges, legislators and administrators; the written instrument being only a means of communication, an Ark of the Covenant, ensuring the integrity of the tradition.

The individual is always cause as well as effect of the institution: he receives the impress of the state whose traditions have enveloped him from childhood, but at the same time impresses his own character, formed by other forces as well as this, upon the state, which thus in him and others like him undergoes change.

If we think carefully about this matter, however, we shall see that there are several somewhat different questions which might be included in a study of the relation between the individual and institutions; and these we ought to distinguish.

One of them is that of the babe to the world, or of the hereditary factor of life, existing in us at birth, to the factor of communication and influence.

Another and quite different one is that of society and personality, or of the relation between the mature individual and the whole of which he is a member.

A third is the question—again a distinct one—of the relation, not between the person and society at large, but between him and particular institutions. This last is the one with which we are more properly concerned, but it may not be amiss to offer some observations on the others.

The child at birth, when, we may suppose for convenience, society has had no direct influence upon him, represents the race stock or hereditary factor in life in antithesis to the factor of tradition, communication and social organization. He also represents an undeveloped or merely biological individuality in contrast to the developed social whole into which he comes.

We think of the social world as the mature, organized, institutional factor in the problem; and yet we may well say that the child also embodies an institution (using the word largely) and one more ancient and stable than church or state, namely the biological type, little changed, probably, since the dawn of history. It cannot be shown in any way that I know of that the children born to-day of English or American parents—leaving aside any question of race mixture—are greatly different in natural outfit from

315

the Saxon boys and girls, their ancestors, who played upon the banks of the Elbe fifteen hundred years ago. The rooted instincts and temperament of races appear to be very much what they were, and the changes of history— the development of political institutions, the economic revolutions, the settlement of new countries, the Reformation, the rise of science and the like—are changes mainly in the social factor of life, which thus appears comparatively a shifting thing.

In the development of the child, then, we have to do with the interaction of two types, both of which are ancient and stable, though one more so than the other. And the stir and generation of human life is precisely in the mingling of these types and in the many variations of each one. The hereditary outfit of a child consists of vague tendencies or aptitudes which get definiteness and meaning only through the communicative influences which enable them to develop. Thus babbling is instinctive, while speech comes by this instinct being defined and instructed in society; curiosity comes by nature, knowledge by life; fear, in a vague, instinctive form, is supposed to be felt even by the fœtus, but the fears of later life are chiefly social fears; there is an instinctive sensibility which develops into sympathy and love; and so on.

Nothing is more futile than general discussions of the relative importance of heredity and environment. It is much like the case of matter *versus* mind; both are indispensable to every phase of life, and neither can exist apart from the other: they are coördinate in importance and incommensurable in nature. One might as well ask whether the soil or the seed predominates in the formation

316

of a tree, as whether nature does more for us than nurture. The fact that most writers have a predilection for one of these factors at the expense of the other (Mr. Galton and the biological school, for example, seeing heredity everywhere, and not much else, while psychologists and sociologists put the stress on influence) means only that some are trained to attend to one class of facts and some to another. One may be more relevant for a given practical purpose than the other, but to make a general opposition is unintelligent.

To the eye of sentiment a new-born child offers a moving contrast to the ancient and grimy world into which it so innocently enters; the one formed, apparently, for all that is pure and good, "trailing clouds of glory" as some think, from a more spiritual world than ours, pathetically unconscious of anything but joy; the other gray and saturnine, sure to prove in many ways a prison-house, perhaps a foul one.

"Full soon thy soul shall have her earthly freight." *

No doubt, however, the pathos of this contrast arises in part from somewhat fallacious preconceptions. The imagination idealizes the child, reading its own visions into his innocence as it does into the innocence of the sea and the mountains, and contrasting his future career not with what he is, but with an ideal of what he might become. In truth the child already feels, in his own way, the painful side of life; he has the seeds of darkness in him as well as those of light, and cannot in strictness be said to be any

* Wordsworth, Ode on the Intimations of Immortality, etc.

317

better than the world. The good of life transcends his imagination as much as does the evil, and he could not become anything at all except in a social world. The pity of the matter, which may well move every one who thinks of it to work for better homes, schools and playgrounds, is simply that we are about to make so poor a use of a plastic material, that he might be so much better and happier if we would prepare a better place for him.

It is true, in a sense, as Bacon says, that youth has more of divinity, but perhaps we might also say that it has more of deviltry; the younger life is, the more unbound it is, not yet in harness, with more divine insight and more reckless passion, and adolescence is the period of criminality as well as of poetry.

There is a natural affinity between childhood and democracy; the latter implying, indeed, that we are to become more as little children, more simple, frank and human. And it is a very proper part of the democratic movement that more and more prestige is attaching to childhood, that it is more studied, cherished and respected. Probably nothing else gives such cogency to the idea of reform as to think of what it means to children. We wish to know that all the children of the land are happily unfolding their minds and hearts at home, school and play; and that there is a gradual induction into useful work, which also proceeds regularly and happily. This calls for better homes and neighborhoods, and the overcoming of conditions that degrade them; it implies better schools, the suppression of child-labor, regular industrial education, wholesome and fairly paid work and reasonable security of position. While the child is not exactly better than the world, his possibilities make us feel that the world ought to be better for his sake.

As fast as a child becomes a person, he also becomes a member of the existing social order. This is simply a case of a whole and one of its differentiated parts; having so often insisted that society and the individual are aspects of the same thing, I need not enlarge upon it here. Even the degenerate, so far as they have faculty enough to be human, live in the social order and are as much one with it as the rest of mankind. We simply cannot separate the individual from society at large; to get a contrast we must pass on to consider him in relation to particular institutions, or to institutions in general as distinguished from more plastic phases of life.

An institution is a mature, specialized and comparatively rigid part of the social structure. It is made up of persons, but not of whole persons; each one enters into it with a trained and specialized part of himself. Consider, for instance, the legal part of a lawyer, the ecclesiastical part of a church member or the business part of a merchant. In antithesis to the institution, therefore, the person represents the wholeness and humanness of life; he is, as Professor Alfred Lloyd says,* "a corrector of partiality, and a translator and distributor of special development." A man is no man at all if he is merely a piece of an institution; he must stand also for human nature, for the instinctive, the plastic and the ideal.

* In a paper on The Personal and the Factional in the Life of Society. The Journal of Philosophy, Psychology and Scientific Methods, 1905, p. 337.

The saying that corporations have no soul expresses well enough this defect of all definite social structures, which gives rise to an irrepressible conflict between them and the freer and larger impulses of human nature. Just in proportion as they achieve an effective special mechanism for a narrow purpose, they lose humanness, breadth and adaptability. As we have to be specially on our guard against commercial corporations, because of their union of power and impersonality, so we should be against all institutions.

The institution represents might, and also, perhaps, right, but right organized, mature, perhaps gone to seed, never fresh and unrecognized. New right, or moral progress, always begins in a revolt against institutions.

I have in mind a painting which may be said to set forth to the eye this relation between the living soul and the institution. It represents St. James before the Roman Emperor.* The former is poorly clad, beautiful, with rapt, uplifted face; the latter majestic, dominant, assured, seated high on his ivory chair and surrounded by soldiers.

Of course the institutional element is equally essential with the personal. The mechanical working of tradition and convention pours into the mind the tried wisdom of the race, a system of thought every part of which has survived because it was, in some sense, the fittest, because it approved itself to the human spirit. In this way the individual gets language, sentiments, moral standards and all kinds of knowledge: gets them with an exertion of the

* By Mantegna.

320

will trifling compared with what these things originally cost. They have become a social atmosphere which pervades the mind mostly without its active participation. Once the focus of attention and effort, they have now receded into the dimness of the matter-of-course, leaving energy free for new conquests. On this involuntary foundation we build, and it needs no argument to show that we could accomplish nothing without it.

Thus all innovation is based on conformity, all heterodoxy on orthodoxy, all individuality on solidarity. Without the orthodox tradition in biology, for instance, under the guidance of which a store of ordered knowledge had been collected, the heterodoxy of Darwin, based on a reinterpretation of this knowledge, would have been impossible. And so in art, the institution supplies a basis to the very individual who rebels against it. Mr. Brownell, in his work on French Art, points out, in discussing the relation of Rodin the innovating sculptor to the French Institute, that he owes his development and the interest his non-conformity excites largely to "the very system that has been powerful enough to popularize indefinitely the subject both of subscription and revolt."* In America it is not hostile criticism but no criticism at all—sheer ignorance and indifference—that discourages the artist and man of letters and makes it difficult to form a high ideal. Where there is an organized tradition there may be intolerance but there will also be intelligence.

Thus choice, which represents the relatively free action of human nature in building up life, is like the coral insect,

* Page 30. See also the last chapter.

always working on a mountain made up of the crystallized remains of dead predecessors.

It is a mistake to suppose that the person is, in general, *better* than the institution. Morally, as in other respects, there are advantages on each side. The person has love and aspiration and all sorts of warm, fresh, plastic impulses, to which the institution is seldom hospitable, but the latter has a sober and tried goodness of the ages, the deposit, little by little, of what has been found practicable in the wayward and transient outreachings of human idealism. The law, the state, the traditional code of right and wrong, these are related to personality as a gray-haired father to a child. However world-worn and hardened by conflict, they are yet strong and wise and kind, and we do well in most matters to obey them.

A similar line of reasoning applies to the popular fallacy that a nation is of necessity less moral in its dealings with other nations than an individual with other individuals. International morality is on a low plane because it is recent and undeveloped, not from any inevitable defect in its nature. It is slow to grow, like anything else of an institutional character, but there is no reason why it should not eventually express the utmost justice and generosity of which we are capable. All depends upon the energy and persistence with which people try to effectuate their ideals in this sphere. The slowness of an institution is compensated by its capacity for age-long cumulative growth, and in this way it may outstrip, even morally, the ordinary achievement of individuals—as the Christian Church, for example, stands for ideals beyond the attain-

322

ment of most of its members. If we set our hearts on having a righteous state we can have one more righteous than any individual.

The treatment of Cuba by the United States and the suppression of the slave-trade by the British are examples of nations acting upon generous principles which we may reasonably expect to extend as time goes on. As the need of international justice and peace becomes keenly felt, its growth becomes as natural as the analogous process in an individual.

Whenever the question is raised between choice and mechanism,* the advocates of the latter may justly claim that it saves energy, and may demand whether, in a given case, the results of choice justify its cost.

Thus choice, working on a large scale, is competition, and the only alternative is some mechanical principle, either the inherited status of history or some new rule of stability to be worked out, perhaps, by socialism. Yet the present competitive order is not unjustly censured as wasteful, harassing, unjust and hostile to the artistic spirit. Choice is working somewhat riotously, without an adequate basis of established principles and standards, and so far as socialism is seeking these it is doing well.

Carlyle and others have urged with much reason that the mediæval workman, hemmed in as he was by mechanical and to us unreasonable restrictions, was in some respects better off than his modern successor. There was less freedom of opportunity, but also less strain, ugliness and

* I mean by mechanism anything in the way of habit, authority or formula that tends to dispense with choice.

323

despair; and the standards of the day were perhaps better maintained than ours are now.

We need a better discipline, a more adequate organization; the competent student can hardly fail to see this; but these things do not exist ready-made, and our present task seems to be to work them out, at the expense, doubtless, of other objects toward which, in quieter times, choice might be directed.

Thus it is from the interaction of personality and institutions that progress comes. The person represents more directly that human nature which it is the end of all institutions to serve, but the institution represents the net result of a development far transcending any single personal consciousness. The person will criticise, and be mostly in the wrong, but not altogether. He will attack, and mostly fail, but from many attacks change will ensue.

It is also true that although institutions stand, in a general way, for the more mechanical phase of life, they yet require, within themselves, an element of personal freedom. Individuality, provided it be in harness, is the life of institutions, all vigor and adaptability depending upon it.

An army is the type of a mechanical institution; and yet, even in an army, individual choice, confined of course within special channels, is vital to the machine. In the German army, according to a competent observer, there is a systematic culture of self-reliance, a "development of the individual powers by according liberty to the utmost extent possible with the maintenance of the necessary system and discipline." "To the commandant of the company is left the entire responsibility for the instruction

324

of his men, in what mode and at what hour he may see fit," and "a like freedom is accorded to every officer charged with every branch whatsoever of instruction," while "the intelligence and self-reliance of the soldier is constantly appealed to." * In American armies the self-reliant spirit of the soldier and the common-sense and adaptability developed by our rough-and-ready civilization have always been of the utmost value. Nor are they unfavorable to discipline, that "true discipline of the soldiers of freedom, a discipline which must arise from individual conviction of duty and is very different from the compulsory discipline of the soldier of despotism."† Thus, in the battle of Gettysburg, when Pickett's charge broke the Federal line, and when for the moment, owing to the death of many officers, the succession of command was lost, it is said that the men without orders took up a position which enabled them to crush the invading column.

As the general character of organization becomes freer and more human, both the mechanical and the choosing elements of the institution rise to a higher plane. The former ceases to be an arbitrary and intolerant law, upheld by fear, by supernatural sanctions and the suppression of free speech; and tends to become simply a settled habit of thought, settled not because discussion is stifled but because it is superfluous, because the habit of thought has so proved its fitness to existing conditions that there is no prospect of shaking it.

Thus in a free modern state, the political system, funda-

* Baring-Gould, Germany, i, 350 *ff*.
† Garibaldi's Autobiography, i, 105.

mental property rights and the like are settled, so far as they are settled, not because they are sacred or authoritative, but because the public mind is convinced of their soundness. Though we may not reason about them they are, so to speak, potentially rational, inasmuch as they are believed to rest upon reason and may at any time be tested by it.

The advantages and disadvantages of this sort of institutions are well understood. They do not afford quite the sharp and definite discipline of a more arbitrary system, but they are more flexible, more closely expressive of the public mind, and so, if they can be made to work at all, more stable.

The free element in institutions also tends to become better informed, better trained, better organized, more truly rational. We have so many occasions to note this that it is unnecessary to dwell upon it here.

CHAPTER XXIX

INSTITUTIONS AND THE INDIVIDUAL—*Continued.*

INNOVATION AS A PERSONAL TENDENCY—INNOVATION AND CON-
SERVATISM AS PUBLIC HABIT—SOLIDARITY—FRENCH AND
ANGLO-SAXON SOLIDARITY—TRADITION AND CONVENTION—
NOT SO OPPOSITE AS THEY APPEAR—REAL DIFFERENCE, IN
THIS REGARD, BETWEEN MODERN AND MEDIÆVAL SOCIETY
—TRADITIONALISM AND CONVENTIONALISM IN MODERN LIFE.

THE time-worn question of conservatism as against
change has evidently much in common with that of personality as against institutions.   Innovation, that is, is bound
up with the assertion of fresh personality against mechanism; and the arguments for and against it are the same
as I have already suggested.   Wherever there is vigor and
constructive power in the individual there is likely to be
discontent with the establishment.   The young notoriously
tend to innovation, and so do those of a bold and restless
temperament at any age; the old, on the contrary, the
quiet, the timid, are conservative.   And so with whole
peoples; in so far as they are enfeebled by climate or
other causes they become inert and incapable of constructive change.

What may not be quite so obvious, at least to those who
have not read M. Tarde's work on the Laws of Imitation,*

* Gabriel Tarde, Les lois de l'imitation; English translation
The Laws of Imitation.

is that innovation or the opposite may be a public habit, independently of differences in age or vigor. The attitude toward change is subject to the same sort of alteration as public opinion, or any other phase of the public mind. That a nation has moved for centuries in the deepest ruts of conservatism, like China or India, is no proof of a lack of natural vigor, but may mean only that the social type has matured and hardened in isolation, not encountering any influence pungent enough to pierce its shell and start a cycle of change. Thus it is now apparent that lack of incitement, not lack of capacity, was the cause of the backwardness of Japan, and there is little doubt that the same is true of China.

Energy and suggestion are equally indispensable to all human achievement. In the absence of the latter the mind easily spends itself in minor activities, and there is no reason why this should not be true of a whole people and continue for centuries. Then, again, a spark may set it on fire and produce in a few years pregnant changes in the structure of society. The physical law of the persistence of energy in uniform quantity is a most illusive one to apply to human life. There is always a great deal more mental energy than is utilized, and the amount that is really productive depends chiefly on the urgency of suggestion. Indeed, the higher activities of the human mind are, in general, more like a series of somewhat fortuitous explosions than like the work of a uniform force.

There may also be a habit of change that is mere restlessness and has no constructive significance. In the early history of America a conspicuous character on the frontier was the man who had the habit of moving on.

He would settle for two or three years in one locality and then, getting restless, sell out and go on to another. So at present, those whom ambition and circumstance, in early manhood, have driven rapidly from one thing to another, often continue into old age the habit so acquired, making their families and friends most uncomfortable. I have noticed that there are over-strenuous people who have come to have an ideal of themselves as making an effort, and are most uneasy when this is not the case. To "being latent feel themselves no less" is quite impossible to them.

In our commercial and industrial life the somewhat feverish progress has generated a habit, a whole system of habits, based on the expectation of change. Enterprise and adaptability are cultivated at the expense of whatever conflicts with them; each one, feeling that the procession is moving on and that he must keep up with it, hurries along at the expense, perhaps, of health, culture and sanity.

This unrest is due rather to transition than to democracy; the ancient view that the latter is in its nature unstable being, as I have said, quite discredited. Even De Tocqueville, about 1835, saw that the political unrest of America was in minor affairs, and that a democratic polity might conceivably "render society more stationary than it has ever been in our western part of the world."* Tarde has expounded the matter at length and to much the same effect. A policy is stable when it is suited to prevailing conditions; and every year makes it more apparent that for peoples of European stock, at least, a

* Democracy in America, vol. ii, book iii, chap. 21.

polity essentially democratic is the only one that can permanently meet this test.

A social group in which there is a fundamental harmony of forces resulting in effective coöperation may be said, I suppose, to be *solidaire*, to adopt a French word much used in this connection. Thus France with its comparatively homogeneous people has no doubt more solidarity —notwithstanding its dissensions—than Austria; England more than Russia, and Japan more than China.

But if one thinks closely about the question he will find it no easy matter to say in just what solidarity consists. Not in mere likeness, certainly, since the difference of individuals and parts is not only consistent with but essential to a harmonious whole—as the harmony of music is produced by differing but correlated sounds. We want what Burke described as "that action and counteraction, which in the natural and in the political world, from the reciprocal struggle of discordant powers draws out the harmony of the universe."*

So far as likeness is necessary it is apparently a likeness of essential ideas and, still more, of sentiments, appropriate to the activity in question. Thus a Japanese writer explains the patriotic unity of his countrymen by their common devotion to the Mikado and the imperial family.

"When a Japanese says 'I love my country,' a great or even the greater part of his idea of his 'country' is taken up by the emperor and the imperial family . . . his forefathers and descendants are also taken into account." "In joy and in sorrow he believes that they (his own ancestors) are with him. He serves them as if they were living. And these ancestors whom he loves and reveres were

* The Works of Edmund Burke (Boston, 1884), vol. iii, p. 277.

all loyal to their emperors in their days; so he feels *he* must be loyal to *his* emperor.

"Nothing is so real to him as what he feels; and he feels that with him are united the past, the present and the future generations of his countrymen." "Thus fully conscious of the intense sympathy of his compatriots, both 'dead and living, and swelled with lofty anticipations of his glorious destiny, no danger can appall and no toil can tire the real Japanese soldier."*

In America unity of spirit is intense, and yet singularly headless and formless. There is no capital city, no guiding upper class, no monarch, no creed, scarcely even a dominating tradition. It seems to be a matter of common allegiance to vague sentiments of freedom, kindliness and hope. And this very circumstance, that the American spirit is so little specialized and so much at one with the general spirit of human nature, does more than anything else to make it influential, and potent in the assimilation of strange elements.

The only adequate proof of a lack of solidarity is inefficiency in total action. There may be intense strife of parties and classes which has nothing really disintegrating in it; but when we see, as was apparently the case in Russia not long ago, that the hour of conflict with an external enemy does not unite internal forces but increases their divergence, it is clear that something is wrong.

It is sometimes said that France has more solidarity than Great Britain or the United States, the ground being that we have a less fluent unity of the social mind, a more vigorous self-assertion of the individual. But this is as

* Amenomori in the Atlantic Monthly, Oct., 1904.

dubious as to say that the contention of athletes among themselves will prevent their uniting to form a strong team. Yet there does seem to be an interesting difference in kind between the sort of unity, of common discipline and sentiment, which exists among the French and that of English or Americans—these latter, however different, being far more like each other in this respect than either to the French. The contrast seems to me so illuminating, as a study of social types, that I will spend a few pages in attempting to expound it.

French thought—as to this I follow largely Mr. Brownell's penetrating study*—seems to be not only more centralized in place, that is, more dominated by the capital, but also, leaving aside certain notorious divisions, more uniform, more authoritative, more intolerant, more obviously *solidaire*. There is less initiative, less aggressive non-conformity. French sentiment emphasizes equality much more than individual freedom and is somewhat intolerant of any marked departure from the dominant types of thought. There is more jealousy of personal power, especially in politics, and less of that eager yet self-poised sympathy with triumphant personality which we find in England or America. There is, in fact, more need to be jealous of a personal ascendency, because, when it once gains sway, there is less to check it. And with all this goes the French system of public education, whose well-known uniformity, strictness of discipline and classical conservatism is both cause and effect of the trend toward formal solidarity.

* French Traits. P. G. Hamerton's works, especially his French and English, are also full of suggestion.

There is also an intolerance of the un-French and an inability to understand it even greater, perhaps, than the corresponding phenomenon in other nations. The French are self-absorbed and care little for the history of other peoples. Nor are they sympathetic with contemporaries. "In Paris, certainly," says Mr. Brownell, "the foreigner, hospitably as he is invariably treated, is invariably treated as the foreigner that he is."*

The relative weakness of individuality in France is due, of course, not to any lack of self-feeling, but to the fact that the Frenchman identifies himself more with the social whole, and, merged in that, does not take his more particular self so seriously. It is rather a we-feeling than an I-feeling, and differentiates France more sharply from other nations than it does the individual Frenchman from his compatriots. "He does not admire France because she is his country. His complacence with himself proceeds from the circumstance that he is a Frenchman; which is distinctly what he is first, being a man afterward." †
"One never hears the Frenchman boast of the character and quality of his compatriots as Englishmen and ourselves do. He is thinking about France, about her different *gloires*, about her position at the head of civilization."‡

As there is less individuality in general, so there is a happy lack of whimsical and offensive oddity, of sharp corners and bad taste. Mr. Brownell finds nothing more significant than the absence in France of prigs. "One infers at once in such a society a free and effortless play of the faculties, a large, humorous and tolerant view of

* French Traits, page 284.　　† Page 295.　　‡ Page 295.

333

oneself and others, leisure, calm, healthful and rational vivacity, a tranquil confidence in one's own perceptions and in the intelligence of one's neighbors."*

With this partial irresponsibility, this tendency not to take one's private self too seriously, goes a lack of moral extremes of all kinds. Their goodness is not so good, their vice not so vicious as ours. Both are more derived from immediate intercourse. "What would be vice among us remains in France social irregularity induced by sentiment.†"

These traits have an obvious connection with that more eager and facile communicativeness that strikes us so in the French: they have as a rule less introspection, live more immediately and congenially in a social stream from which, accordingly, they are less disposed to differentiate themselves.

France is, no doubt, as truly democratic in its way as the United States; indeed, in no other country, perhaps, is the prevalent sentiment of the people in a given group so *cratic*, so immediately authoritative. Such formalism as prevails there is of a sort with which the people themselves are in intelligent sympathy, not one imposed from above like that of Russia, or even that of Germany. But it is a democracy of a type quite other than ours, less differentiated individually and more so, perhaps, by groups, more consolidated and institutional. The source of this divergence lies partly in the course of history and partly, no doubt, in race psychology. Rooted dissensions, like that between the Republic and the Church, and the need of keeping the people in readiness for sudden war, are

* *Idem*, page 304. † Page 64.

among the influences which make formal unity more necessary and tolerable in France than in England.

The French kind of solidarity has both advantages and disadvantages as compared with the Anglo-Saxon. It certainly facilitates the formation of well-knit social groups; such, for instance, as the artistic "schools" whose vigor has done so much toward giving France its lead in æsthetic production. On the other hand, where the Anglo-Saxon type of structure succeeds in combining greater vigor of individuality with an equally effective unity of sentiment, it would seem to be, in so far, superior to a type whose solidarity is secured at more expense of variation. It is the self-dependence, the so-called individualism, of the Teutonic peoples which has given them so decided a lead in the industrial and political struggles of recent times.

Perhaps the most searching test of solidarity is that loyalty of the individual to the whole which ensures that, however isolated, as a soldier, a pioneer, a mechanic, a student, he will cherish that whole in his heart and do his duty to it in contempt of terror or bribes. And it is precisely in this that the Anglo-Saxon peoples are strong. The Englishman, though alone in the wilds of Africa, is seldom other than an Englishman, setting his conscience by English standards and making them good in action. This moral whole, possessing the individual and making every one a hero after his own private fashion, is the solidarity we want.

Tradition comes down from the past, while convention arrives, sidewise as it were, from our contemporaries; the fireside tales and maxims of our grandparents illustrate the one, the fashions of the day the other. Both indicate continuity of mind, but tradition has a long extension in time and very little, perhaps, in place, while convention extends in place but may endure only for a day.

This seems a clear distinction, and a great deal has been made of it by some writers, who regard "custom imitation" and "fashion imitation,"* to use the terms of Tarde, the brilliant French sociologist, as among the primary traits that differentiate societies.

Thus mediæval society, it is said, was traditional: people lived in somewhat isolated groups and were dominated by the ideas of their ancestors, these being more accessible than those of their contemporaries. On the other hand, modern society, with its telegraphs, newspapers and migrations, is conventional. Thought is transmitted over vast areas and countless multitudes; ancestral continuity is broken up; people get the habit of looking sidewise rather than backward, and there comes to be an instinctive preference of fashion over custom. In the time of Dante, if you travelled over Europe you would find that each town, each district, had its individual dress, dialect and local custom, handed down from the fathers. There was much change with place, little with time. If you did the same to-day, you would find the people everywhere dressed very much alike, dialects passing out of use and men eager to identify themselves with the common stir of contemporary life. And you would also find that the dress, behavior and objects of current interest, though much the same for whole nations and having a great deal in common the

* *Imitation-coutume* and *imitation-mode*.

336

world over, were somewhat transient in character, changing much with time, little with place.

There is, truly, a momentous difference in this regard between modern and mediæval life, but to call it a change from tradition to convention does not, I think, indicate its real character. Indeed, tradition and convention are by no means the separate and opposite things they may appear to be when we look at them in their most contrasted phases. It would be strange if there were any real separation between ideas coming from the past and those coming from contemporaries, since they exist in the same public mind. A traditional usage is also a convention within the group where it prevails. One learns it from other people and conforms to it by imitation and the desire not to be singular, just as he does to any other convention. The quaint local costume that still prevails in out-of-the-way corners of Europe is worn for the same reasons, no doubt, that the equally peculiar dress-suit and silk hat are worn by sophisticated people the world over; one convention is simply more extended than the other. In old times the conforming group, owing to the difficulty of intercourse, was small. People were eager to be in the fashion, as they are now, but they knew nothing of fashions beyond their own locality. Modern traditions are conventional on a larger scale. The Monroe Doctrine, to take a dignified example, is a tradition, regarded historically, but a convention as to the manner in which it enters into contemporary opinion.

In a similar manner we may see that conventions must also be traditions. The new fashions are adaptations of

337

old ones, and there are no really new ideas of any sort, only a gradual transformation of those that have come down from the past.

In a large view, then, tradition and convention are merely aspects of the transmission of thought and of the unity of social groups that results from it. If our mind is fixed upon the historical phase of the matter we see tradition, if upon the contemporary phase we see convention. But the process is really one, and the opposition only particular and apparent. All influences are contemporary in their immediate origin, all are rooted in the past.

What is it, then, that makes the difference between an apparently traditional society, such as that of mediæval Europe, and an apparently conventional society, like that of our time? Simply that the conditions are such as to make one of these phases more obvious than the other. In a comparatively small and stable group, continuous in the same locality and having little intercourse with the world outside, the fact that ideas come from tradition is evident; they pass down from parents to children as visibly as physical traits. Convention, however, or the action of contemporary intercourse, is on so small a scale as to be less apparent; the length and not the breadth of the movement attracts the eye.

On the other hand, in the case of a wide-reaching group bound into conscious unity by facile communication, people no longer look chiefly to their fathers for ideas; the paternal influence has to compete with many others, and is further weakened by the breaking up of family associations which goes with ease of movement. Yet men are not less dependent upon the past than before; it is only that tradition is so intricate and so spread out over the face of things that its character as tradition is hardly to be discovered. The obvious thing now is the lateral movement; influences seem to come in sidewise and fashion rules over custom. The difference is something like that between a multitude of disconnected streamlets and a single wide river, in which the general downward movement is obscured by numerous cross-currents and ed'dies.

In truth, facile communication extends the scope of tradition as much as it does that of fashion. All the known past becomes accessible anywhere, and instead of the cult of immediate ancestors we have a long-armed, selective appropriation of whatever traditional ideas suit our tastes. For painting the whole world goes to Renaissance Italy, for sculpture to ancient Greece, and so on. Convention has not gained as against tradition, but both have been transformed.

In much the same way we may distinguish between traditionalism and conventionalism; the one meaning a dominant type of thought evidently handed down from the past, the other a type formed by contemporary influence—but we should not expect the distinction to be any more fundamental than before.

Traditionalism may be looked for wherever there are long-established groups somewhat shut out from lateral influence, either by external conditions or by the character of their own system of ideas—in isolated rural communities, for example, in old and close-knit organizations like the

church, or in introverted nations such as China used to
be. Conventionalism applies to well-knit types not evidently traditional, and describes a great part of modern
life.

The fact that some phases of society are more dominated by settled types, whether traditional or conventional,
than others, indicates, of course, a certain equilibrium
of influences in them, and a comparative absence of com-
peting ideas. This, in turn, is favored by a variety of
causes. One is a lack of individuality and self-assertive-
ness on the part of the people—as the French are said to
conform to types more readily than the English or Americans. Another requisite is the lapse of sufficient time
for the type to establish itself and mould men's actions
into conformity; even fashion cannot be made in a minute. A third is that there should be enough interest in
the matter that non-conformity may be noticed and dis-
approved; and yet not enough interest to foster originality. We are most imitative when we notice but do not
greatly care. Still another favoring condition is the habit
of deference to some authority, which may impose the
type by example.

Thus the educated classes of England are, perhaps,
more conventional in dress and manner than the corresponding classes in the United States. If so, the explanation is probably not in any intrinsic difference of individuality, but in conditions more or less favorable to the
ripening of types; such as the comparative newness and
confusion of American civilization, the absence of an acknowledged upper class to set an authoritative example,
and a certain lack of interest in the externals of life which

our restlessness seems to foster.* On the other hand, it must be said that the insecurity of position and more immediate dependence upon the opinion of one's fellows, which exist in America, have a tendency toward conventionalism, because they make the individual more eager to appear well in the eyes of others. It is a curious fact, which may illustrate this principle, that the House of Commons, the more democratic branch of the British legislature, is described as more conventional than the House of Lords. Probably if standards were sufficiently developed in America there would be no more difficulty in enforcing them than in England.

Perhaps we should hit nearest the truth if we said that American life had conventions of its own, vaguer than the British and putting less weight on forms and more on fellow-feeling, but not necessarily less cogent.

* Americans should notice that what they are apt to call the snobbishness of the English middle class—their anxiety to imitate those whom they regard as social superiors—has its good result in producing a discipline in which many of us are somewhat grossly lacking. It may be better, in manners for instance, that people should adopt a standard from questionable motives than that they should have no standard at all. The trouble with us is the prevalence of a sprawling, gossiping self-content that does not know or care whether such things as manners, art and literature exist or not.

CHAPTER XXX

FORMALISM AND DISORGANIZATION

THE NATURE OF FORMALISM—ITS EFFECT UPON PERSONALITY—
FORMALISM IN MODERN LIFE—DISORGANIZATION, "INDIVID-
UALISM"—HOW IT AFFECTS THE INDIVIDUAL—RELATION TO
FORMALISM—"INDIVIDUALISM" IMPLIES DEFECTIVE SYMPATHY
—CONTEMPORARY "INDIVIDUALISM"—RESTLESSNESS UNDER
DISCOMFORT—THE BETTER ASPECT OF DISORGANIZATION.

Too much mechanism in society gives us something for
which there are many names, slightly different in meaning,
as institutionalism, formalism, traditionalism, conventionalism, ritualism, bureaucracy and the like. It is by
no means easy, however, to determine whether mechanism is in excess or not. It becomes an evil, no doubt,
when it interferes with growth and adaptation, when it
suppresses individuality and stupefies or misdirects the
energies of human nature. But just when this is the case
is likely not to be clear until the occasion is long past and
we can see the matter in the perspective of history.

Thus, in religion, it is well that men should adhere to
the creeds and ritual worked out in the past for spiritual
edification, so long as these do, on the whole, fulfil their
function; and it is hard to fix the time—not the same for
different churches, classes or individuals—when they cease
to do this. But it is certain that they die, in time, like
all tissue, and if not cleared away presently rot.

It has been well said that formalism is "an excess of
the organ of language."* The aim of all organization is

* The Poet. Emerson.

342

to express human nature, and it does this through a system
of symbols, which are the embodiment and vehicle of the
idea. So long as spirit and symbol are vitally united
and the idea is really conveyed, all is well, but so fast
as they are separated the symbol becomes an empty
shell, to which, however, custom, pride or interest may
still cling. It then supplants rather than conveys the
reality.

Underlying all formalism, indeed, is the fact that it is
psychically cheap; it substitutes the outer for the inner
as more tangible, more capable of being held before the
mind without fresh expense of thought and feeling, more
easily extended, therefore, and impressed upon the multitude. Thus in our own architecture or literature we have
innumerable cheap, unfelt repetitions of forms that were
significant and beautiful in their time and place.

The effect of formalism upon personality is to starve
its higher life and leave it the prey of apathy, self-complacency, sensuality and the lower nature in general.
A formalized religion and a formalized freedom are,
notoriously, the congenial dwelling-place of depravity
and oppression.

When a system of this sort is thoroughly established,
as in the case of the later Roman Empire, it confines the
individual mind as in a narrow cage by supplying it with
only one sort of suggestions. The variation of ideas and
the supplanting of old types by new can begin only by
individuals getting hold of suggestions that conflict with
those of the ruling system; and in the absence of this an
old type may go on reproducing itself indefinitely, indi-

viduals seeming no more to it than the leaves of a tree, which drop in the autumn and in the spring are replaced by others indistinguishable from them. It "breeds true" on the same principle that wild pigeons, long kept to a fixed type by natural limitations, are less variable than domestic species, in whose recent past there have been elements of change.

Among the Hindoos, for instance, a child is brought up from infancy in subjection to ceremonies and rites which stamp upon him the impression of a fixed and immemorial system. They control the most minute details of his life, and leave little room for choice either on his part or that of his parents. There is no attempt to justify tradition by reason: custom as such is obligatory.

Intolerance goes very naturally with formalism, since to a mind in the unresisted grasp of a fixed system of thought anything that departs from that system must appear irrational and absurd. The lowest Chinaman unaffectedly despises the foreigner, of whatever rank, as a vulgar barbarian, just as Christians used to despise the Jews, and the Jews, in their time, the Samaritans. Tolerance comes in along with peaceful discussion, when there is a competition of various ways of thinking, no one of which is strong enough to suppress the others.

In America and western Europe at the present day there is a great deal of formalism, but it is, on the whole, of a partial and secondary character, existing rather from the inadequacy of vital force than as a ruling principle. The general state of thought favors adaptation, because we are used to it and have found it on the whole beneficial.

344

We expect, for example, that a more vital and flexible form of organization will supplant the rigid systems of Russia and the Orient, and whatever in our own world is analogous to these.

But dead mechanism is too natural a product of human conditions not to exist at all times, and we may easily find it to-day in the church, in politics, in education, industry and philanthropy; wherever there is a lack of vital thought and sentiment to keep the machinery pliant to its work.

Thus our schools, high and low, exhibit a great deal of it. Routine methods, here as everywhere, are a device for turning out cheap work in large quantities, and the temptation to use them, in the case of a teacher who has too much to do, or is required to do that which he does not understand or believe in, is almost irresistible. Indeed, they are too frequently inculcated by principals and training schools, in contempt of the fact that the one essential thing in real teaching is a personal expression between teacher and pupil. Drill is easy for one who has got the knack of it, just because it requires nothing vital or personal, but is a convenient appliance for getting the business done with an appearance of success and little trouble to any one.

Even universities have much of this sort of cant. In literature, for instance, whether ancient or modern, English or foreign, little that is vital is commonly imparted. Compelled by his position to teach *something* to large and diverse classes, the teacher is led to fix upon certain matters—such as grammar, metres, or the biographies of the authors—whose definiteness suits them for the didactic purpose, and drill them into the student; while the real thing, the sentiments that are the soul of literature, are not communicated. If the teacher himself feels them, which is often the case, the fact that they cannot be reduced to formulas and tested by examinations discourages him from dwelling upon them.

In like manner our whole system of commerce and industry is formal in the sense that it is a vast machine grinding on and on in a blind way which is often destructive of the human nature for whose service it exists. Mammon—as in the painting by Watts—is not a fiend, wilfully crushing the woman's form that lies under his hand, but only a somewhat hardened man of the world, looking in another direction and preoccupied with the conduct of business upon business principles.

A curious instance of the same sort of thing is the stereotyping of language by the cheap press and the habit of hasty reading. The newspapers are called upon to give a maximum of commonplace information for a minimum of attention, and in doing this are led to adopt a small standard vocabulary and a uniform arrangement of words and sentences. All that requires fresh thought, either from reader or writer, is avoided to the greater comfort of both. The telegraph plays a considerable part in this, and an observer familiar with its technique points out how it puts a premium on long but unmistakable words, on conventional phrases (for which the operators have brief signs) and on a sentence structure so obvious that it cannot be upset by mistakes in punctuation.*

* See the article by R. L. O'Brien in the Atlantic Monthly, Oct., 1904.

In this way our newspapers, and the magazines and books that partake of their character, are the seat of a conventionalism perhaps as destructive of the spirit of literature as ecclesiasticism is of the spirit of Christianity.

The apparent opposite of formalism, but in reality closely akin to it, is disorganization or disintegration, often, though inaccurately, called "individualism."* One is mechanism supreme, the other mechanism going to pieces; and both are in contrast to that harmony between human nature and its instruments which is desirable.

In this state of things general order and discipline are lacking. Though there may be praiseworthy persons and activities, society as a whole wants unity and rationality, like a picture which is good in details but does not make a pleasing composition. Individuals and special groups appear to be working too much at cross purposes; there is a "reciprocal struggle of discordant powers" but the "harmony of the universe" does not emerge. As good actors do not always make a good troupe nor brave soldiers a good army, so a nation or a historical epoch—say Italy in the Renaissance—may be prolific in distinguished persons and scattered achievements but somewhat futile and chaotic as a system.

Disorganization appears in the individual as a mind without cogent and abiding allegiance to a whole, and without the larger principles of conduct that flow from such allegiance. The better aspect of this is that the lack

* Inaccurately, because the full development of the individual requires organization

347

of support may stimulate a man to greater activity and independence, the worse that the absence of social standards is likely to lower his plane of achievement and throw him back upon sensuality and other primitive impulses: also that, if he is of a sensitive fibre, he is apt to be overstrained by the contest with untoward conditions. How soothing and elevating it is to breathe the atmosphere of some large and quiet discipline. I remember feeling this in reading Lord Roberts' Forty-one Years in India, a book pervaded with one great and simple thought, the Anglo-Indian service, which dominates all narrow considerations and gives people a worthy ideal to live by. How rarely, in our day, is a book or a man dominated by restful and unquestioned faith in anything!

The fact that great personalities often appear in disordered times may seem to be a contradiction of the principle that the healthy development of individuals is one with that of institutions. Thus the Italian Renaissance, which was a time of political disorder and religious decay, produced the greatest painters and sculptors of modern times, and many great personalities in literature and statesmanship. But the genius which may appear in such a period is always, in one point of view, the fruitage of a foregoing and traditional development, never a merely personal phenomenon. That this was true of Renaissance art needs no exposition; like every great achievement it was founded upon organization.

It is no doubt the case, however, that there is a spur in the struggles of a confused time which may excite a few individuals to heroic efforts and accomplishment, just as a fire or a railroad disaster may be the occasion of heroism;

and so the disorder of the Renaissance was perhaps one cause of the men of genius, as well as of the demoralization which they did not escape.

It looks at first sight as if formalism and disorganization were as far apart as possible, but in fact they are closely connected, the latter being only the next step after the former in a logical sequence—the decay of a body already dead. Formalism goes very naturally with sensuality, avarice, selfish ambition, and other traits of disorganization, because the merely formal institution does not enlist and discipline the soul of the individual, but takes hold of him by the outside, his personality being left to torpor or to irreverent and riotous activity. So in the later centuries of the Roman Empire, when its system was most rigid, the people became unpatriotic, disorderly and sensual.

In the same way a school whose discipline is merely formal, not engaging the interest and good-will of the scholar, is pretty certain to turn out unruly boys and girls, because whatever is most personal and vital in them becomes accustomed to assert itself in opposition to the system. And so in a church where external observance has been developed at the expense of personal judgment, the individual conforms to the rite and then feels free for all kinds of self-indulgence. In general the lower "individualism" of our time, the ruthless self-assertion which is so conspicuous, for example, in business, is not something apart from our institutions but expresses the fact that they are largely formal and unhuman, not containing and enlarging the soul of the individual.

349

The real opposite of both formalism and disorder is that wholesome relation between individuality and the institution in which each supports the other, the latter contributing a stable basis for the vitality and variation of the former.

From one point of view disorganization is a lack of communication and social consciousness, a defect in the organ of language, as formalism is an excess. There is always, I suppose, a larger whole; the question is whether the individual thinks and feels it vividly through some sort of sympathetic contact; if he does he will act as a member of it.

In the writings of one of the most searching and yet hopeful critics of our times* we find that "individualism" is identified primarily with an isolation of sentiment, like that of the scholar in his study, the business man in his office or the mechanic who does not feel the broader meaning of his work. The opposite of it is the life of shoulder-to-shoulder sympathy and coöperation, in which the desire for separate power or distinction is lost in the overruling sense of common humanity. And the logical remedy for "individualism" is sought in that broadening of the spirit by immediate contact with the larger currents of life, which is the aim of the social settlement and similar movements.

This is, indeed, an inspiring and timely ideal, but let us hold it without forgetting that specialized and lonesome endeavor, indeed even individual pride and self-seeking, have also their uses. If we dwell too exclusively upon the

* Jane Addams.

350

we-feeling and the loss of the one in the many, we may lapse into a structureless emotionalism. Eye-to-eye fellowship and the pride of solitary achievement are both essential, each in its own way, to human growth, and either is capable of over-indulgence. We need the most erect individual with the widest base of sympathy.

In so far as it is true of our time that the larger interests of society are not impressed upon the individual, so that his private impulses coöperate with the public good, it is a time of moral disintegration. A well-ordered community is like a ship in which each officer and seaman has confidence in his fellows and in the captain, and is well accustomed to do his duty with no more than ordinary grumbling. All hangs together, and is subject to reason in the form of long-tried rules of navigation and discipline. Virtue is a system and men do heroic acts as part of the day's work and without self-consciousness. But suppose that the ship goes to pieces—let us say upon an iceberg—then the orderly whole is broken up and officers, seamen and passengers find themselves struggling miscellaneously in the water. Rational control and the virtue that is habit being gone, each one is thrown back upon his undisciplined impulses. Survival depends not upon wisdom or goodness—as it largely does in a social system—but upon ruthless force, and the best may probably perish.

Here is "individualism" in the lowest sense, and it is the analogue of this which is said, not without some reason, to pervade our own society. Old institutions are passing away and better ones, we hope, are preparing to take their

351

place, but in the meantime there is a lack of that higher discipline which prints the good of the whole upon the heart of the member. In a traditional order one is accustomed from childhood to regard usage, the authority of elders and the dominant institutions as the rule of life. "So it must be" is one's unconscious conviction, and, like the seaman, he does wise and heroic things without knowing it. But in our own time there is for many persons, if not most, no authoritative canon of life, and for better or worse we are ruled by native impulse and by that private reason which may be so weak when detached from a rational whole. The higher morality, if it is to be attained at all, must be specially thought out; and of the few who can do this a large part exhaust their energy in thinking and do not practise with any heartiness the truths they perceive.

We find, then, that people have to make up their own minds upon their duties as wives, husbands, mothers and daughters; upon commercial obligation and citizenship; upon the universe and the nature and authority of God. Inevitably many of us make a poor business of it. It is too much. It is as if each one should sit down to invent a language for himself: these things should be thought out gradually, coöperatively each adding little and accepting much. That great traditions should rapidly go to pieces may be a necessary phase of evolution and a disguised blessing, but the present effect is largely distraction and demoralization.

In particular, we notice that few who have burdens to bear are much under the control of submissive tradition, but every one asks "Why must I bear this?" and the pain of trying to see why is often worse than the evil itself. There is commonly no obvious reason, and the answer is often a sense of rebellion and a bitterness out of which comes, perhaps, recklessness, divorce, or suicide.

Why am I poor while others are rich? Why do I have to do work I do not like? Why should I be honest when others are unscrupulous? Why should I wear myself out bearing and rearing children? Why should I be faithful to my husband or wife when we are not happy together, and another would please me better? Why should I believe in a good God when all I know is a bad world? Why should I live when I wish to die? Never, probably, were so many asking such questions as this and finding no clear answer. There have been other times of analogous confusion, but it could never have penetrated so deeply into the masses as it does in these days of universal stir and communication.

How contemptible these calculations seem in comparison with the attitude of the soldier, who knows that he must suffer privation and not improbably death, and yet faces the prospect quite cheerfully, with a certain pride in his self-devotion. In this spirit, evidently, all the duties of life ought to be taken up. But the soldier, the seaman, the fireman, the brakeman, the doctor and others whose trade leads them into obvious peril have one great advantage: they know what their duty is and have no other thought than to do it; there is no mental distraction to complicate the situation. And as fast as principles become settled and habits formed, people will be as heroic in other functions as they are in these.

353

We may apply to many in our own time the words of Burckhardt in describing the disorganization of the Renaissance: "The sight of victorious egoism in others drives him to defend his own right by his own arm. And, while thinking to restore his inward equilibrium, he falls, through the vengeance which he executes, into the hands of the powers of darkness." That is, we think we must be as selfish as other people, but find that selfishness is misery. I notice that many men, even of much natural sympathy and fellow-feeling, have accepted "every man for himself" as a kind of dogma, making themselves believe that it is the necessary rule of a competitive society, and practising it with a kind of fanaticism which goes against their better natures. Perhaps the sensitive are more apt to do this than others—because they are more upset by the spectacle of "victorious egoism" around them. But the true good of the individual is found only in subordinating himself to a rational whole; and in turning against others he destroys himself.

The embittered and distracted individual must be a bad citizen. There is the same kind of moral difference between those who feel life as a rational whole, and so have some sort of a belief in God, as there is between an army that believes in its commander and one that does not. In either case the feeling does much to bring about its own justification.

The fact that the breaking up of traditions throws men back upon immediate human nature has, however, its good as well as its bad side. It may obscure those larger truths that are the growth of time and may let loose pride,

sensuality and scepticism; but it also awakens the child
in man and a childlike pliability to the better as well as the
worse in natural impulse. We may look, among people
who have lost the sense of tradition, for the sort of virtues,
as well as of vices, that we find on the frontier: for plain
dealing, love of character and force, kindness, hope, hospitality and courage. Alongside of an extravagant growth
of sensuality, pride and caprice, we have about us a general cult of childhood and womanhood, a vast philanthropy, and an interest in everything relating to the welfare of the masses of the people. The large private gifts
to philanthropic and educational purposes, and the fact
that a great deal of personal pride is mingled with these
gifts, are equally characteristic of the time.

And, after all, there is never any general state of extreme disintegration. Such as our time suffers from in
art and social relations is chiefly the penalty of a concentration of thought upon material production and physical
science. In these fields there is no lack of unified and
cumulative endeavor—though unhuman in some aspects
—resulting in total achievement. If we have not Dante
and gothic architecture, we have Darwin and the modern
railway. And as fast as the general mind turns to other
aims we may hope that our chaotic material will take on
order.

CHAPTER XXXI

DISORGANIZATION: THE FAMILY

OLD AND NEW RÉGIMES IN THE FAMILY—THE DECLINING BIRTH-
RATE—"SPOILED" CHILDREN—THE OPENING OF NEW CAREERS
TO WOMEN—EUROPEAN AND AMERICAN POINTS OF VIEW—
PERSONAL FACTORS IN DIVORCE—INSTITUTIONAL FACTORS—
CONCLUSION.

THE mediæval family, like other mediæval institutions,
was dominated by comparatively settled traditions which
reflected the needs of the general system of society.
Marriage was thought of chiefly as an alliance of interests,
and was arranged by the ruling members of the families
concerned on grounds of *convenance*, the personal congeniality of the parties being little considered.

We know that this view of marriage has still considerable force among the more conservative classes of European society, and that royalty or nobility, on the one hand,
and the peasantry, on the other, adhere to the idea that
it is a family rather than a personal function, which should
be arranged on grounds of rank and wealth. In France
it is hardly respectable to make a romantic marriage,
and Mr. Hamerton tells of a young woman who was indignant at a rumor that she had been wedded for love, in-
sisting that it had been strictly a matter of *convenance*.
He also mentions a young man who was compelled to ask
his mother which of two sisters he had just met was to be
his wife.*

* French and English, 357.

Along with this subordination of choice in contracting marriage generally went an autocratic family discipline. Legally the wife and children had no separate rights, their personality being merged in that of the husband and father, while socially the latter was rather their master than their companion. His rule, however—though it was no doubt harsh and often brutal, judged by our notions —was possibly not so arbitrary and whimsical as would be the exercise of similar authority in our day; since he was himself subordinate not only to social superiors, but still more to traditional ideas, defining his own duties and those of his household, which he felt bound to carry out. The whole system was authoritative, admitting little play of personal choice.

Evidently the drift of modern life is away from this state of things. The decay of settled traditions, embracing not only those relating directly to the family but also the religious and economic ideas by which these were supported, has thrown us back upon the unschooled impulses of human nature. In entering upon marriage the personal tastes of the couple demand gratification, and, right or wrong, there is no authority strong enough to hold them in check. Nor, if upon experience it turns out that personal tastes are not gratified, is there commonly any insuperable obstacle to a dissolution of the tie. Being married, they have children so long as they find it, on the whole, agreeable to their inclinations to do so, but when this point is reached they proceed to exercise choice by refusing to bear and rear any more. And as the spirit of choice is in the air, the children are not slow to inhale it and to exercise their own wills in accordance with the same law of impulse their elders seem to follow. "Do as you please so long as you do not evidently harm others" is the only rule of ethics that has much life; there is little regard for any higher discipline, for the slowly built traditions of a deeper right and wrong which cannot be justified to the feelings of the moment.

Among the phases of this domestic "individualism" or relapse to impulse are a declining birth-rate among the comfortable classes, some lack of discipline and respect in children, a growing independence of women accompanied by alleged neglect of the family, and an increase of divorce.

The causes of decline in the birth-rate are clearly psychological, being, in general, that people prefer ambition and luxury to the large families that would interfere with them.

Freedom of opportunity diffuses a restless desire to rise in the world, beneficent from many points of view but by no means favorable to natural increase. Men demand more of life in the way of personal self-realization than in the past, and it takes a longer time and more energy to get it, the consequence being that marriage is postponed and the birth-rate in marriage deliberately restricted. The young people of the well-to-do classes, among whom ambition is most developed, commonly feel poorer in regard to this matter than the hand-workers, so that we find in England, for instance, that the professional men marry at an average age of thirty-one, while miners marry at twenty-four. Moreover, while the hand-working classes, both on the farms and in towns, expect to make their children more than pay for themselves after they are fourteen years old, a large family thus becoming an investment for future profit, the well-to-do, on the contrary, see in their children a source of indefinitely continuous expense. And the trend of things is bringing an ever larger proportion of the people within the ambitious classes and subject to this sort of checks.

The spread of luxury, or even comfort, works in the same direction by creating tastes and habits unfavorable to the bearing and rearing of many children. Among those whose life, in general, is hard these things are not harder than the rest, and a certain callousness of mind that is apt to result from monotonous physical labor renders people less subject to anxiety, as a rule, than those who might appear to have less occasion for it. The joy of children, the "luxury of the poor," may also appear brighter from the dulness and hardship against which it is relieved. But as people acquire the habit, or at least the hope, of comfort they become aware that additional children mean a sacrifice which they often refuse to make.

These influences go hand-in-hand with that general tendency to rebel against trouble which is involved in the spirit of choice. In former days women accepted the bearing of children and the accompanying cares and privations as a matter of course; it did not occur to them that anything else was possible. Now, being accustomed to choose their life, they demand a reason why they should undergo hardships; and since the advantages which are to follow are doubtful and remote, and the suffering near and obvious, they are not unlikely to refuse. Too com-

359

monly they have no inwrought principles and training that dispose them to submit.

The distraction of choice grievously increases the actual burden and stress upon women, for it is comparatively easy to put up with the inevitable. What with moral strain of this sort and the anxious selection among conflicting methods of nurture and education it possibly costs the mother of to-day more psychical energy to raise four children than it did her grandmother to raise eight.

It would be strange if children were not hospitable to the modern sentiment that one will is as good as another, except as the other may be demonstrably wiser in regard to the matter in hand. Willing submission to authority as such, or sense of the value of discipline as a condition of the larger and less obvious well-being of society, is hardly to be expected from childish reasoning, and must come, if at all, as the unconscious result of a training which reflects general sentiment and custom. It is institutional in its nature, not visibly reasonable.

But the child, in our day, finds no such institution, no general state of sentiment such as exists in Japan and existed in our own past, which fills the mind from infancy with suggestions that parents are to be reverenced and obeyed; nor do parents ordinarily do much to instil this by training. Probably, so great is the power of general opinion even in childhood, they would hardly succeed if they tried, but as a rule they do not seriously try. Being themselves accustomed to the view that authority must appeal to the reason of the subject, they see nothing strange

in the fact that their children treat them as equals and demand to know "Why?"

The fond attention which parents give to their children
is often of a sort to overstimulate their self-consequence.
This constantly asking them, What would you like? Shall
we do this or that? Where do you want to go? and so on,
though amiable on our part, does the child little good.
The old practice of keeping children at a distance, whatever its evils, was more apt to foster reverence.

Among hand-workers, especially in the country, the
work being more obvious and often shared by the whole
family, the pressure of necessary labor makes a kind of
discipline for all, and the children are more likely to see
that there are rules and conditions of life above their immediate pleasure. Social play, as we have seen, may also
do much for this perception. But this visible control of
a higher law has a decreasing part in modern life, especially with the well-to-do classes, whose labors are seldom
such as children may share, or even understand.

In this, as in so many other respects, we are approaching a higher kind of life at the cost of incidental demoralization. The modern family at its best, with its intimate
sympathy and its discipline of love, is of a higher type
than the family of an older *régime*. "I never," said
Thackeray, "saw people on better terms with each other,
more frank, affectionate, and cordial, than the parents and
the grown-up young folks in the United States. And
why? Because the children were spoiled, to be sure."*
But where this ideal is not reached, there is apt to be a somewhat disastrous failure which makes one regret the auto-

* Philip, chapter 28.

cratic and traditional order. Not merely is discipline lacking, but the affection which might be supposed to go with indulgence is turned to indifference, if not contempt. As a rule we love those we can look up to, those who stand for the higher ideal. In old days parents shared somewhat in that divinity with which tradition hedged the great of the earth, and might receive a reverence not dependent upon their personality; and even to-day they are likely to be better loved if they exact respect—just as an officer is better loved who enforces discipline and is not too familiar with his soldiers. Human nature needs something to look up to, and it is a pity when parents do not in part supply this need for their children.

In short, the child, like the woman, helps to bear the often grievous burden of disorganization; bears it, among the well-to-do classes, in an ill-regulated life, in lack of reverence and love, in nervousness and petulance; as well as in premature and stunting labor among the poor.

The opening of new careers to women and a resulting economic independence approaching that of men is another phase of "individualism" that has its worse and better aspects. In general it has, through the fuller self-expression of women, most beneficial reactions both upon family life and society at large, but creates some trouble in the way of domestic reluctance and discontent.

The disposition to reject marriage altogether may be set aside as scarcely existent. The marriage rate shows little decline, though the average age is somewhat advanced. The wage-earning occupations of women are mostly of a temporary character, and the great majority of domestic servants, shop and factory girls, clerks, typewriters and teachers marry sooner or later. There is no reason to doubt that a congenial marriage continues to be the almost universal feminine ideal.

A more real problem, perhaps, is found in the excessive requirements, in the way of comfort and refinement, that young women are said to cherish. In the United States their education, so far as general culture is concerned, outstrips that of men, something like three-fifths of our high school pupils being girls, while even in the higher institutions the study of history, foreign languages and English literature is largely given over to women. A certain sense of superiority coming from this state of things probably causes the rejection of some honest clerks or craftsmen by girls who can hardly look for a better offer; and it has a tendency toward the cultivation of refinement at the expense of children where marriage does occur. It need hardly be said, however, that aggressive idealism on the part of women is in itself no bad thing, and that it does harm only where ill-directed. Hardly anything, for instance, would be more salutary than the general enforcement by women of a higher moral standard upon the men who wish to marry them.

And certainly nothing in modern civilization is more widely and subtly beneficent than the enlargement of women in social function. It means that a half of human nature is newly enfranchised, instructed and enabled to become a more conscious and effective factor in life. The ideals of home and the care of children, in spite of pessimists, are changing for the better, and the work of women in independent careers is largely in the direction of much-needed social service—education and philanthropy in the largest sense of the words. Any one familiar with these movements knows that much of the intellectual and most of the emotional force back of them is that of women. One may say that the maternal instinct has been set free and organized on a vast scale, for the activities in which women most excel are those inspired by sympathy with children and with the weak or suffering classes.

To the continental European, accustomed to a society in which the functions and conventions of men and women are sharply distinguished and defined by tradition, it seems that Americans break down a natural and salutary differentiation, making women masculine and men feminine by a too indiscriminate association and competition. No doubt there is some ground for distinct standards and education, and in the general crumbling of traditions and sway of a somewhat doctrinaire idea of equality some "achieved distinctions" of value may have been lost sight of. Like other social differentiations, however, this is one that can no longer be determined by authority, but must work itself out in a free play of experiment. As Mr. Ellis says, "The hope of our future civilization lies in the development, in equal freedom, of both the masculine and feminine elements in life."*

Perhaps, also, the masculine element, as being on the whole more rational and stable, should be the main source of government, keeping in order the emotionality more commonly dominant in women: and it may appear that this controlling function is ill-performed in America. It

* Man and Woman, 396.

should be remembered, however, that with us the emancipation of women comes chiefly from male initiative and is a voluntary fostering of *das ewig Weibliche* out of love and respect for it. And also that most European societies govern women by coercive laws or conventions and, in the lower classes, even by blows. Americans have almost wholly foregone these extrinsic aids, aiming at a higher or voluntary discipline, and if American women are, after all, quite as well guided, on the whole, as those of Europe, it is no mean achievement.

There are in general two sorts of forces, one personal and one institutional, which hold people together in wedlock. By the personal I mean those which spring more directly from natural impulse, and may be roughly summed up as affection and common interest in children. The institutional are those that come more from the larger organization of society, such as economic interdependence of husband and wife, or the state of public sentiment, tradition and law.

As regards affection, present conditions should apparently be favorable to the strength of the bond. Since personal choice is so little interfered with, and the whole matter conducted with a view to congeniality, it would seem that a high degree of congeniality must, on the whole, be secured. And, indeed, this is without much doubt the case: nowhere probably, is there so large a proportion of couples living together in love and confidence as in those countries where marriage is most free. Even if serious friction arises, the fact that each has chosen the other without constraint favors a sense of responsibility for the relation, and a determination to make it succeed that might be lacking in an arranged marriage. We know that if we do not marry happily it is our own fault, and the more character and self-respect we have the more we try to make the best of our venture. There can hardly be a general feeling that marriage is one thing and love another, such as may prevail under the rule of *convenance*.

Yet it is not inconsistent to say that this aim at love increases divorce. The theory being that the contracting parties are to be made happy, then, if they are not, it seems to follow that the relation is a failure and should cease: the brighter the ideal the darker the fact by contrast. Where interest and custom rule marriage those who enter into it may not expect congeniality, or, if they do, they feel that it is secondary and do not dream of divorce because it is not achieved. The woman marries because her parents tell her to, because marriage is her career, and because she desires a wedding and to be mistress of a household; the man because he wants a household and children and is not indifferent to the dowry. These tangible aims, of which one can be fairly secure beforehand, give stability where love proves wanting.

And while freedom in well-ordered minds tends toward responsibility and the endeavor to make the best of a chosen course, in the ill-ordered it is likely to become an impulsiveness which is displayed equally in contracting and in breaking off marriage without good cause. The conditions of our time give an easy rein to undisciplined wills, and one index of their activity is the divorce rate. Bad training in childhood is a large factor in this, neglected or spoiled children making bad husbands or wives, and

366

probably furnishing the greater number of the divorced. Common observation seems to show that the latter are seldom people of thoroughly wholesome antecedents.

It may not be amiss to add that personal affection is at the best an inadequate foundation for marriage. To expect that one person should make another happy or good is requiring too much of human nature. Both parties ought to be subject to some higher idea, in reverence for which they may rise above their own imperfection: there ought to be something in the way of religion in the case. A remark which Goethe made of poetry might well be applied to personal love: "It is a very good companion of life, but in no way competent to guide it";* and because people have no higher thought to shelter them in disappointment is frequently the reason that marriage proves a failure.

As regards institutional bonds there is of course a great relaxation.

Thus economic interdependence declines with the advance of specialization. The home industries are mostly gone, and every year more things are bought that used to be made in the house. Little is left but cooking, and that, either as a task of the wife or in the shape of the Domestic Service Question, is so troublesome that many are eager to see it follow the rest. At one time marriage was, for women, about the only way to a respectable maintenance, while to men a good housewife was equally an economic necessity. Now this is true only of the farming population,

* Die Muse das Leben zwar gern begleitet, aber es keineswegs zu leiten versteht.

and less true of them than it used to be: in the towns the economic considerations are mostly opposed to married life.

Besides making husband and wife less necessary to each other, these changes tend to make married women restless. Nothing works more for sanity and contentment than a reasonable amount of necessary and absorbing labor; disciplining the mind and giving one a sense of being of use in the world. It seems a paradox to say that idleness is exhausting, but there is much truth in it, especially in the case of sensitive and eager spirits. A regular and necessary task rests the will by giving it assurance, while the absence of such a task wearies it by uncertainty and futile choice. Just as a person who follows a trail through the woods will go further with less exertion than one who is finding his way, so we all need a foundation of routine, and the lack of this among women of the richer classes is a chief cause of the restless, exacting, often hysterical, spirit, harassing to its owner and every one else, which tends toward discontent, indiscretion and divorce.

The old traditional subordination on the part of the wife had its uses, like other decaying structures of the past; and however distasteful to modern ideas of freedom, was a factor in holding the family together. For, after all, no social organization can be expected to subsist without some regular system of government. We say that the modern family is a democracy; and this sounds very well; but anarchy is sometimes a more correct description. A well-ordered democracy has a constitution and laws, prescribing the rights and duties of the various members of the state, and providing a method of determining controversies: the family, except as we recognize within reasonable limits the authority of the husband and father, has nothing of the sort. So long as the members are one in mind and feeling there is an unconscious harmony which has nothing to do with authority; but with even slight divergence comes the need of definite control. What would happen on shipboard if the captain had to govern by mere personal ascendency, without the backing of maritime law and custom? Evidently there would be mutinies, as among pirate crews, which only an uncommonly strong man could quell; and the family is often in a similar condition.*

The relaxation of moral sentiment regarding marriage by migrations and other sorts of displacement is easily traced in statistics, which show that divorce is more frequent in new countries, in cities—peopled by migration —and in the industrial and commercial classes most affected by economic change. To have an effective public opinion holding people to their duty it is important that men should live long in one place and in one group, inheriting traditional ideas and enforcing them upon one

---

* That the increase of divorces is due chiefly to the initiative of the wife is seen in the fact that as they become more numerous an increasing proportion is granted at the instance of the woman. Under the old *régime* the divorcing of a husband was almost unknown, the first case in England occurring in 1801. (See the essay on Marriage and Divorce in Mr. Bryce's Studies in History and Jurisprudence.) In the United States a great preponderance are now granted to wives, and the greater the total rate the greater this preponderance. In those states where the rate is highest the proportion is from two-thirds to three-fourths. It is not far wrong to say that the old idea of divorce was to rid the husband of an unfaithful wife, the new is to rid the wife of an uncongenial or troublesome husband.

another. All breaking up of old associations involves an "individualism" which is nowhere more active than in family relations.

The same principles go to explain diminished control by the law and the church. Thus we notice that the states of the American Union, having made their marriage laws in comparative independence of the English tradition and in harmony with a relaxing public sentiment, have much divorce; while in Canada the restraining hand of that tradition has kept the law conservative and made divorce difficult and rare. The surprising contrast in this regard between the two sides of the Detroit or St. Lawrence rivers is only partly explained by the different social traits of the people.

Christian teaching is the chief source of the ideal of marriage as a sacred and almost indissoluble bond, and church organization has been the main agent in enforcing this ideal. The Roman Catholic church has never admitted the possibility of absolute divorce, and to her authority, chiefly, is due its absence in Spain and Italy; while in England the Established Church, not much behind Rome in strictness, has been perhaps the chief cause of conservatism in English law and sentiment. And the other Protestant churches, though more liberal, are conservative in comparison with the drift of popular feeling. So the fact, needless to discuss in this connection, that the disciplinary authority of the church has declined, makes directly for the increase of divorce.

The relaxation of the family is due, then, to changes progressive on the whole, but involving much incidental demoralization; being in general those arising from a somewhat rapid decay of old traditions and disciplines and a consequent dependence upon human impulse and reason.

The evil involved is largely old evil in a new form; it is not so much that new troubles have arisen between husband and wife as that a new remedy is sought for old ones. They quarreled and marriage vows were broken quite as much in former times as now, as much in England today as in America: the main difference is in the outcome.

Moreover, the matter has its brighter side; for divorce, though full of evils, is associated with a beneficent rise in the standing of women, of which it is to a certain degree the cause. The fact that law and opinion now permit women to revolt against the abuse of marital power operates widely and subtly to increase their self-respect and the respect of others for them, and like the right of workmen to strike, does most of its good without overt exercise.

CHAPTER XXXII

DISORGANIZATION: THE CHURCH

THE PSYCHOLOGICAL VIEW OF RELIGION—THE NEED OF SOCIAL STRUCTURE—CREEDS—WHY SYMBOLS TEND TO BECOME FORMAL—TRAITS OF A GOOD SYSTEM OF SYMBOLS—CONTEMPORARY NEED OF RELIGION—NEWER TENDENCIES IN THE CHURCH.

IN religion, too, our day is one of confusion in institutions and falling back upon human nature. The most notable books of the day in this field are, first of all, studies in religious psychology. Perceiving that the question has come to be one of the very being and function of religion, they ignore the discussion of particular doctrines, polities or sacraments, and seek a foundation in the nature of the human mind.

I do not wish to follow these researches in detail: their general outcome is reassuring. They seem to show that religion is a need of human nature, centring, perhaps, in the craving to make life seem rational and good. As thought it is belief regarding the power underlying life and our relation to it; our conceptions of God and of other divine agents serving as symbols—changing like other symbols with the general state of thought—of this hidden reality. As feeling it is a various body of passion and sentiment associated with this belief; such as the sense of sin and of reconciliation; dread, awe, reverence, love and

372

faith. And religious action is such as expresses, in one way or another, this sort of thought and feeling.

Like all our higher life, religion lives only by communication and influence. Its sentiments are planted in instinct, but the soil in which they grow is some sort of fostering community life. Higher thought—call it intellectual, spiritual, or what you will—does not come to us by any short and easy road, its nature being to require preparation and outlay, to be the difficult and culminating product of human growth. And this is quite as much a growth of the social order as of individuals, for the individual cut off from that scaffolding of suggestion that the aspiration of the race has gradually prepared for him is sure to be lawless and sensual: his spiritual impulse can hardly be more than a futile unrest, just as the untaught impulse of speech in a deaf person produces only inarticulate cries. Much has been said of natural religion; but if this means a religion achieved *de novo* by the individual mind, there is no such thing, all religion and religious sentiment being more or less distinctly traditional.

We find, then, that the religious life always rests upon a somewhat elaborate social structure—not necessarily a church, but something which does in fact what the church aims to do. The higher sentiments now possible to us are subtly evoked and nourished by language, music, ritual and other time-wrought symbols. And even more obviously are ideas—of God and of the larger being, of religious observance, government and duty—matters of communal and secular growth.

The root problem of the church—as, in a sense, of all

373

organization—is to get the use of the symbol without the abuse. We cannot hold our minds to the higher life without a form of thought; and forms of thought come by traditions and usages which are apt to enchain the spirit. "Woe unto thee thou stream of human custom"; cries St. Augustine, "Who shall stay thy course? How long shall it be before thou art dried up? How long wilt thou carry down the sons of Eve into that huge and formidable ocean, which even those who are embarked on the Tree can scarce pass over?"*

The iconoclastic fervor against formalism that usefully breaks out from time to time should not make us imagine that religion can dispense with institutions. There is in religious thought at present much of a kind of anarchism which, in the justifiable revolt against the pretensions of authority, is inclined to overlook the importance of tradition and structure. Perhaps we may cite Emerson as an anarchist of this sort; he saw the necessity of institutions, but was inclined by temperament and experience to distrust them, and to dwell almost wholly upon freedom.

Is it not the fact, however, that the progress of religion has been less in the perception of new truth than in bringing it home to the many by organization? There is perhaps little in religious thought that was not adequately expressed by occasional thinkers millenniums ago; the gain has been in working this thought into the corporate life. The great religions—Buddhism, Judaism, Christianity, Mohammedanism—are nothing if not systems; that is to say, although based on primary needs of human nature, their very being as widespread religions consists

* Confessions, book i, chap. 16.

in a social structure, adapted to the changing state of society, through which these needs are met and fostered. Thus the appeal of Christianity to the human mind may be said to have rested, in all periods, partly on the symbolic power of a personality—so idealized and interpreted as to be in effect a system as well as a man—and partly on a changing but always elaborate structure of doctrines, ritual, polity, preaching and the like. Take away these symbols and there is nothing distinctive left. And if the whole is to go on, the system of symbols, again renewed, must go on, too. No more in religion than in any other phase of life can we have an inside without an outside, essence without form.

The existing creeds, formulated in a previous state of thought, have lost that relative truth they once had and are now, for most of us, not creeds at all, since they are incredible; but creeds of some sort we must have. A creed may, perhaps, be defined as a settled way of thinking about matters which are beyond the reach of positive knowledge, but which the mind must and will think of in some way—notably, of course, about the larger life and our relation to it. For the majority, who are not metaphysicians, it is mere waste and distraction to struggle unaided with these problems; we need a chart in this sea, a practicable form of thought to live by. That competent men should devise such forms of thought, consistent with the state of knowledge, and that other symbols should grow up about them, is as natural and useful as any other kind of invention. We need to believe, and we shall believe what we can. John Addington Symonds declared that "health of soul results from possessing a creed," and his own sufferings in trying to make one out of the scattered materials of his time are typical of those of a great number of sensitive minds, many of whom have been harassed into despair and degradation.* Without some regular and common service of the ideal, something in the way of prayer and worship, pessimism and selfishness are almost sure to encroach upon us.

Those who teach truth in its mere abstractness can never take much hold of the general mind, and success awaits a teaching which is intellectually sound (that is, consistent with the clearer thought of the day), and at the same time able, by a wealth of fit symbols, to make itself at home in all sorts of plain minds. And it is just this that is apt to be destructively wanting in a time of intellectual and social change.

Why is it that the symbol encroaches and persists beyond its function? Evidently just because it is external, capable of imitation and repetition without fresh thought and life, so that all that is inert and mechanical clings to it. All dull and sensual persons, all dull and sensual moods in any person, see the form and not the substance. The spirit, the idea, the sentiment, is plainly enough the reality *when one is awake to see it*, but how easily we lose our hold upon it and come to think that the real is the tangible. The symbol is always at command: we can always attend church, go to mass, recite prayers, contribute money, and the like; but kindness, hope, reverence, humility, courage, have no string attached to them; they come and go as the spirit moves; there is no insurance on them.

* See his life by H. F. Brown, *passim*.

Just as in the schools we teach facts and formulas rather than meanings, because the former can be received by all and readily tested, so religion becomes external in seeking to become universal.

It is perhaps hardly necessary to recall the application of this to Christianity. Jesus himself had no system: he felt and taught the human sentiments that underly religion and the conduct that expresses them. The Sermon on the Mount appears paradoxical only to sluggish, sensual, formal states of mind and the institutions that embody them. In our times of clearer insight it is good sense and good psychology, expressing that enlargement of the individual to embrace the life of others which takes place at such times. This natural Christianity, however, is insecure in the best people, and most of us have only a fleeting experience of it; so the teachers who wished to make a popular system, valid for all sorts of persons and moods, were led to vulgarize it by grounding it on miracles and mystic authority and enforcing it by sensual rewards and punishments.

The perennial truth of what Christ taught comes precisely from the fact that it was not a system, but an intuition and expression of higher sentiments the need of which is a central and enduring element in our best experience. It is this that has made it possible, in every age, to go back to his life and words and find them still alive and potent, fit to vitalize renewed systems. The system makers did well, too, but their work was transient.

A good system of symbols is one which, on the whole, stands to the group or to the individual for a higher life:

377

merit in this matter being relative to the particular state of mind that the symbol is to serve.   It is quite true that—

"Each age must worship its own thought of God,
   More or less earthy, clarifying still
   With subsidence continuous of the dregs."*

Crude men must have crude symbols—even "rod or candy for child-minded men" †—but these should be educational, leading up from lower forms of thought to higher.   A system that keeps men in sensualism when they are capable of rising above it, or in dogmatism when they are ready to think, is as bad as one that does not reach their minds at all.

At the present time all finality in religious formulas is discredited philosophically by the idea of evolution and of the consequent relativity of all higher truth, while, practically, free discussion has so accustomed people to conflicting views that the exclusive and intolerant advocacy of dogma is scarcely possible to the intelligent.   It is true, of course, that philosophical breadth and free discussion have flourished before, only to be swept under by the forces making for authority; but they were never so rooted in general conditions—of communication and personal freedom—as they are now.   It seems fairly certain that the formulas of religion will henceforward be held with at least a subconsciousness of their provisional character.

The creeds of the future are likely, also, to be simple. In all institutions there is nowadays a tendency to exchange formulas for principles, as being more flexible and so

* J. R. Lowell, The Cathedral.   † Ibid.

378

more enduring. The nearer you can get to universal human nature without abandoning concreteness the better. There is coming to be a clearer distinction of functions between metaphysics and worship, which may enable each to be enjoyed to the utmost without being unnecessarily mixed with the other.

The less intellectual a religious symbol is the better, because it less confines the mind. Personality is the best symbol of all; and after that music, art, poetry, festivity and ceremony are more enduring and less perilous symbols than formulas of belief. Sentiments change like ideas, but not so much and not so evidently; and the essential exercises of religion for the mass of men are those which awaken higher sentiment, especially those good works, in which, chiefly, the founder of Christianity and his real followers have expressed their religious impulse. These also are symbols, and the most potent and least illusive of all.

It is indeed a general truth that sentiment is nearer to the core of life than definable thought. As the rim of a wheel whirls about its centre, so ideas and institutions whirl about the pivotal sentiments of human nature. To define a thing is to institutionize it, to draw it forth from the pregnant obscurity of the soul and show just how it appears in the transient color of our particular way of thinking. Definitions are, in their nature, short-lived.

We need religion, probably, as much as any age can have needed it. The prevalent confusion, "the tumult of the time disconsolate," is felt in every mind not wholly inert as a greater or less distraction of thought, feeling and will;

and we need to be taught how to live with joy and calm in the presence of inevitable perplexities. A certain natural phlegm is a great advantage in these days, and better still, if we could get it, would be religious assurance. Never was it more urgent or more difficult to justify the ways of God to men. Our material betterment is a great thing, and our comparative freedom a greater, but these rather increase than diminish the need of a higher discipline in the mind that is to use them profitably: the more opportunities the more problems. Social betterment is like the advance of science in that each achievement opens up new requirements. There is no prospect that the world will ever satisfy us, and the structure of life is forever incomplete without something to satisfy the need of the spirit for ideas and sentiments that transcend and reconcile all particular aims whatsoever. Mediæval religion is too unworldly, no doubt, for our use, but all real religion has its unworldly side, and Thomas à Kempis and the rest were right in holding that no sort of tangible achievement can long assuage the human soul.

Still more evident is the need of religion in the form of "social salvation," of the moral awakening and leadership of the public mind. Society is in want of this, and the agency that supplies the want will have the power that goes with function—if not the church, then some secular and perhaps hostile agency, like socialism, which is already a rival to the church for the allegiance of the religious spirit.

Perhaps, also, there was never an age in which there was.more vital, hopeful religious aspiration and endeavor than the present—notwithstanding that so many are astray. It is, of course, a great advantage of the decline of forms that what survives is the more likely to be real. The church is being transformed in the persons of its younger and more adaptive members, and the outcome can be nothing else than a gradual readjustment of the tradition to the real spiritual needs of the time. It is notable that the severest critics of the institution are reformers within its own body, and their zeal overlooks nothing in the way of apathy or decadence.

As a matter of historical comparison the irreligion of our time is often exaggerated. Any reader of history may perceive that formalism, materialism and infidelity have flourished in all epochs, and as regards America we are assured by Mr. Bryce that Christianity influences conduct more here than in any other modern country, and far more than in the so-called ages of faith.* In fact it is just because this age is Christian in its aspirations that we hear so much of the inadequacy of the church. People are taking religion seriously and demanding true function in its instruments.

The church is possibly moving toward a differentiated unity, in which the common element will be mainly sentiment—such sentiments as justice, kindness, liberty and service. These are sufficient for good-will and coöperation, and leave room for all the differentiation of ideas and methods that the diversity of life requires.

With whatever faults the church is one of the great achievements of civilization. Like the body of science or our system of transportation and manufacture, it is

* The American Commonwealth, chap. 80.

the cumulative outcome of human invention and endeavor, and is probably in no more danger of perishing than these are. If certain parts of it break up we shall no doubt find that their sound materials are incorporated into new structures.

CHAPTER XXXIII

DISORGANIZATION: OTHER TRADITIONS

DISORDER IN THE ECONOMIC SYSTEM—IN EDUCATION—IN HIGHER
CULTURE——IN THE FINE ARTS.

THIS same idea, of confusion and inefficiency in social
functions arising from the breaking up of old structures,
might find illustration in almost any phase of life which
one might choose to investigate. The economic system,
for example, is in a state somewhat analogous to that of
the family and the church, and indeed the "industrial
revolution" is the chief seat of those phases of decay and
reconstruction which most affect the daily life of the people.

Location itself—to begin with man's attachment to the
soil—has been so widely disturbed that possibly a majority of the people of the civilized world are of recent migra-
tory origin; they themselves or their parents having
moved from one land to another or from country to city.
With this goes a severing of traditions and a mixture of
ideas and races.

Still more subversive, perhaps, is the change in occupations, which is practically universal, so that scarcely
anywhere will you find people doing the things which
their grandparents did. The quiet transmission of handi-
crafts in families and neighborhoods, never much in-
terrupted before, is now cut off, and the young are driven
to look for new trades. Nor is this merely one change, to

383

which the world may adapt itself once for all, but a series, a slide, to which there is no apparent term. Seldom is the skill learned in youth available in age, and thousands of men have seen one trade after another knocked out of their hands by the unforeseen movement of invention. Even the agriculturist, heretofore the symbol for traditionalism, has had to supple his mind to new devices.

I need not point out in detail how the old legal and ethical relations—the whole social structure indeed—of industry have mostly broken down; how the craftsman has lost control of his tools and is struggling to regain it through associations; how vast and novel forms of combination have appeared; how men of all classes are demoralized by the lack of standards of economic justice; these are familiar matters which I mention only to show their relation to the principle under discussion.

In general, modern industry, progressing chiefly in a mechanical sense, has attained a marvellous organization in that sense; while the social and moral side of it remains in confusion. We have a promising plant but have not yet learned how to make it turn out the desired product of righteousness and happiness.

Wherever there is power which has outstripped the growth of moral and legal standards there is sure to be some kind of anarchy; and so it is with our commerce and finance. On these seas piracy flourishes alongside of honest trade; and, indeed, as in the seventeenth century, many merchants practise both of these occupations. And the riches thus gained often go to corrupt the state.

In the inferior strata of the commercial order we find that human nature has been hustled and trodden under foot: "Things are in the saddle and ride mankind." The hand-worker, the clerk and the small tradesman, generally insecure in the tenure of their occupations and homes, are anxious and restless, while many classes suffer special and grievous wrongs, such as exhaustion and premature old age, due to the nervous strain of certain kinds of work, death and mutilation from machinery, life in squalid tenements, and the debasement of children by bad surroundings and premature work.

Although the individual, in a merely mechanical sense, is part of a wider whole than ever before, he has often lost that conscious membership in the whole upon which his human breadth depends: unless the larger life is a moral life, he gains nothing in this regard, and may lose. When children saw the grain growing in the field, watched the reaping and threshing and grinding of it, and then helped their mother to make it into bread, their minds had a vital membership in the economic process; but now that this process, by its very enlargement, has become invisible, most persons have lost the sense of it.* And this is a type of modern industry at large: the workman, the man of business, the farmer and the lawyer are contributors to the whole, but being morally isolated by the very magnitude of the system, the whole does not commonly live in their thought.

Is it not a universal experience that we cannot do anything with spirit or satisfaction unless we know what it is for? No one who remembers the tasks of childhood will doubt this; and it is still my observation that so soon as I lose a sense of the bearing of what I am doing upon gen-

* This illustration is used by Miss Jane Addams.

eral aims and the common life, I get stale and discouraged and need a fresh view. Yet a great part not only of hand labor but of professional work and business is of this character. The world has become so complicated that we know not what we do, and thus suffer not only in our happiness but in our moral steadfastness and religious faith. There is no remedy short of making life a moral and spiritual as well as a mechanical whole.

Education is another matter that might be discussed at much length from this point of view. That radical changes are taking place in it is hardly more obvious than that these changes are not altogether beneficent. We may say of this department as of others that there is a spirit of freedom and vigor abroad, but that its immediate results are somewhat anarchical.

The underlying reason for the special growth of educational institutions in our time is the free and conscious character of our system, which demands a corresponding individual to work it. Thus democracy requires literacy, that the voter may learn what he is voting about, and this means schools. Under the plan of free competition the son need not follow his father's occupation, but may take the open sea of life and find whatever work suits him; and this renders obsolete household instruction in trades. Indeed, our whole life is so specialized and so subject to change that there is nothing for it but special schools.

We may probably learn also, as time goes on, that the enlarged sphere of choice and the complexity of the relations with which it deals call for a social and moral education more rational and explicit than we have had in the past. There are urgent problems with which no power can deal but an instructed and organized public conscience, for the source of which we must look, in part, to public education.

In striving to meet new requirements our schools have too commonly extended their system rather than their vital energies; they have perhaps grown more rapidly in the number of students, the variety of subjects taught, and in other numerable particulars, than in the inner and spiritual life, the ideals, the traditions and the *personnel* of the teaching force. In this as in other expanding institutions life is spread out rather thin.

In the country the schools are largely inefficient because of the falling off in attendance, the poor pay and quality of the teachers, and the persistence of a system of instruction that lacks vital relation to country life, tending in fact to discredit it and turn children toward the towns. In cities the schools are overcrowded—often insufficient even to contain the children who swarm in the poorer districts—and the teachers often confused, overworked and stupefied by routine. Very little, as yet, is done to supply that rational training for industry which is the urgent need of most children, and which industry itself no longer furnishes. The discipline, both of pupils by teachers and of teachers by officials, is commonly of a mechanical sort, and promising innovations often fail because they are badly carried out.

Our common schools no doubt compare well enough, on the whole, with those of the past or of other countries; but when we think of what they might and should do in the way of bringing order and reason into our society,

387

and of the life that is going to waste because they do not nourish and guide it, there is no cause for congratulation.

In our higher education there is a somewhat similar mixture of new materials, imperfectly integrated, with fragments of a decadent system. The old classical discipline is plainly going, and perhaps it is best that it should go, but surely nothing satisfactory has arisen to take its place. Among the many things that might be said in this connection I will touch upon only one consideration, generally overlooked, namely the value of a *common* type of culture, corresponding in this respect to what used to be known as "the education of a gentleman." Since the decay of the classical type set in our higher education, notwithstanding so much that is excellent in it, has had practically no common content to serve as a medium of communication and spiritual unity among the educated class. In this connection as in so many others the question arises whether even an inadequate type of culture is not better than no type at all.

Not only was the classical tradition the widest and fullest current of higher thought we had, but it was also a treasury of symbols and associations tending to build up a common ideal life. Beginning with Dante all imaginative modern literature appeals to the mind through classical allusion and reverberation, which, mingling with newer elements, went to make up a continuing body of higher feeling and idea, upon which was nourished a continuing fellowship of those competent to receive and transmit it. All that was best in production came out of it and was unconsciously disciplined by its standards.

It would indeed be stupid to imagine that any assort-

388

ment of specialties can take the place of the culture stream from which all civilization has been watered: to lose that would be barbarism. And, in fact, it is a question whether we are not, in some degree and no doubt temporarily, actually relapsing into a kind of barbarism through the sudden decay of a culture type imperfectly suited to our use but much better than none.

If one has an assembly of university graduates before him, what, in the way of like-mindedness, can he count on their having? Certainly not Latin, much less Greek; he would be rash indeed to venture a quotation in these tongues, unless for mystification: nor would allusions to history or literature be much safer. The truth is that few of the graduates will have done serious work outside of their specialty; and the main thing they have in common is a collective spirit animated by the recollection of football victories and the like.

I suspect that we may be participating in the rise of a new type of culture which shall revise rather than abandon the old traditions, and whose central current will perhaps be a large study of the principles of human life and of their expression in history, art, philanthropy and religion. And the belief that the new discipline of sociology (much clarified and freed from whatever crudeness and pretension may now impair it) is to have a part in this may not be entirely a matter of special predilection.

Not very long since a critic, wrote of contemporary art as follows:

"Every one who is acquainted with technical matters in the fine arts is aware that the *quietly perfect* art of oil painting is extinct or

389

nearly so, and that in its place we have a great variety of extremely clever and dexterous substitutes, resulting in skilful partial expressions of artistic beauty, but not reaching that calm divine harmony of aim and method which we find in Titian and Giorgione, and even in such work as that of Velasquez. The greatest painting of past times had one quality which no modern one really possesses—it had *tranquillity.*" *

This touches upon something which—as we have already had occasion to observe—impairs nearly all in the way of higher spiritual achievement that our time produces—a certain breathlessness and lack of assured and quiet power. And this is connected with that confusion which does not permit the unquestioned ascendency of any one type, but keeps the artist choosing and experimenting, in the effort to make a whole which tradition does not supply ready-made.

In times of authoritative tradition a type of art grows up by accretion, rich and pregnant after its kind, which each artist unconsciously inherits and easily expresses. His forerunners have done the heavy work, and all that he needs to do is to add the glamour of personal genius. The grandeur of great literature—like the Bible, or Homer, or even, though less obviously, Dante, Shakespeare and Goethe—is largely that of traditional accumulation and concentration. The matter is old; it has been worked over and over and the unessential squeezed out, leaving a pregnant remainder which the artist enlivens with creative imagination. And the same is true of painting and sculpture.

So in architecture: a mediæval cathedral was the culmination of a long social growth, not greatly dependent upon

* Philip Gilbert Hamerton, Thoughts about Art, page 99.

individual genius. "Not only is there built into it," says Mr. Ferguson in his History of Modern Architecture, "the accumulated thought of all the men who had occupied themselves with building during the preceding centuries . . . but you have the dream and aspiration of the bishop, who designed it, of all his clergy, who took an interest in it, of the master-mason, who was skilled in construction; of the carver, the painter, the glazier, of the host of men who, each in his own craft, knew all that had been done before them, and had spent their lives in struggling to surpass the work of their forefathers. . . . You may wander in such a building for weeks or for months together and never know it all. A thought or a motive peeps out through every joint, and is manifest in every moulding, and the very stones speak to you with a voice as clear and as easily understood as the words of the poet or the teaching of the historian. Hence, in fact, the little interest we can feel in even the stateliest of modern buildings, and the undying, never satisfied interest with which we study over and over again those which have been produced under a different and truer system of art."*

In the same way the Greek architect of the time of Pericles "had before him a fixed and sacred standard of form. . . . He had no choice; his strength was not wasted among various ideals; that which he had inherited was a religion to him. . . . Undiverted by side issues as to the general form of his monument, undisturbed by any of the complicated conditions of modern life, he was able to concentrate his clear intellect upon the perfection of his details; his sensitiveness to harmony of proportion was

* Page 24.

391

refined to the last limits: his feeling for purity of line reached the point of a religion."*

The modern artist may have as much personal ability as the Greek or the mediæval, but, having no communal tradition to share in his work, he has to spread his personality out very thin to cover the too broad task assigned to it, and this thinness becomes the general fault of contemporary æsthetic production. If he seeks to avoid it by determined concentration there is apt to be something strained and over-conscious in the result.

* Van Brunt, Greek Lines, 95 ff.

PART VI
PUBLIC WILL

CHAPTER XXXIV

THE FUNCTION OF PUBLIC WILL

PUBLIC AND PRIVATE WILL—THE LACK OF PUBLIC WILL—SOCIAL
WRONGS COMMONLY NOT WILLED AT ALL.

WHAT I shall say about Public Will—which is only another phase of the Democratic Mind—might well have been introduced under Part III; but I put it here because in a sense it rounds off our whole inquiry, involving some general conclusions as to the method and possibility of social betterment.

By public will we may understand the deliberate self-direction of any social group. There is, of course, nothing mysterious about it, for it is of the same nature as public opinion, and is simply that so informed and organized as to be an effective guide to the life of the group. Nor can we say just when this state is reached—it is a matter of degree—but we may assume that when a group intelligently pursues a steadfast policy some measure, at least, of public will has been achieved. Many savage tribes have it in a small way; the Jews developed it under the leadership of Moses and Joshua; the mediæval church and the Venetian aristocracy displayed it. It is capable, like individual will, of indefinite improvement in insight, stability and scope.

Just as public and private opinion are general and

395

particular phases of the same thing, so will is a single complex activity with individual and collective aspects. But there is this difference between public and private will—just as there is between other individual and collective phases of mind—that the activity usually appears less conscious when looked at in its larger aspect than when considered in detail. I mean that we generally know a great deal better what we are about as individuals than we do as members of large wholes: when one sits down to dinner he is conscious of hunger and has a will to appease it; but if his action has any bearing upon the community, as no doubt it has, he is unaware of the fact. In the same way the activities of business have much consciousness and purpose when looked at in detail, but little when taken collectively. A thousand men buy and sell in the market, each with a very definite intention regarding his own transaction, but the market price which results from their bargaining is an almost mechanical outcome, not a matter of conscious intention at all. On the other hand, there are conscious wholes in which the general result may be as clearly purposed as the particular; as when an intelligent crew is working a vessel, each attending to his own work but understanding perfectly what the general purpose is and how he is contributing to it.

So if we restrict the word will to that which shows reflective consciousness and purpose there is a sense in which a certain choice (as of the purchaser in the market) may express individual will but not public will: there is a public side to it, of course, but of an involuntary sort.

We must remember, also, that although large wholes are, as a rule, much inferior to individuals in explicit consciousness and purpose, they are capable of rational structure and action of a somewhat mechanical sort far transcending that of the individual mind. This is because of the vast scope and indefinite duration they may have, which enables them to store up and systematize the work of innumerable persons, as a nation does, or even an industrial corporation. A large whole may and usually does display in its activity a kind of rationality or adaptation of means to ends which, as a whole, was never planned or purposed by anybody, but is the involuntary result of innumerable special endeavors. Thus the British colonial empire, which looks like the result of deliberate and farsighted policy, is conceded to have been, for the most part, the unforeseen outcome of personal enterprise. An institution, as we have seen in previous chapters, is not fully human, but may, nevertheless, be superhuman, in the sense that it may express a wisdom beyond the grasp of any one man. And even in a moral aspect it is by no means safe to assume that the personal is superior to the collective. This may or may not be the case, depending, among other things, upon whether there has been a past growth of collective moral judgment upon the point in question. The civil law, for example, which is the result of such a growth, is for the most part a much safer guide regarding property rights than the untrained judgment of any individual.

But after all public thought and will have the same superiority over unconscious adaptation (wonderful as the results of that often are) as private thought and will have over mere instinct and habit. They represent a higher principle of coördination and adaptation, one which, properly employed, saves energy and prevents mistakes. The British may have succeeded on instinct, but probably they would have succeeded better if more reason had been mixed with it; and the latter may save them from the decay which has attacked other great empires.

It is quite plain that the social development of the past has been mostly blind and without human intention. Any page of history will show that men have been unable to foresee, much less to control, the larger movements of life. There have been seers, but they have had only flashes of light, and have almost never been men of immediate sway. Even great statesmen have lived in the present, feeling their way, and having commonly no purpose beyond the aggrandizement of their country or their order. Such partial exceptions as the framing of the American constitution by the light of history and philosophy, and with some prevision of its actual working, are confined to recent times and excite a special wonder.

In particular the democratic movement of modern times has been chiefly unconscious. As De Tocqueville says of its course in France, ". . . it has always advanced without guidance. The heads of the state have made no preparation for it, and it has advanced without their consent or without their knowledge. The most powerful, the most intelligent and the most moral classes of the nation have never attempted . . . to guide it."*

Will has been alive only in details, in the smaller courses of life, in what each man was doing for himself and his neighbors, while the larger structure and movement

* Democracy in America, vol. i, Introduction.

have been subconscious, and for that reason erratic and wasteful. For it is just as true of large wholes as of individuals that if they blunder on without knowing what they are doing much of their energy is lost. No doubt it is better to go ahead even blindly than to stand still, and remarkable things have been achieved in this way, but they are little to what might be done if we could work out our highest human nature intelligently, with assurance and prevision, and on a large scale. A society which did this would have the same sort of superiority to present society as man to his sub-human progenitors.

The very idea of Progress, of orderly improvement on a great scale, is well known to be of recent origin, or at least recent diffusion, the prevalent view in the past having been that the actual state of things was, in its general character, unalterable.*

Even at the present day social phenomena of a large sort are for the most part not willed at all, but are the unforeseen result of diverse and partial endeavors. It is seldom that any large plan of social action is intelligently drawn up and followed out. Each interest works along in a somewhat blind and selfish manner, grasping, fighting and groping. As regards general ends most of the energy is wasted; and yet a sort of advance takes place, more like the surging of a throng than the orderly movement of troops. Who can pretend that the American people, for instance, are guided by any clear and rational plan in their economic, political and religious development? They

* Of course the Greeks had the philosophical conception of general flux, but I do not know that they applied it to society with such distinctness as to give anything worth calling an idea of progress.

399

have glimpses and impulses, but hardly a will, except on a few matters of near and urgent interest.

In the same way the wrongs that afflict society are seldom willed by any one or any group, but are by-products of acts of will having other objects; they are done, as some one has said, rather with the elbows than the fists. There is surprisingly little ill-intent, and the more one looks into life the less he finds of that vivid *chiaroscuro* of conscious goodness and badness his childish teaching has led him to expect.

Take, for instance, a conspicuous evil like the sweating system in the garment trades of New York or London. Here are people, largely women and children, forced to work twelve, fourteen, sometimes sixteen hours a day, in the midst of dirt, bad air and contagion, suffering the destruction of home life and decent nurture; and all for a wage hardly sufficient to buy the bare necessities of life. But if one looks for sin dark enough to cast such a shadow he will scarcely find it. "Neither hath this man sinned nor his parents." The "sweater" or immediate employer, to whom he first turns, is commonly himself a workman, not much raised above the rest and making but little profit on his transactions. Beyond him is the large dealer, usually a well-intentioned man, quite willing that things should be better if they can be made so without too much trouble or pecuniary loss to himself. He is only doing what others do and what, in his view, the conditions of trade require. And so on; the closer one gets to the facts the more evident it is that nowhere is the indubitable wickedness our feelings have pictured. It is quite the

400

same with political corruption and the venal alliance between wealth and party management. The men who control wealthy interests are probably no worse intentioned than the rest of us; they only do what they think they are forced to do in order to hold their own; and so with the politician: he finds that others are selling their power, and easily comes to think of it as a matter of course. In truth the consciously, flagrantly wicked man is, and perhaps always has been, a fiction, for the most part, of denunciation. The psychologist will hardly find him, but will feel that most sorts of badness are easily enough comprehensible, and will perhaps agree with the view ascribed to Goethe, that he never heard of a crime which he might not himself have committed.

Naturally the more mechanical the system is the less of will and of live human nature there is in its acts. So in Russia, says Tolstoy, "Some make the laws, others execute them; some train men by discipline to autocratic obedience; and these last, in their turn, become the instruments of coercion, and slay their kind without knowing why or to what end." * In our reading and thinking democracy there is at least the feeling that the working of the whole *ought* to be the fulfilment of some humane purpose, and a continual protest that this is not more the case.

I cannot hold out a prospect of the early appearance of an adequate public will; it is a matter of gradual improvement, but it seems clear that there is a trend this way, based, mechanically, on recent advances in communication, and, as regards training, on the multiform disciplines in voluntary coöperation which modern life affords.

* My Religion, 45.

401

CHAPTER XXXV

GOVERNMENT AS PUBLIC WILL

GOVERNMENT NOT THE ONLY AGENT OF PUBLIC WILL—THE RELA-
TIVE POINT OF VIEW; ADVANTAGES OF GOVERNMENT AS AN
AGENT—MECHANICAL TENDENCY OF GOVERNMENT—CHAR-
ACTERISTICS FAVORABLE TO GOVERNMENT ACTIVITY—MUNICI-
PAL SOCIALISM—SELF-EXPRESSION THE FUNDAMENTAL DEMAND
OF THE PEOPLE—ACTUAL EXTENSION OF STATE FUNCTIONS.

IN the growth of public will any agency amenable to
public opinion may serve as an instrument; and this means,
of course, any sort of rational activity, personal as well as
institutional. Thus the work of a secluded scientist, like
Pasteur or Edison, taken together with the general acceptance and application of his results, is as much an act
of public will as the proceedings of a legislature, and often
more—because they may show a more public spirit and a
wider knowledge and foresight. What is necessary is
that somewhere there shall be effectual purpose and endeavor based on a large grasp of the situation. In short,
public will is simply a matter of the more efficient organization of the general mind: whatever in the way of leadership or mechanism contributes to the latter has a share in
it; and we may naturally expect it to progress rather by
the quickening and coördination of many agencies than by
the aggrandizement of any particular one.*

The view which many hold that public will must be
chiefly if not wholly identified with the institution of gov-

* If the reader is not clear as to what I mean by public will, I beg
to refer him to chapters I, XII and XXXIV.

ernment is a just one only in a certain narrow sense. That is to say, the mechanism of government is indeed the most definite and authoritative expression of public choice, and if public will is to be limited to what is decided by a count of voices and carried out, if necessary, by force, then the government is its only agent. But only a small part of the will of society is of this sort. In a larger sense it is a diversified whole, embracing the thought and purpose of all institutions and associations, formal and informal, that have any breadth of aim, and even, as I have said, of secluded individuals. Surely the true will of humanity never has been and is not likely to be concentrated in a single agent, but works itself out through many instruments, and the unity we need is something much more intricate and flexible than could be secured through the state alone. Like other phases of organization, government is merely one way of doing things, fitted by its character for doing some things and unfitted for doing others.

As to what these things are, we must, of course, take the relative point of view and hold that the sphere of government operations is not, and should not be, fixed, but varies with the social condition at large. Hard-and-fast theories of what the state may best be and do, whether restrictive or expansive, we may well regard with distrust. It is by no means impossible that the whole character of the political state and of its relation to the rest of life is undergoing change of an unforeseeable kind which will eventually make our present dogmas on this point quite obsolete.

The most evident advantage of government as a social

instrument—that which makes it the logical recourse of those who seek a short way to regeneration—is its power and reach. It is the strongest and most extensive of our institutions, with elaborate machinery ready to undertake almost anything, and power limited, in the long run, only by public opinion.

Moreover, under a democratic system, it is *definitely* responsible to the people. Not that it always serves them: we know too well how apt it is to respect particular rather than general interests: but there is always a definite means of bringing it into line with public thought, always reins which the people may grasp if they will. This has the momentous effect that there is less jealousy of a democratic government, other things equal, than of any other form of power. Feeling that it is potentially at least their own, the people will endure from it with patience abuses that would be intolerable from any other source. The maddening thing about the oppression of private monopolies is the personal subjection, the humiliation of being unable to assert oneself, while in public life the free citizen has always a way of regular and dignified protest. He appeals not to an alien but to a larger self.

The most general defect of government is that which goes with its good qualities. Just because it is the most ancient and elaborate machine we have, it is apt to be too mechanical, too rigid, too costly and unhuman. As the most institutional of institutions it has a certain tendency toward formalism, and is objectionable on grounds of red-tape, lack of economy and remoteness from the fresher needs of the people.

404

It is easy, however, for one impressed with this idea to be too indiscriminate in its application. Much depends upon the kind of government actually in question, upon the interest the people take in it, and many other conditions.

In the United States, for instance, each of us lives under three somewhat distinct kinds of government—federal, state and local—each of which has a large measure of practical independence of the others, and may be treated as a separate agent of public will. Moreover, it is often the case that the larger systems—say the federal post-office—allow a great deal of local autonomy in their administration, making it flexible to local opinion.

Under this system, a township, village or small city is no unwieldy machine, but pretty much what the people see fit to make it, and the fact that it is a phase of government is no sufficient reason why any affairs it may choose to undertake may not be as humanly and flexibly administered as those of a non-political association of equal extent. They often are so administered, and the same is true of great cities wherever a vigorous civic consciousness exists and has had time to work out its instruments. The question is only one of organization, and this confronts non-political associations as well as political; large private incorporations having notoriously about the same experience of formalism, extravagance and malfeasance as the state.

There are certain characteristics whose presence in a given function is favorable to state activity, though they cannot be said to indicate clearly where it should begin or end.

405

One of these, naturally, is the inadequacy or harmfulness of other agencies. The fact that a work is deemed necessary and that there is no other adequate way of doing it is the real basis of most state functions; not only the primary ones of waging war and keeping order, but of issuing money, building roads, bridges and harbors, collecting statistics, instituting free schools, controlling monopolies, and so on.

Another is that the work in question should be susceptible of comparatively simple and uniform methods; since the more various and intricate a function is, the more difficulty will be found in getting it properly done by the powerful but usually somewhat clumsy mechanism of the state. The reasons that may justify a state post or telegraph, for instance, do not necessarily suffice for the assumption of the far more complicated business of the railways.

Again, whatever the state undertakes should be something likely to be watched by public opinion; not necessarily by the whole public, but at least by some powerful group steadfastly interested in efficiency and capable of judging whether it is attained. In the United States, certainly, the successes or failures of government are largely explicable on this ground. Public education works well, in spite of a constant leaning toward formalism, because the people take a close and jealous interest in it, while the monetary and financial functions are in like manner safeguarded by the scrutiny of the commercial world. But in the matter of tariffs the scrutiny of the latter, inadequately balanced by that of any other interest, has produced what is practically class legislation; and some-

406

thing similar may be said of many phases of government action.*

From such considerations it seems that local government, because it is on a small scale and because the people will presumably be more able and willing to watch the details of its operation, should be the sphere in which extension of functions has the most chance of success. The more the citizen feels that government is close to him and amenable to his will, the more, other things equal, he should be inclined to trust it and to put himself into it. In spite of much disappointing experience, it seems reasonable to expect that small units, dealing with the every-day interests of the people, will, in the long run, enlist an ample share of their capacity and integrity.

And yet the nearness of the whole to the will of the member is psychical, not spatial, so that if the citizen for some reason feels closer to the central government and trusts it more, he may be more willing to aggrandize it. In the United States the people often have more interest and confidence in the federal system than in their particular states and cities; one reason being that the constant enlargement of private organization—as in the case of railways and the so-called trusts—puts it beyond the power of local control. Of course there is a natural sphere of development for each of the various phases of government.

Municipal socialism has the great advantage over other sorts of state extension of being optional by small units, and of permitting all sorts of diversity, experiment and

* These principles are much the same as those put forth by W. S. Jevons. See his Methods of Social Reform, 355.

comparison. There is nothing in it of that deadening uniformity and obliteration of alternatives involved in the blanket socialism of the central state. The evils we suffer from private monopolies—against which we may always invoke the state if not other competitors—are as nothing compared with those to be feared from an all-embracing state-monopoly; and I feel sure that common-sense, a shrewd attachment to the principle of "checks and balances," and the spirit of local individuality will preserve the English-speaking nations, at least, from serious danger of the latter. In countries like France, where there is a great traditional preponderance of the central authority, it may be among the possibilities, though the probable decline of war—the main cause of mechanical consolidation—should work in the opposite direction.

There are few things that would be more salutary to the life of our people than a lively and effective civic consciousness in towns, villages and rural communities. I trust this is growing and feel no dread of any socialism which it may prove to involve. One of the best things I have known Ann Arbor to do was to hold a public-school carnival on the occasion of the opening of a new high school. There were all sorts of performances by the children, largely of their own devising, and the people were interested and brought together as never, perhaps, before. It was communal, it was *ours*, and the social spirit it evoked was a common joy. Enterprises of the same nature on a larger and more permanent scale, such as the recreation centres of Chicago, are beginning to arise in various parts of the country.

It seems probable that the plain citizen must look largely

to the communal life to supply that chance for self-expression which town residence and the specialized nature of modern industry have so largely restricted. Urban life is inevitable, and instead of regretting the country the city-dwellers had better make the most of the new situation, through playgrounds, public amusements, socialized schools, recreation centres, and, in general, a more vital and human civic organization.*

The fundamental need of men is for self-expression, for making their will felt in whatever they feel to be close to their hearts; and they will use the state in so far and in such a manner as they find it helpful in gratifying this need.

The more self-expression, therefore, there is in other spheres of life, the less need, relatively, people will feel of acting through government—a principle which should remind those who dread the growth of the latter that the only sure way to restrict it is by developing a real, affirmative freedom in other relations. Political democracy plus social and economic oppression is pretty sure to equal state socialism, because men will look to political control as a refuge. But if general conditions are free and open, men will be the more sensible, by contrast, of the unfree aspects of state activity.

A lack of economy in government will not much check its aggrandizement if the need of it is strongly felt on other grounds, since human nature, on the whole, cares very little for economy in comparison with freedom and justice.   One will more willingly pay a water-tax of twenty

* Compare Simon N. Patten, The New Basis of Civilization, 124.

dollars to a city government in which he has a voice than
of ten to an alien and overbearing corporation.

In our day there is a tendency toward extension of state
functions which after all is perhaps no more than symmet-
rical in view of the general expansion of larger structures
in every sphere. It does not seem to outstrip the growth,
for instance, of private corporations, or labor unions, or
of individual wealth. It is easy to see a tendency to state
socialism if you look only at the new functions of the state;
easy to see an opposite tendency if you fix your attention
on private organization. Whether or not the state is
relatively increasing its sphere is not easy to decide. The
new conditions of life bring men closer together, creating
a general need of wider organization; and, so far as now
appears, this need is to be met by the simultaneous development of various structures already well begun; such
as popular government and education, private industrial
and commercial corporations, labor unions, mutual-aid
societies, philanthropical associations, and so on.

The special demand for state extension seems to spring
chiefly from two conditions: the need to control the ex-
orbitant power of private economic associations, and the
need of meeting novel problems arising from life in great
cities. In these and similar directions an intelligent and
practised democracy will proceed tentatively, "with the
firm foot below," always balancing the loss against the
gain. Experiments in political socialism are sure to be tried,
which will prove instructive and perhaps beneficial. How
far they will be carried no man can say, but I see no special
reason to fear that they will go to any pernicious extreme.

410

CHAPTER XXXVI

SOME PHASES OF THE LARGER WILL

GROWING EFFICIENCY OF THE INTELLECTUAL PROCESSES—ORGANIC
IDEALISM—THE LARGER MORALITY—INDIRECT SERVICE—
INCREASING SIMPLICITY AND FLEXIBILITY IN SOCIAL STRUCTURE
—PUBLIC WILL SAVES PART OF THE COST OF CHANGE—HUMAN
NATURE THE GUIDING FORCE BEHIND PUBLIC WILL.

THE main source of a more effective public will is to
be sought not, peculiarly, in the greater activity of government, but in the growing efficiency of the intellectual and
moral processes as a whole. This general striving of the
public mind toward clearer consciousness is too evident
to escape any observer. In every province of life a multiform social knowledge is arising and, mingling with the
higher impulses of human nature, is forming a system of
rational ideals, which through leadership and emulation
gradually work their way into practice.

Compare, for instance, the place now taken in our
universities by history, economics, political science, sociology and the like with the attention given them, say, in
1875, when in fact some of these studies had no place at
all. Or consider the multiplication since the same date
of government bureaus—federal, state and local—whose
main function is to collect, arrange and disseminate social
knowledge. It is not too much to say that governments
are becoming, more and more, vast laboratories of social
science. Observe, also, the number of books and period-

411

icals seriously devoted to these subjects. No doubt much of this work is feverish and shallow—as must be expected in a time of change—but there is, on the whole, nothing more certain or more hopeful than the advance in the larger self-knowledge of mankind.

One result of this clearer consciousness is that idealism is coming to be organic; that is to say each particular ideal is coming to be formed and pursued in subordination to a system of ideals based on a large perception of fact. While putting a special enthusiasm into his own work, the idealist is learning that he needs to have also a general understanding of every good work, and of the whole to which all contribute. For him to imagine that his is the only work worth doing is as unfortunate as for the captain of a company to imagine that he is conducting the whole campaign. Other things equal, the most effective idealists are those who are most sane, and who have a sense for the complication, interdependence and inertia of human conditions.

A study of the ideals and programmes that have had most acceptance even in recent years would make it apparent that our state of mind regarding society has been much like that which prevailed regarding the natural world when men sought the philosopher's stone and the fountain of perpetual youth. Much energy has been wasted, or nearly wasted, in the exclusive and intolerant advocacy of special schemes—single tax, prohibition, state socialism and the like—each of which was imagined by its adherents to be the key to millennial conditions. Every year, however, makes converts to the truth that no isolated scheme can be

412

a good scheme, and that real progress must be an advance all along the line. Those who see only one thing can never see that truly, and so must work, even at that, in a somewhat superficial and erratic manner.

For similar reasons our moral schemes and standards must grow larger and more commensurate with the life which they aim to regulate.* The higher will can never work out unless it is as intelligently conceived and organized as commerce and politics. Evidently if we do not see how life really goes and what good and ill *are* under actual conditions, we can neither inculcate nor follow the better courses. There is nothing for it but to learn to feel and to effectuate kinds of right involving a sense of wider and remoter results than men have been used to take into account. As fast as science enables us to trace the outcome of a given sort of action we must go on to create a corresponding sense of responsibility for that outcome.

The popular systems of ethics are wholly inadequate, and all thinking persons are coming to see that those traits of decency in the obvious relations of life that we have been accustomed to regard as morality are in great part of secondary importance. Many of them are of somewhat the same character as John Woolman's refusal to wear dyed hats—we wonder that people do not see something more important to exercise their consciences upon. When the larger movements of life were subconscious and the good and ill flowing from them were

* This line of thought is developed by Professor E. A. Ross in his book, Sin and Society.

413

ascribed to an inscrutable providence, morality could not be concerned with them; but the more we understand them the more they must appear the chief field for its activity.

We still have to do with obvious wrong—the drunkard, the housebreaker, the murderer, and the like—but these simple offences are easy to deal with, comparatively, as being evident and indubitable, so that all normal people condemn them. No great ability or organization upholds them; they are like the outbreaks of savages or children in that they do not constitute a formidable menace to society. And, moreover, we are coming to see that they are most effectually dealt with by indirect and preventive methods.

The more dangerous immorality is, of course, that which makes use of the latest engines of politics or commerce to injure the community. Wrong-doers of this kind are usually decent and kindly in daily walk and conversation, as well as supporters of the church and other respectable institutions. For the most part they are not even hypocrites, but men of a dead and conventional virtue, not awake to the real meaning of what they are and do. A larger morality requires that they should be waked up, that a public conscience, based on knowledge, should judge things by their true results, and should know how to make its judgments effectual.

Moreover, this is not a matter merely of the bad men whom we read about in the newspapers, but one of personal guilt in all of us. It is my observation that the same wrongs which are held up to execration in the magazines are present, under appropriate forms, among teachers, lawyers, ministers, reputable tradesmen, and others who

414

come under my immediate notice. We are all in it: the narrow principles are much the same, the differences being largely in the scale of operations, in being or not being found out, in more or less timidity in taking risks, and so on.

A somewhat similar problem is that of energizing indirect service. The groups we serve—the nation, the educational institution, the oppressed class, for instance—have come to be so vast, and often so remote from the eye, that even the ingenuity of the newspaper and magazine press can hardly make them alive for us and draw our hearts and our money in their direction. The "we" does not live in face-to-face contact, and though photo-engravings and stereopticons and exhibitions and vivid writing are a marvelous substitute, they are often inadequate, so that we do not feel the cogency of the common interest so immediately as did the men of the clans. "Civilization," says Professor Simon Patten, "spares us more and more the sight of anguish, and our imaginations must be correspondingly sharpened to see in the check-book an agent as spiritual and poetic as the grime and blood-stain of ministering hands." * How far this may come to pass it is hard to say: for myself, I do not find it easy to write checks for objects that are not made real to me by some sort of personal contact. No doubt, however, our growing system of voluntary institutions—churches, philanthropic societies, fraternal orders, labor unions and the like—are training us in the habit of expressing ourselves through the check-book and other indirect agents.

I expect, however, that the best results will flow not

* The New Basis of Civilization, 61.

merely from an intelligent general benevolence that writes checks for all sorts of good causes, but from a kind of specialization in well-doing, that will enable one by familiarity to see through the tangle of relations at a particular point and act in the view of truth. In philanthropy, for instance, an increasing number of men and women of wealth and ability will devote not only their checks but trained thought and personal exertion to some particular sort of work which takes hold of their interest— to the welfare of dependent children, of the blind, and so on—making this their business, giving it the same close and eager attention they would any other business, and so coming to understand it through and through. These, along with salaried workers, will be the leaders in each special line, and will draw after them the less personal support of those who have confidence in them; but people will never send much of their treasure where their heart does not go first. Every city and neighborhood has its urgent social needs which the resident may study and devote himself to with much better results to the world and to his own character than if he limits himself to the writing of checks. And for that matter every occupation—as law, medicine, teaching and the various sorts of business and hand-labor—has its own philanthropies and reforms into which one may put all the devotion he is capable of. If each of us chooses some disinterested form of public service and puts himself thoroughly into it, things will go very well.

Another tendency involved in the rise of public will is that toward a greater simplicity and flexibility of structure in every province of life: principles are taking the place of formulas.

In the early history of a science the body of knowledge consists of a mass of ill-understood and ill-related observations, speculations and fancies, which the disciple takes on the authority of the master: but as principles are discovered this incoherent structure falls to pieces, and is replaced by a course of study based on experiment and inference. So in the early growth of every institution the truth that it embodies is not perceived or expressed in simplicity, but obscurely incarnated in custom and formula. The perception of principles does not do away with the mechanism, but tends to make it simple, flexible, human, definitely serving a conscious purpose and quick to stand or fall according to its success. Under the old system everything is preserved, because men do not know just where the virtue resides; under the new the essential is kept and the rest thrown away.

Or we may say that the change is like the substitution of an alphabet for picture writing, with the result that language becomes at the same time more complex in its structure and simpler in its elements. When once it is discovered that all speech may be reduced to a few elementary sounds the symbols of these, being sufficient to express all possible words, are more efficient and less cumbersome than the many characters that were used before.

The method of this change is that struggle for existence among ideas which is implied in the wide and free intercourse of modern life. In this only the vital, human and indispensable can survive, and truth is ever casting off superfluity and working itself down to first principles.

417

We have remarked this in the case of religion, and it would be easy to find the same process at work in other traditions.

The modern world, then, in spite of its complexity, may become fundamentally simpler, more consistent and reasonable. Apparently formalism can never more be an accepted and justified condition, any more than reason can be exchanged for the blind instinct of the lower animals. It will exist wherever thought and feeling are inadequate to create a will—as is much the case at present—but people will not be content with it as in the past. There will be creeds, but they will affirm no more than is really helpful to believe, ritual, but only what is beautiful or edifying; everything must justify itself by function.

Public will, like individual will, has the purpose of effecting an adaptation to conditions that is rational and economical instead of haphazard and wasteful. In general it should greatly diminish, though it can hardly obviate, the cost of social change. In commerce, for instance, it has already rendered crises less sudden and destructive —in spite of the enormous scale of modern transactions —and the time should not be very far away when trouble of this sort will be so foreseen and discounted and so provided against by various sorts of insurance as to do but little damage. In the same way the vast problem of poverty, and of the degeneracy that springs from it, can be met and in great part conquered by a long-sighted philanthropy and education. In religion there is apparently no more need of that calamitous overthrow of the foundations of belief from which many suffered in the passing generation. In the state violent revolution seems likely

418

to disappear as fast as democracy is organized; while in international relations it will be strange if we do not see a rapid diminution of war. In all these matters, and in many others, social costs are capable of being foreseen and provided against by rational measures expressing an enlightened public will.

The guiding force back of public will, now as ever, is of course human nature itself in its more enduring characteristics, those which find expression in primary groups and are little affected by institutional changes. This nature, familiar yet inscrutable, is apparently in a position to work itself out more adequately than at any time in the past.

INDEX

ABBOTT, LYMAN, 187.
Achilles, 110.
Addams, Jane, 25, 137, 190, 191, 244, 350, 385.
Agreement, not essential to public opinion, 122.
Alphabet, 417.
Amenomori, 331.
Anarchism, 196; in the church, 374.
Anarchy and spoliation, fear of, 276.
Anderson, W. L., 83.
Ann Arbor, school carnival in, 408.
Architecture, as communication, 79, 172; disorganization in, 390 ff.
Aristocracy, hereditary, 210, 257, 282 f.
Army, German, 324; American, 325.
Art, visible society a work of, 21; collective judgments on, 125; in relation to democracy, 157 ff.; spirit of, 244 f.; 321, disorganization in, 390 ff.
Arts, non-verbal, as communication, 77 ff.
Assemblage, public, 109.
Athletic sports, 163, 199.
Attenuation of sentiment, 178.
Augustine, 374.
Austen, Jane, 102.
Autocratic control of industry, 262 ff.
Average-theory of group action, 123 ff.

BACON, FRANCIS, 76, 318.
Bagehot, W., 178.
Baring-Gould, 325.
Biological type, the, 315 f.
Birth-rate, decline of, 358 ff.
Blame, 15 ff, 201 ff.
Bourget, Paul, 160, 171.
Brooks, John G., 45.
Brotherhood, sentiment of, 189 ff.
Browne, Sir T., 70, 153.
Brownell, W. C., 161, 166, 321, 332 ff.
Bryce, James, 85, 136, 182, 276, 280, 369, 381.

Buck, Winifred, 43.
Burckhardt, 354.
Burke, 330.
Burne-Jones, 168.
Burroughs, John, 93.

CAMP-FIRE, Assembly around, 109 f.
Carlyle, 167, 323.
Carnegie, A., views of on wealth, 281.
Capitalist class, ascendency of, 256 ff.
Caste, 209 ff.
Change, social, in relation to caste, 217, 225, 231.
Check-book, in social reform, 415 f.
Chicago, 212; recreation centres in, 408.
Child, the, his relation to the world, 315 ff.
Children, development of social consciousness in, 7 ff., 72; reforms in the interest of, 318 f.; "spoiled," 358 ff.
China, lack of communication in, 86.
Chinese, 186, 198.
Chivalry, 224.
Choice, excessive, 172; versus mechanism, 323; spirit of, 359 ff., 365 ff.
Christianity, 52, 73, 136, 166, 203 ff., 253, 304, 373 ff.
Church, the, 204, 322, 342, 347, 370; disorganization in, 372 ff.
City life, 94, 178 f., 409.
Class animosity, 301 ff.
Class atmosphere, 272.
Class-consciousness, 240 ff., 275, 284 ff., 305.
Class struggle, the, 241, 277, 286.
Classes, social, 179 f., 209–309; open, 239 ff.; open, in relation to wealth, 248 ff.; capitalist, 256 ff.; organization of the ill-paid, 284 ff.; hostile feeling between, 301.
Classical culture, 388 f.
Clergymen, facial expression of, 67.

Commercialism, 167; in relation to art, 173 f., 261, 346, 383 ff.
Commons, J. R., 286.
Communication, 54; significance of, 61 ff.; growth of, 66 ff.; modern, a cause of enlargement and animation, 80 ff.; modern, in relation to individuality, 91 ff.; in relation to superficiality and strain, 98 ff.; in relation to crowds, 151, 180, 191; in realtion to caste, 226 f., 338 f.
Community ideal, the, 33 ff., 52, 305. See also We-feeling and Moral unity.
Compensation, principle of, in social organization, 55 ff., 115, 118.
Competition, 35, 56, 158, 199 ff., 210, 226 f., 235, 239 f., 244, 323. See also Survival of the fittest.
Comte, 237.
Conflict. See Competition.
Confusion, in relation to art and literature, 162 ff.; to sentiment, 193. See also Disorganization.
Conquest, a cause of caste, 221.
Conscience, public, 387.
Consciousness, growth of in history, 107 ff.
Consciousness, public, 10 ff., 82, 411 ff.
Consciousness, social, 4 ff.; development of in children, 7 ff., 71, 350.
Conservatism, 327 ff.
Constitution of the United States, 314, 398.
Convention and tradition, 335 ff.
Conventionalism, 339 ff.
Cornish, F. W., 224.
Cost of change, 418 f.
Country life, effects of, 93 f., 178 f.
Courage, 187.
Creeds, 375 ff., 418.
Crime, 202 f.
Crises, commercial, 418.
Crowd excitement, in relation to democracy, 149 ff.
Crowds, psychology of, 149 ff.
Cuba, 322.
Culture groups and types, 163 ff., 243, 388 f.

Dante, 36, 70, 165, 173, 190, 388.
Darwin, 29, 67, 189, 295, 321.
Dead-level theory, 93, 159 ff.
Declaration of Independence, 48, 134.

Dellenbaugh, F. S., 108.
Demand, economic, often degrading, 141.
Democracy, among children, 45; source of its ideals, 51; dependent upon printing, 75; relation to modern communication, 85 ff.; an inadequate name, 86; as mental organization, 105–205; a discipline in self-control, 152; and distinction, 157 ff.; in relation to wealth, 278 ff.; to childhood, 318, 329, 334, 398.
Descartes, 5 ff.
Determinism, moral value of, 19 f.
De Tocqueville, Alexis, 27, 92, 99, 101, 116, 159, 172, 175, 235, 329, 398.
Devine, E. T., 297.
Dialects, revival of, 96.
Diffusion, a result of modern communication, 81; possibilities of, 87; not opposed to selection, 88; zeal for, 174; the age of, 175.
Dill, Samuel, 114.
Discussion. See Opinion.
Disorganization, spiritual, 162 ff., 347 ff.; in the family, 356 ff.; in the church, 372 ff.; in industry, 383 ff.; in education and culture, 386 ff.; in fine art, 389 ff.
Distinction, apt to cause isolation, 138 f.; in relation to democracy 157 f.
Divorce, 365 ff.
Domestic service, 367.
Donovan, J., 109.
Dorsey, J. O., 111.
Dress, 305.
Drink, 293 f.

Economic Interpretation of History, 255.
Economic system, confusion in, 383.
Education, 48, 87, 117, 227, 234; formalism in, 345 f., 349; of women, 363 ff.; disorganization in, 386 ff.; public, 406.
Efficiency, social, depends upon freedom, 234 f.
Ellis, H., 364.
Emerson, 125, 167, 176, 246, 342, 385.
Emulation, 307.
Energy, persistence of, 328.
England, 274, 281, 301, 302, 340, 358, 397 f.
Ennui, 99.

INDEX

Environment, 214 f., 230, 291 ff., 316 f.
Equality, 180, 257, 301 f.
Ethics. See Morality.
Eugenics, 296.

FACIAL EXPRESSION, 66 f.
Family, 10 f.; as a primary group, 24; as a source of primary ideals, 24, 48, 52; traditional careers in, 236 f.; disorganization in, 356 ff.
Fashion, 336 ff.
Fellowship, 174 f., 242 ff.
Ferguson, on architecture, 391.
Feudal system, 223 ff.
Formalism, 56, 198, 342 ff., 376 ff., 418.
Fort Sumter, attack on, 154.
France, 155, 166, 275, 330, 331 ff., 398, 408.
Frederick the Great, 86.
Freedom, as a primary ideal, 46; two aspects of in relation to classes 245 f.; 275, 325.
Free-will, 20.

GALTON, FRANCIS, 214, 317.
"Gangs" of boys, as primary groups, 49.
Garibaldi, 325.
Genius, 348.
Germany, 27, 248, 306, 324.
Gesture, 66, 69.
Gibbon, Edward, 73, 77.
God, 188, 196, 203, 205, 352, 353, 354, 372, 373, 380.
Goethe, 78, 165, 367, 401.
Gossip, organized, 84 f.
Government, as public will, 402 ff.; sphere of, 403 ff.; transformation of, 411.
Greece, refinement in, 180.
Greed of gain, 36, 254.
Green, J. R., 108.
Groups, primary, 23 ff. See also Types, Classes and Institutions.
Gummere, F. B., 107, 222.

HAMERTON, P. G., 140, 356, 390.
Hartt, R. L., 94.
Haste, 170 ff.
Heine, 95.
Herbert, Geo., 287.
Heredity and environment, 294 f., 316.
Higginson, T. W., 127, 136, 282.

History, organic view of, 255.
Holbein, 67.
Honesty and policy, 184.
Hopefulness, 187.
Horace (Q. Horatius Flaccus), 110.
Hostile feeling, 199 ff., 301 ff.
House of Commons, 341.
Howard, Geo. E., 24.
Howells, W. D., 271.
Human nature, relation to primary groups, 28 ff.; dependent upon communication, 62 f., 419.
Humanism of sentiment, 178, 180 ff.
Huxley, 190.

IDEALISM, Organic, 412 f.
Ideals, primary, 32 ff., 51 ff., 113; of groups, 126 f.; 165 f.
Imitation, two kinds of, 336.
Immigrants, 294, 295.
Immigration, 169, 220 f., 369.
India, caste in, 224.
Indians, American, kindness among, 41; individuality among, 110 f.
Individual, in relation to institutions, 313 ff.
Individualism, in art, 166, 243, 347 ff.; domestic, 357 ff. See also Disorganization.
Individuality, how affected by modern communication, 91 ff.; in tribal life, 110; development of in history, 112, 116 ff.; in relation to democracy, 160 ff.; moral, 201 f.; enjoyment of, 307; in harness, 324, 332 ff.
Inheritance principle, 209 ff.
Institutions, in relation to privileged classes, 140 f., 186, 313–392; and the individual, 313 ff.
Intolerance, 344.
Introspection, sympathetic, 7.
Italy, 167, 185, 186, 347, 348.

JAMES, HENRY, 84, 171, 174.
James, William, 20, 138, 253.
Japan, 328, 330.
Jesus, 16, 203 ff., 377.
Jevons, W. S., 407.
Johnson, Doctor, 93.
Johnson, Samuel (the orientalist), 225.
Justice, sentiment of, 181.

KELLER, HELEN, 62 f.
Kempis, Thomas à, 137, 138.

422

INDEX

Kindness, 40 ff., 189 ff.
Kropotkin, P. A., 41, 189.

LABOR MOVEMENT, 196, 242, 243, 258, 275, 284 ff.
Labor troubles, 308.
Lamb, Charles, 88.
Latin language, 74.
Law students, 141.
Lawfulness as a primary ideal, 42 ff.
Lawyers, 269.
Leadership, 135 f., 402.
LeBon, G., 149, 153.
Lecky, W. H. H., 96, 144.
Lee, H. C., 75.
Lee, Joseph, 34, 43.
Lincoln, 76.
Lindsey, Judge, 39.
Literature, in relation to democracy, 157 ff.; growth of refinement in, 179; disorganization in, 390; of social knowledge, 411 f.
Lloyd, A. H., 319.
Lloyd, H. D., 140, 263, 264.
Longinus, 115.
Lowell, J. R., 101, 378.
Loyalty, 38 f., 182.
Luther, 75.
Luxury, 306, 359.

MACAULAY, on democracy, 143 f.
Macchiavelli, 184.
Mackenzie, J. S., 92.
Maladjustment, as a cause of poverty, 293 f.
Malthus, 295.
Manners, tendency of, 197 ff.
Mantegna, 320.
Manual training, 304.
Marriage, 282, 356 ff. See also Family.
Masses, in relation to public opinion, 135 ff.
Middle ages, caste in, 222 ff., 267.
Might and right, 320.
Milton, 76.
Mind, organic view of, 3 ff.; democratic, 107–207.
Mind-cure doctrines, 297.
Mir, Russian, 26.
Mob. See Crowd.
Money-value, nature of, 265 f.
Montesquieu, 86, 116, 142, 261, 302.
Moral aspect, of the organic view of mind, 13 ff.; of institutions, 322; of public will, 397.

Moral principles, need of settled, 200 f., 307.
Moral unity, 33, 133, 182, 385.
Morality, of group action, 124; specialization in, 130; mode of progress in, 131; of capitalists, 259 f.; international, 322; the larger, 413 ff.
Music as communication, 77, 79.

NAPOLEON, 184.
Nationality, persistence of, 96.
Natural Right, doctrine of, relation to primary ideals, 47 f.
Natural selection, 189, 294 ff.
Nature and nurture, 214.
Negro question, 218 ff.
Negroes, 295.
Neighborhood, the, 24 ff., 49.
Newspaper, in modern communication, 83 ff., 151, 192 f., 270 f., 346.
North Carolina, mountain people of, 94.

O'BRIEN, R. L., 346.
Omahas, war party among, 110 f.
Opinion, public, 10 f., 85, 108, 121 ff., 144 f., 307 f., 406. See also Democracy.
Opportunity, freedom of, 233 ff., 245 f., 257 f.
Opposition, morality of, 37. See also Competition.
Organic conception of society, 3 ff., 13 ff., 255. See also table of contents.
Organic idealism, 412 f.
Organization, social, 3, 21, 22. See also table of contents.
Organizing capacity, 266.
Originality of masses, 135.
Ostrogorski, 99.

PAINTING, 77 ff., 179, 389 f.
Paralysis, general, 103.
Pater, Walter, 14, 79.
Patten, Simon N., 299, 409, 415.
Paul, St., on truth, 182.
Personality, relation of to social organization, 53; to specialization, 130 f.; interest in at elections, 143; 161, 214 f. See also Individuality.
Persons, judgment of by the masses, 142 ff.
Philanthropy, 48, 195, 299, 355, 416.
Plato, 86, 125, 159.
Play-group, the, 24 ff., 34 ff.

423

INDEX

Politics, rule of public opinion in, 132 ff.
Portraits, old and new, 101 f.
Poverty, 290 ff., 418.
Power, the deepest of instincts, 251; social nature of, 264 ff.
Prestige of wealth, 271 f.
Prigs, lack of in France, 333.
Primary groups, 23 ff.
Primary ideals, 32 ff. See also Ideals.
Principles, supplanting formulas, 417.
Printing, the basis of democracy, 71 ff.
Privilege, apt to cause isolation, 138.
Professional classes, 269 f.
Progress, irregularity of, 114; a modern idea, 399; cost of, 418.
Public opinion. See Opinion, public.
Punishment, 15 ff., 202 f.

RACE QUESTION, 218 ff.
Race-capacity, 28 f., 44 f.
Realism, 183 ff.
Refinement, tendency toward, 179 f.
Religion, 372 ff. See also Christianity.
Renaissance, 179, 348.
Resentment, 202 f.
Responsibility, 18 ff.
Roberts, Lord, 348.
Rodin, 321.
Roman Empire, 114 f., 349.
Roscommon, Earl of, 153.
Ross, E. A., on the mob-mind, 149; on the larger morality, 413.
Rules of the game, 43 ff., 200, 307.
Ruskin, 167.
Russia, 183.

SARGENT, 101.
Schiller, 266.
Sculpture, 77, 339.
Sedgwick, H. D., 101 f.
Self-consciousness, inseparable from social consciousness, 5 ff.
Self-expression, the fundamental need, 304, 409.
Self-words, a study of the early use of, 8.
Sentiment, how affected by communication, 88; individuality of, 97; leadership in by the masses, 135 ff., 142 ff.; meaning and trend of, 177 ff.; religious, 372, 379.

Service, as a primary ideal, 39; spirit of, 196, 260 f.; ideal of, 302 f.; indirect, 415 f.
Sexes, differentiation of, 364 f.
Sighele, 149.
Sill, E. W., 97.
Smiles, Samuel, 246.
Smith, A. H., 198.
Social consciousness. See Consciousness.
Social salvation, 380.
Social structure, increasing simplicity and flexibility of, 416 f.
Socialism, 51, 196, 276 ff., 285, 308; municipal, 407 ff.; state, 409 ff., 412.
Sociology, 197, 389, 411.
Solidarity, of classes, 276 f.; of nations, 330 ff.
Spahr, Charles, 309.
Spain, class feeling in, 301.
Specialization, of opinion, 126 ff.; not opposed to democracy, 147 f., in philanthropy, 416.
Speech, origin and growth of, 68; mental and social functions of, 69 ff., 109, 417.
Spencer, Herbert, 92.
Spencer and Gillen, 29, 41.
Spinoza, 19, 20.
Strain, 98 ff., 170 ff.
Strike, general, 277.
Struggle for existence, among ideas, 417. See also Competition, Class struggle, Survival of the fittest.
Students, university, 274.
Sturgis, Russell, 174.
Suffrage, popular, 146.
Suggestion, 150 ff., 328.
Suicide, 103.
Sullivan, Miss, Helen Keller's teacher, 62 f.
Superficiality, 98 ff., 117, 170 ff.
Survival of the fittest, 189, 258, 294 ff. See also Competition.
Sweating system, 400 f.
Symbols, religious, 373 ff.
Symonds, J. A., 375.
Sympathy, as the basis of reform, 14 f.

TARDE, GABRIEL, 327, 329, 336.
Tariff, 406.
Telegraph, effect of on language, 346.
Tennyson, 167.
Thackeray, 361.

INDEX

Thoreau, 34, 164 f., 176, 195, 249, 253.
Tolstoi, 167, 401.
Tout, T. F., 223.
Tradition and convention, 335 ff.
Traditionalism, 339 ff.
Tranquillity, lack of in art, 390.
Transition, distinguished from democracy, 158 f.
Truth, as a primary ideal, 39; sentiment of, 182 ff.
Types, social, 22, 163, 340.

UNCONSCIOUS SOCIAL RELATIONS, 4, 112.
Unfit, are the poor the?, 295 f.
Uniformity of American life, 166 f.
Unions. See Labor movement.
University of Michigan, supported by popular suffrage, 145.

VAN BRUNT, HENRY, 172, 391.
Variation of ideas, 343.
Veblen, T. V., 119.
Vulgarity of wealth and privilege, 139 f.

WATTS' MAMMON, 346.
Wealth, 136; inheritance of, 229, 236; as the basis of open classes, 248 ff.; comparative ascendency of, 278 f.; prestige of, 303 f.; use of, 304 f.
We-feeling, 23, 31, 33 ff., 189 ff.. 298, 333, 351, 415.
Westermarck, Edward, 24, 40 f.
Wharton, Edith, 102.
Whateley, 150.
Whitman, 176, 195 f., 303.
Will, public, 395–419; government as, 402 ff.; some phases of, 411 ff. See also Opinion, public.
Winckelmann, 78.
Women, opening of new careers to, 362 ff.
Woods, Robert, 43, 49.
Woolman, John, 413.
Wordsworth, 165, 317.
Worry, a cause of poverty, 297.
Writing, social function of, 72 ff.
Wrongs, social, not willed, 400 f.

YOUNG MEN, in relation to classes, 223, 273 f., 327.